The Crowdsourced Panopticon

The Crowdsourced Panopticon

Conformity and Control on Social Media

Jeremy Weissman

ROWMAN & LITTLEFIELD
Lanham • Boulder • New York • London

Published by Rowman & Littlefield
An imprint of The Rowman & Littlefield Publishing Group, Inc.
4501 Forbes Boulevard, Suite 200, Lanham, Maryland 20706
www.rowman.com

6 Tinworth Street, London SE11 5AL, United Kingdom

Copyright © 2021 by Jeremy Weissman

All rights reserved. No part of this book may be reproduced in any form or by any electronic or mechanical means, including information storage and retrieval systems, without written permission from the publisher, except by a reviewer who may quote passages in a review.

British Library Cataloguing in Publication Data

A catalogue record for this book is available from the British Library

ISBN: HB 978-1-5381-4431-2
PB 978-1-5381-4432-9

Library of Congress Control Number: 2020950817

ISBN 978-1-5381-4431-2 (cloth)
ISBN 978-1-5381-7409-8 (pbk)
ISBN 978-1-5381-4433-6 (electronic)

For Becky, Mom, Dad, Lauren, Mike, Amanda, Matthew, Grandma Mary, Grandpa Abe, Grandma Jeanie, Grandpa Milt, Grandpa Lowell, my aunts, uncles, and cousins, my in-laws, Shaina, Maggie, and all my friends old and new.

Contents

Acknowledgments — ix

Introduction — 1

PART I: CONFORMITY — 5

1 The Human Animal in Civilized Society — 7

2 Social Media as an Escape from Freedom — 25

3 Meaninglessness in the Present Age — 43

PART II: CONTROL — 63

4 The Spectacular Power of the Public — 65

5 P2P Surveillance — 83

6 The Net of Normalization — 101

PART III: RESISTANCE — 119

7 Freedom from the Public Eye — 121

8 Strategies of Resistance — 139

Works Cited — 159

Index — 171

Acknowledgments

I cannot be grateful enough for George Khushf who dedicated an unbelievable amount of care and attention to this work and who strongly influenced many of the arguments herein through our extensive conversations on the subject matter and on my earlier drafts. I am also deeply grateful to Justin Weinberg, Jerry Wallulis, and Evan Selinger who all played extremely important roles in guiding this work.

Thank you to Rowman & Littlefield International, Frankie Mace, Isobel Cowper-Coles, University of South Carolina and the Department of Philosophy, Heike Sefrin-Weis, Brian Murchison, Amy Jarrett, The Roger Mudd Center for Ethics, Washington and Lee University and the Department of Philosophy, and all the folks at Rosewood Market in Columbia, SC, for letting me hang out and write so much of this on their patio.

Portions of this text were first published in *Ethics and Information Technology* in the article "P2P Surveillance in the Global Village" by Jeremy Weissman.

Introduction

If you look around the world today, you may feel like the great sci-fi works of the twentieth century missed the mark or were at least off by several decades. The technological promises that were supposed to have emerged by now, the jetpacks, robot maids, are basically nowhere to be found. We don't live underwater, nor do we live on the moon. Nobody's made it to Mars, and there are *no* flying cars, let alone hoverboards. Just by glancing around it would appear that we are very far from the Jetsons-like future previous generations were confident would arise by now, already two decades into the new millennium. Rather, for the moment at least, things look relatively the same as they have for a long time, with rolling cars, brick houses firmly planted on the ground, and no one floating in the sky. But, as the cyberpunk godfather William Gibson is famously reported to have once said: "The future is already here—it's just not very evenly distributed."

We are indeed already *deep* into "the future," and by now it is finally being spread about a little more evenly. You just have to look a little harder. The biggest change is basically invisible. It is the Internet, and it is all around us. All of us are swimming in its waves nearly all the time. The next dramatic change has to do with the little universal computing devices in everybody's pockets which we still antiquatedly refer to as phones. Here the changes are truly extraordinary. Today, around the world billions of people, even in the least technologically developed countries, carry in their pockets a technology that is light years beyond the most advanced computing power of the most advanced governments and corporations in the world from just a few decades ago, for a fraction of the cost. Through these powerful devices, we have become constantly plugged, *en masse*, into a vast global network. From there, we can universally transmit practically any information to anyone around the world instantaneously. This combination of a greatly expanding World Wide Web, combined with ubiquitous high-powered computing devices, represents perhaps the most dramatic science-fiction scenario that has already become a reality. It may be smaller and harder to see than flying cars, but it is utterly transforming society and the nature of being human in a way that flying cars will barely touch.

We are today merging with our technologies, becoming more deeply intertwined with them than ever before. From out of our pockets, the resting place of the smartphone, the network is now creeping onto our wrists with smartwatches, and the network will soon likely settle squarely upon our faces with augmented reality glasses, literally immersing our senses in the information of the web. We will then virtually live inside the network. Soon enough from there these networked devices will likely creep inside many if not most people's bodies. It's a smooth continuum from on the body at all times to in the body at all times.

What does it mean for the nature of human existence and social relations to be constantly plugged into a global network, one that is getting closer and closer technologically to the very source of our thoughts? At DEF CON 25, one of the world's largest hacker conventions, the hacker "father-figure" Richard Thieme offered what might amount to a partial answer:

> At the heart of internet culture is a force that wants to know everything about you. We think of privacy as a human right, but we live in a Facebook age, when all that matters is publicity.... Privacy has meaning only for an individual. And we are no longer individuals. We believe in ourselves, but our selves are no longer our selves. We are not the same people who we once were.[1]

No longer ourselves? No longer individuals? That's a rather shocking statement, and seems to fly in the face of common notions about the allegedly self-absorbed "i" generation. Yet maybe there is something to what he is saying. If we are completely intertwined with our devices, if information about us practically down to the level of our thoughts is constantly being transmitted to the global network, if we are just inches away from these devices being embedded directly into our brains, into our minds, becoming neurologically plugged into a global system, then where do we draw the line between the individual and society? That fundamental boundary seems to be dissolving.

For some that might feel like a welcome relief, a relief from the burden of choice, a relief from the quest to be oneself, and a comforting dissolution of one's individual being into the interconnected primordial soup of an ambiently aware global community. But for those of us who see individuality as being essential to liberty, and liberty being essential to self-realization and happiness, resisting this emerging techno-collective existence is imperative.

This book is one attempt at such a resistance, of a resistance to an Internet cultural force that "wants to know everything about you," and in a sense dissolve individuality into an amorphous collectivity. To be clear, while privacy is disturbingly being whittled away in our technological society through multiple interlocking entities, including government and corporate agencies, this work is focused on the public of millions or billions of ordinary people around the globe, networked together, and able to peer into each other's lives in a way that was never possible before.

The networked crowd, through the Internet, has quickly grown larger than the population of any nation on Earth. At the same time, behind our screens, the crowd has become rather invisible and anonymous in digitized form. On the flipside, in front of our cameras, individuals are becoming hyper-exposed in a global broadcast that allows the networked collective to watch other people's lives in often great detail on an ongoing basis. It is the interplay of these two forces, of the invisibility of the anonymous crowd, and the exposure of the individual before that crowd, boosted up exponentially through the power of our information and communication technologies (ICTs), that is a central focus herein.

This book is a deep criticism of our current technological society and the culture surrounding the Internet, social media, and our "smart" devices. It is also a loud warning over the apparent trajectory we are heading toward based on current trends extrapolated out to the near future. I focus on the negative much more than the positive, but this is not to deny the many benefits these technologies may hold, but rather it is to raise alarm in order to mitigate dangers and strengthen whatever goods there might be. Right now we are not in desperate need of more praise for these existing and emerging ICTs. The majority of people on the planet have already adopted the Internet, social media, and smartphones arguably faster than any other technologies in history and use them constantly throughout their days. If anything we badly need a reality check, to slow down, and to take stock of how these technologies are rapidly transforming society, and in what ways they may be changing things for the worse.

I also paint some highly pessimistic socio-technological scenarios, especially in the latter half of the book where we look at some technologies that are still relatively early in development like augmented reality glasses. I hope society does not become as chilling as some of the scenarios I portray, and I do not think such scenarios are technologically determined to occur. However, I think we can all admit that sometimes what would have seemed an almost unthinkably pessimistic possibility does come true. While some of the more dire scenarios I present have a lower risk of materializing than others, their dystopian nature warrants serious concern precisely so that we can attempt to act preemptively to mitigate their worst potentials while these technologies are still early in development and there is still time to prevent such problematic outcomes.

This book is divided into three parts. Part I provides a normative critique of conformity in past and current institutions. I draw upon the works of Plato, Mill, Fromm, and Kierkegaard to see how their thinking can help shed light on the conformity effects of the Internet, social media, and smart devices. Part II is especially focused on emerging socio-technological trends and future scenario forecasts. Relying heavily on the work of Foucault, I provide less of a normative critique and more of an analysis of how the power of the public is beginning to be deployed through ICTs in a manner that infringes upon liberty through encroaching on privacy. Finally, in part III, I move to offering solutions as to how to resist this encroachment at individual, community, and broader collective levels including through the power of the state.

NOTE

1. Paul Wagenseil, "Your Privacy Is Gone. You Just Don't Know It Yet," *tom's guide*, last modified July 31, 2017, https://www.tomsguide.com/us/privacy-lost-defcon25,news-25558.html.

Part I
CONFORMITY

Chapter 1

The Human Animal in Civilized Society

We begin with recounting the tale of the Ring of Gyges from Plato's *Republic*. This ancient story provides perhaps the earliest philosophical dialogue on the ethical, legal, and social implications of surveillance. Of particular relevance to our discussion regarding privacy and social media, it highlights the way in which conformity to conventional morality and customs is maintained largely through ordinary people keeping an eye on one another, social pressure, and the power of reputation.

According to the legend, Gyges was a lowly shepherd serving the ruler of Lydia, an Iron Age kingdom in ancient Greece. One day while out tending to his flock, Gyges stumbled upon a mysterious hole in the ground torn wide open from a powerful earthquake. Venturing inside Gyges discovered a gigantic tomb holding the remains of an inhumanly large man wearing a golden ring. Compelled by the ring's otherworldly quality, Gyges slid it off the enormous dead man's finger and slipped it upon his own.

At first nothing happened, but then with a little twist and turn of the ring, he suddenly completely vanished from sight. Gyges, this ordinary shepherd, discovered that he now possessed an extraordinary power beyond even that of the king: the power to become invisible at will. It quickly dawned upon him that invisibility may be the key to living out his wildest and darkest fantasies. So he devised a most devious plan.

Once a month all the king's shepherds would gather together to generate a report on the king's flocks. At these meetings one of the shepherds would be sent to the royal court to deliver the update to him in person. With ring in hand, Gyges volunteered for the job. This was part of his plot.

When he made his way to the castle, he twisted the ring on his finger, and vanished completely out of sight right in the court of the king. With the guards left dumbfounded, Gyges snuck past them and beelined straight to the king's quarters. There he found the queen and seduced her. Now with the queen as his lover, he conspired with her to steal the throne. He thereby slew the king, and took the kingdom of Lydia as his own. Gyges, the once lowly shepherd, got everything he secretly wanted, and all with the aid of his magic ring and its incredible power of invisibility.[1]

In Plato's *Republic*, Glaucon recounts this tale during an encounter with Socrates. Socrates wants to argue that there is a real, fixed, external form of justice, and that to develop oneself in relation to this moral order is intrinsically valuable with virtue its own reward. Glaucon, playing devil's advocate, challenges Socrates with the legend of Gyges, in which he says that the "moral" of the story is that if one could become invisible then "No man would keep his hands off what was not his own when he could safely take what he liked out of the market, or go into houses and lie with anyone at his pleasure, or kill or release from prison whom he would, and in all respects be like a God among men."[2] Socrates must therefore contend with this objection that morality is merely a guise that we use in order to maintain a good reputation among others and get ahead. If we could only become invisible, and thereby unaccountable for our actions, vice would be the true reward. In other words, we would be most happy if we had the power to act freely on our darker animalistic impulses—to act with unremitting aggression and selfishness in the pursuit and satisfaction of our own untold desires. The only reason we do not, he says, the only reason most of us act "morally" at all, is not because we find some ultimate value in being good for goodness sake, but rather because if we all had free reign to do what we *really* wanted, then we *ourselves* would become vulnerable to others seeking the satisfaction of their own selfish, unrestrained appetites in this wolf eat wolf world.

Rather than take that risk, we instead collectively make an implicit compromise with each other that we will not harm one another so that in return we will be afforded mutual protection. Otherwise, despite the temporary maniacal highs of letting loose with our most primal instincts, we'd all be worse for the wear. This, Glaucon says, is the true, and ignoble, origin of justice; it is merely a submission to a lesser evil. It is better to go on a mutual diet than to eat and be eaten. Morality, according to this view, is therefore simply of instrumental value, that which allows one to earn a positive reputation, gain status, and reap the most rewards from society. Being immoral or amoral would probably make us most satisfied, if we could only get away with it.

This contrarian, almost *realpolitik* view of morality, continues to echo across time and across civilizations. We see modern thinkers from Thomas Hobbes to Sigmund Freud defending a similar view on morality as that devilishly presented by Glaucon. For those who wish to think better of human nature, that we are at heart only gentle and loving creatures who want to be "good," these thinkers would implore us to look more soberly at our human history. It is a bitter trail of exploitation, rape, slavery, and genocide, the most brutal atrocities still fresh in our minds, and new ones filling the books daily. Freud says:

> The element of truth behind all this, which people are so ready to disavow, is that men are not gentle creatures who want to be loved, and who at the most can defend themselves if they are attacked; they are, on the contrary, creatures among whose instinctual endowments is to be reckoned a powerful share of aggressiveness. As a result, their neighbour is for them not only a potential helper or sexual object, but also someone who tempts them to satisfy their aggressiveness on him, to exploit his capacity for work without compensation, to use him sexually without his consent, to seize his possessions, to humiliate him, to cause him pain, to torture and to kill him.[3]

We are all too aware of human society's propensity toward breakdown and chaos—toward explosion, war, and carnage: of everyday people, transformed like werewolves, into collective manias of bloodthirsty machete-wielding killers—of Rwanda, Syria, the Holocaust. Freud might say that this is the wild primitive beast contained in humankind, let loose upon each other in an uncontrolled burst of aggression and destruction—*thanatos*, the death instinct in his teachings, the greatest impediment to civilization. Its potential lurks beneath the surface at all times—a monster lying unseen beneath the black ocean. It seethes, knowing no good or evil, not being beyond it, but rather beneath it, and every once in a while, with little warning, it bursts out of the darkness and feeds our collective nightmares: of flesh-eating walking dead trampling over the order and design we've imposed on nature—the fences and walls we've constructed to keep the demons at bay, to tame this bloody instinct for death and destruction.

To push against this entropic nature of the universe, for stability to resolve, for comfort and security to reign for humankind, mass societal organization built on designated roles and programs for carrying out functions of the greater whole are conjured and maintained. Here we find the rules and commands of law and morality that keep our destructive urges in check, that make us tame, controlled, docile, thereby transforming the inner-beast, whipping us into a civilized human being. The collective, that depends on this civilizing effect, thereby overcomes the unruly will of the one, of that satiated brute. Civilization emerges and crawls out from a primitive state of nature. On this view, there is no true justice or real moral order apart from that which is socially imposed.

For Freud, in a prior state of nature, power is exerted through simple brutality—the selfish and aggressive interests of the dominant individual. Civilization, by contrast, and its tamed social order, arises from the power of the majority that constrains all individuals into obeying a "moral" order based on the interests of the greater good:

> Human life in common is only made possible when a majority comes together which is stronger than any separate individual and which remains united against all separate individuals. The power of this community is then set up as "right" in opposition to the power of the individual, which is condemned as "brute force." This replacement of the power of the individual by the power of the community constitutes the decisive step of civilization. The essence of it lies in the fact that the members of the community restrict themselves in their possibilities of satisfaction, whereas the individual knew no such restrictions.[4]

Freud would presumably believe that if individuals were shielded from the power of the majority around them, then one's repressed beastly instincts would spew forth from the *id*, the primal unconscious, and that many if not everyone would ultimately be delighted to kill the king, seduce the queen, and steal the empire, just like Gyges. Today, we have at least *some* empirical evidence that lends support to this view.

THE DIGITAL RING OF GYGES

At the dawn of the Internet age, the sudden vast new power of digital anonymity, to become practically invisible online from those around you, was already apparent. A famous 1993 New Yorker cartoon illustrates this realization with a dog typing on a computer, remarking to his canine companion that "on the Internet, no one knows you're a dog." For over two decades now, netizens have been able to explore the endless digital superhighway of virtual experiences with their "real-world" identities shielded from the society of the "real-world" people around them. In other words, we have all been democratically bestowed our very own digital Ring of Gyges.

In the ancient tale of the magic ring, Gyges' first action upon attaining the power of invisibility was to sneak into the king's bedroom and seduce the queen. This represents, among other things, an enormous de-inhibition of Gyges' sexual impulses. With digital invisibility, or anonymity, we also see a clear de-inhibiting effect on sexuality. Most notably, consumption of hardcore pornographic videos has exploded. What was once relegated to seedy corners of the city where no "decent" person would dare to go, or certainly not be caught dead by anyone he knew, has become essentially a mainstream staple of modern entertainment, albeit consumed in the shadows. Online pornographic sites now receive more web traffic than Netflix, Amazon, and Twitter combined.[5] On Pornhub alone, "In 2016, the human race watched a grand total of 91,980,225,000 videos . . . clocking in 23,000,000,000 total visits to the site and 4,599,000,000 hours of porn watched, enough to last 191,625,000 days, or 5,246 centuries."[6]

Next, as for stealing, Glaucon claimed that if people were made invisible, they would take anything they like out of the market. This appears to have proven correct as well, at least for the market of digital goods. A 2013 study showed that nearly half of Americans actively steal digital media, with that number jumping to a walloping 70 percent with younger demographics.[7] Without an electronic store-keeper keeping a lookout, people take whatever they like, to the tune of 30 billion songs illegally downloaded in the five years from 2004 to 2009 alone.[8] The music in our ears and the movies in our eyes that once would have been paid for are widely stolen when the digital Ring of Gyges is placed on.

Finally, Glaucon foretold that with invisibility we would unleash a wave of violence upon one another, killing anyone we please. Here it is slightly harder to discern this effect since, while sexuality has generally been shunned, a love of violence has always been widely celebrated. Today, young and old alike spend countless hours engaged in realistic and gratuitous simulated carnage in video games like the best-selling franchises *Grand Theft Auto* and *Call of Duty*, and we do so with a relatively clear conscious. We go home and blow the brains out of realistic human simulations. By contrast to this virtual nightmare, in the daily interactions we have with one another, in the light of day, in the office, in the supermarket, around the town, this human aggression is largely contained: thumbs up and smiles all around. The stark contrast between these two sides of the human, between the hidden beast, and the tamed civilian, is made clear.

It is no surprise then that with online anonymity, hidden behind a cloak, an aggressive inner-beast has been widely set free to roam: the troll. The troll is commonly understood to be those for whom online anonymity has brought out some of the worst in humanity with hate speech, harassment, or worse, that knows practically no bounds. The online troll has the potential to be utterly overwhelming, unhinged, hostile, and threatening; they may hunt in packs, in online hit mobs, and they can take a serious toll on other people's lives. In the now-infamous GamerGate controversy, for example, a group of female video game developers and critics spoke out against the widespread misogyny and sexual violence commonly found in video games, which they heavily documented. They subsequently became a target of a massive and aggressively vile online intimidation campaign against them. Anita Sarkeesian, one of the main targets, became harassed online by a virtual mob on a daily basis. Receiving death threats to her and her family, she fled her home after the location of her apartment was revealed online—doxing—which is a typical end result of troll-mob intimidation campaigns.

As if to prove Sarkeesian's point about the impact of violence toward women in video games, here is a small sampling of what people have said to her by the dozens in a typical week: "BITCH . . . I HOPE YOU GET FUCKING RAPED U FUCKING WHORE"; "the only question left is will [she] be raped first or killed first or both or?"; "imma kill u and rape u."[9] If one were to speak this way to someone 'in real life' (IRL), it would likely have substantial repercussions for the perpetrator, and that's partly why you rarely hear it, and if you do hear such verbal assaults and threats, it may become a scandal or violate the law. But, on the Internet such assaults are common, as being anonymous, it has no effect on what others think of you "in real life"—no effect on one's "real world" reputation. One can become irresponsible.

While the GamerGate mob represents some of the worst of the worst trolls, a survey found nearly a third of Millennial Americans confessing to having 'trolled' someone online, a number that in reality is likely higher as this figure represents only those who *admitted* to such behavior.[10] Notably, nearly 80 percent of respondents reported that anonymity contributes to trolling,[11] and nearly 70 percent of eighteen- to twenty-nine-year-olds have experienced online harassment.[12]

Over two thousand years later, perhaps Glaucon's challenge to Socrates about human nature and the origins of justice and morality has new evidence ruling in its favor. Once invisible, it appears that a critical mass of people seem to be, at least digitally, "lying" with whom they want at pleasure, taking whatever they like out of the market, and in a sense killing anyone they like as well, at least in terms of unleashing unremitting violent hostility and aggression online in a way that would be unimaginable for most people amidst the eyes of their peers. Freud might say that shielded from the strength of the majority the instincts for unbridled sex and violence buried within the *id* are collectively unleashed. This is the power of anonymity and, *vice versa*, the power of surveillance and reputation.

One might reasonably object here that it surely can't be anonymity, or invisibility, that has led to this breakdown of civilization in the digital world because in a sense everyone is quite the opposite of being invisible on the net. In most cases every pornographic view, every pirated download, every trollish comment, practically every digital step we take is tracked by some government and/ or corporate entity with a degree of detail unfathomable in analog eras. It is all on our very permanent records somewhere in some cloud linked to our very personal IP addresses.

But that is the salient point that Internet anonymity illustrates about human behavior: people are not so very concerned about what someone out there in some shadowy bureaucracy knows and keeps on file—the porn sites they visit, or the trollish comments they have made online. They are rather much more concerned about what the mass of ordinary people around them think; they care about their reputations which is ultimately Glaucon's conclusion in his devilish challenge to Socrates as to why people act justly at all. In other words, surveillance by one's peers may have a much more inhibiting effect on our everyday speech and behavior than even the massive surveillance and data collection that is being undertaken by government and corporate agents. It is what society thinks of us, of one's reputation, that probably keeps most of us up at night.

Being seen by others, perhaps merely being seen by others, can be enough to turn us from wolves into dogs, from beasts into domesticated animals, from man's worst enemy into man's "best friend." E.L. Godkin, founder of *The Nation*, writes that, "the love of reputation is the most powerful motive to good conduct—perhaps the very strongest guarantee the community has for the good conduct—of the citizen"; social order is maintained, "by the desire for the applause and good will of [one's] neighbors, comparatively very little by the fear of the penal code."[13] In other words, behavior is kept in check, civilization is maintained, the conventions of law and of morality are followed, not just by authorities watching from above, but perhaps more so by all the everyday people watching one another and the judgments we make on each other's speech and behavior.

One might therefore readily conclude from the above portraits of the mayhem that ensues when people become invisible that we need more cameras, more monitoring, that we need to all keep a "loving" watchful eye on each other at all times lest there be a breakdown of the morality and social norms that hold us together, with entropy and chaos as a result. This would not be an unreasonable reaction given the moral regression that clearly can occur when anonymous and shielded from responsibility and accountability for one's words and actions. It helps explain some of the underlying impetus for the strong forces that are being unleashed that work against privacy and anonymity, that seek to shine a much brighter public spotlight on our day-to-day words and actions. I refer to the force of radical transparency that is now marching across the world enabled through our new technologies, in particular social media, search engines, and smart devices.

What is radical transparency? It is a vision of a world where very little privacy remains, where to use the words of Google's former CEO Erich Schmidt, "everything is available, knowable, and recorded by everyone all the time."[14] Advancing society toward a state of radical transparency appears to be a founding ideological vision that has guided some of the most powerful agents in the world of our developing information and communication technologies. For example, David Kirkpatrick in his 2010 book, *The Facebook Effect*, writes that, "Facebook is founded on a radical social premise—that an inevitable enveloping transparency will overtake modern life."[15] Zuckerberg and other key colleagues believed that "In a more 'open and transparent' world, people will be held to the consequences of their actions and be more likely to behave responsibly."[16] In other words, "more visibility makes us better people."[17]

As we will explore below, whether through an inevitable force out of anyone's control, or through the deliberate manipulations of Silicon Valley executives, or a combination of both, we are heading toward an increasingly transparent world, with our lives being made increasingly visible to be watched and judged by each other online. Through the Internet and social media, we are becoming exposed to social pressures on a scale beyond anything before possible. Anonymity and privacy are rapidly being pulled from society as the light of a billion smart devices shines across all social spheres.

The central concern in this book is that the force of social pressure being unleashed through our ICTs can become too great. While some accountability is necessary for a functioning society, social interference in our lives can go too far getting down into the very contours of our likes and dislikes, ultimately becoming oppressive, coercing us toward opinions that are not our own, and conventions and morals that are not good for oneself or one's community, but only for maintaining a positive reputation among the public at large. Being accountable to everyone all the time, without enough refuge of anonymity and privacy in our day-to-day lives, our IRL lives, is harmful to our well-being. I will argue that the force of radical transparency, even if well intentioned as a check on our more beastly instincts, is a threat to our individuality, to the integrity of our communities, and to the pursuit of happiness.

MASS JUDGMENT ON THE WORLD WIDE WEB

In the previous section, we looked at how our new ICTs are enabling anonymity for our actions in cyberspace. We can put on our digital Ring of Gyges and explore and say all sorts of things without any effect on our reputation. But our ICTs are simultaneously giving rise to the polar opposite dynamic at the same time; that is, a culture of "sharing" and surveillance, where our thoughts, words, and actions are broadcast to a global audience for permanent viewing and judgment with possibly devastating consequences.

In some extreme cases of transparency and hyperexposure on the Internet, many of which have already occurred, one's most private moments, intended for either no audience, or for only a very small group, have been ripped out of a private context, and blasted quickly across the entire World Wide Web, the greatest medium of publicity that has ever existed. One's most random private moments may no longer remain private, but can suddenly become public on an unbelievable scale out of one's control.

One of the first, if not *the* first example of this phenomenon, occurred in 2002 when an overweight fourteen-year-old boy left behind a personal video he made of himself performing Star Wars lightsaber moves with a golf ball retriever in a high school TV studio. He had been practicing for a Star Wars parody film that he was creating with other students to be shown at a gala. The video was a very unrefined performance since he was just goofing around, and he never intended for this private video to be seen by others. He reasonably didn't think anyone would care to watch it so he left it on the studio shelf presumably to be referred to later as he made the polished parody film. But when three of his classmates discovered the tape, they converted it into a digital file and shared it on Kazaa, a then-popular peer-to-peer (P2P) file-sharing program.

What started out as school-wide humiliation quickly jumped from those closed physical confines into the amorphous online globally networked public. By 2006, it was uploaded to YouTube, where it has since received, all told, nearly a billion views. The student became a symbol, losing his name, being dubbed "The Star Wars Kid." His video became a frequent staple for parody and ridicule in pop culture both at the grassroots level, with countless YouTube parodies, and at the upper-echelons with prominent late-night hosts performing their own parodies on national television. On top of this global public humiliation, many of the online comments the high schooler received were mercilessly cruel, and he was frequently exhorted to kill himself. The young teenager was understandably devastated by the experience. He quit school and entered a psychiatric ward with severe depression.

Never before was it possible for something like this to have occurred. His trauma was uniquely a product of the Internet and a phenomenon of unwanted publicity of ordinary people in their everyday lives and their random passing occurrences spiraling out of one's control. While the Star Wars Kid is an extreme example, like a nuclear bomb, its threat affects the dynamics of our social actions today as we loom under this very real possibility of unwanted viral exposure on a potentially global scale.

On a smaller, but ubiquitous scale, this dynamic of one's formerly private life being played out in the open, in front of an indefinitely large audience, is becoming a default condition in society. Take, for example, the popular music streaming service Spotify. On the app, we are encouraged to connect our account to social media so that what we are listening to can be viewed by hundreds or thousands of other people in real time. It changes things, perhaps subtly, but pervasively.

Spotify is aware of how this new social dynamic of transparency affects people's personal listening experiences. They therefore offer a "private session" mode in which the user can temporarily turn off the perpetual broadcast of information about what one is listening to for one's social media followers.

Users of course don't have to connect their accounts to social media, but being connected to social media is also increasingly the norm and expectation. In other words, publicity is almost becoming the social default, and privacy from the collective gaze of others becoming the temporary exception.

Spotify is probably one of the more benign examples of this phenomenon of ambient awareness of each other's activities in what privacy scholar David Lyon calls a "culture of surveillance,"[18] where "sharing" is the norm, but it echoes a dynamic that is taking hold in modern society generally via the Internet, social media, search engines, and ubiquitous recording devices. Transparency in our day-to-day lives, in our thoughts and activities, is becoming the new normal. This state of "public by default" represents a fundamental historical shift in our relations as individuals to society. What used to be internal private decision-making is now becoming regularly blasted to an amorphous group for collective judgment in real time thereby blurring the line between individual reflection and choice and decision-making powers by the collective.

Today on the Internet and social media, we are being regularly exposed and judged by a crowd of people on a scale that was never previously possible. For one, billions around the world are now on social media—more so the younger one is, which speaks clearly to the trends of where this is all going in the future. Facebook alone, the largest social network, has over 2.6 billion monthly active users worldwide at the time of this writing—a major percentage of the entire human species, and a much larger population of users than inhabitants of any nation on Earth.[19] The rapid spread of the Internet and social networking has enabled a massive and growing quantitative increase in the *size* of the group by which one may find oneself evaluated and judged.

In addition to the *size* of the group, there is a major jump in the *breadth* of people in this group watching and judging the individual. Whereas in the past people usually said goodbye to most of the acquaintances that surrounded them at various times of their lives, save for a few rare gems, today people carry around practically everyone in their pocket picked up throughout different times of their lives, sometimes pretty randomly, to continually observe and judge them on an ongoing basis. Because one may be subjected to exposure from *anyone* on the net, the *breadth* of people that one may be potentially judged by is, practically speaking, endless. An ordinary person's thought or behavior captured on the net can be easily spread to an entire city, state, a nation, or practically the whole of Earth's human population (and potentially beyond). Even with deliberate efforts made to control the spread of information, such as Snapchat's disappearing pictures paradigm, because of the nature of digital media—its ability to be captured and spread virally—digital media is never really fully containable by the individual or impermanent.

While never before have ordinary people been regularly subject to this sheer *size* and *breadth* of peer evaluation enabled by our new ICTs, people have additionally never been subject to this *frequency* of collective evaluation. We are literally plugged into our devices from the moment we wake until we sleep. Nearly three-quarters of all Americans sleep by their smartphones[20] with 90 percent of eighteen- to twenty-nine-year-olds reporting they have slept by their smartphone.[21] Over 80 percent of all consumers check their phones within an hour before going to sleep and nearly 90 percent check their phone within an hour of waking up.[22] And once awake, we check our phones constantly. Gen Zers check their phone on average every three minutes,[23] while phone users as a whole check their phones on average over 150 times a day.[24] We are glued to our devices, constantly plugging into the global network, continuously connected to hundreds or thousands of other people, indirectly to the whole world, and frequently given opportunity to collectively watch, judge, rate, and rank our peers, and have the same done to us in return.

Our ICTs enable not only a major increase in the *frequency* of collective evaluation, but there is also a major increase in the *clarity* of that evaluation. Everywhere on the net there is a convenient "one-click" button for the ordinary person to instantly render judgment on one another. Every thought one posts, every word one says, every picture shared, even one's basic existence on the net, is given an aggregated score, and we constantly check on our status to see how we fare in the eyes of the networked collective. Social media renders social judgments hyper-apparent for us in a way they never were before, quantified as a numerical grade often on a digital scoreboard available for all to see.

Never before has so much about us—our thoughts, words, and actions—been witnessed by so many others and subject to their judgment. The *scope* of peer exposure and evaluation has increased to an unprecedented level. Globally, we are collectively posting a whopping 1.8 billion digital images to Facebook, Instagram, Flickr, Snapchat, and WhatsApp *every day*.[25] That is 657 billion photos a year,[26] or "the rough equivalent of one photo for every person on the planet—including billions of people in the developing world who have no access to technology—in less than a week."[27] It is estimated that 8,796 photos are shared per *second* on Snapchat.[28] Meanwhile, over a billion users upload more than 400 hours of video to YouTube each *minute,* the equivalent of 1,000 days of video every hour.[29] What these statistics illustrate is a sense of just how much data on people is collectively being shared to a global audience every day—a mind-boggling amount of detailed information. As has been said, a picture says a thousand words—and these are just the transference of photos and videos, not to mention posts of people's locations, who they are with, what they are listening to, watching, reading, thinking, and so forth.

Finally, there is a digital *permanency* to both what is made available for judgment and often the results of the judgment itself. Unlike memories, digital media does not fade, its reels do not decay, and it can resurface in crystal clear form, reborn anew with each post, at any time. Media uploaded today may be around for practically eternity and the rendered judgments, and their effects on one's reputation, may be permanently stamped. The embarrassing things that one was judged for in the past are not forgotten. They do not fade with time. What happened at any time might as well have happened today.

Through huge quantitative increases in the *size* and *breadth* of the group by which one may be evaluated, the *frequency* with which one is watched and judged, the *clarity* by which those crowdsourced judgments are rendered, the *scope* of one's thought, speech, and activities that are monitored and evaluated, and the *permanency* with which one's life is exposed and judged, there is evidence that we are at the early stages of the sort of radically transparent society many Silicon Valley acolytes had imagined. The intensity of the pressures of the crowd upon the individual, of a collectivity that can span across oceans, is being technologically ratcheted up to a degree and scale that were simply unfathomable in the past.

Meanwhile, as the individual is made increasingly transparent, hypervisible as our day-to-day lives are broadcast or threaten to be broadcast online, the digital crowd watching on the other end becomes collectively invisible. Because of the anonymous nature of being in a crowd, especially online, the result is often that the basest instincts of human nature, unleashed through the digital Ring of Gyges, give rise to a hostile mass that can be as brute a beast collectively as the invisible wolfish individual. Anonymous, collective, and invisible power online, is exercised with relatively little restraint against the individual who becomes hypervisible, whose words and actions are exposed to the world in a way never possible before. This forms an extremely asymmetrical relation of power that makes individuals or small groups extremely vulnerable before this massive collective entity. The individual can in turn watch and judge others as part of a crowd themselves, but one's interactions online maintain this fundamental asymmetric dynamic of the individual radically exposed before an indefinitely large, anonymous, and characteristically hostile crowd for lasting judgment.

EXPOSURE AND CONFORMITY

To begin to understand why radical transparency is problematic, we need to understand how too much exposure of our lives before the crowd can begin to affect one's liberty. To think about how this may occur there is perhaps no better place to start than John Stuart Mill's "On Liberty." Extolling the virtues of freedom of speech, and freedom of action, the essay is best known for its articulation of what the proper limits of government interference ought to be. Yet, what is commonly lost in evaluations of this work is the overwhelming concern that Mill expressed, not just for the kind of infringements on liberty that the state poses, but more so for the threat to individual liberty posed by the masses of ordinary people. This threat of social overreach by ordinary citizens comes about not through legal coercion, as with the state, but through the power of insidious social pressures that push an individual to conform to a shared public opinion on how we should live our lives. Through the power of public opinion, Mill says:

> Society can and does execute its own mandates: and if it issues wrong mandates instead of right, or any mandates at all in things with which it ought not to meddle, it practises a social tyranny more formidable than many kinds of political oppression, since, though not usually upheld by such extreme penalties, it leaves fewer means of escape, penetrating much more deeply into the details of life, and enslaving the soul itself.[30]

If we become too subject to what other people think and other people try too hard to impose their opinion upon us, then facing these pressures, we may abnegate our choice and self-determination, instead following the will of the crowd, even if technically we have the liberty to do what we will without external restraint. We in a sense come to restrain and censor *ourselves*.

To be truly free then, in Mill's view, one must not only be free from unjustifiable coercion, but also to have the inner capacity to be able to choose one's path for oneself even if others disapprove. This requires the development of an inner strength and will which can be easily stifled starting at a very young age in a society that actively discourages and attempts to stomp out any deviation from its conventions. This is not to say that any path an individual may choose is a good one, or that what others think should always be ignored. But Mill stresses we need the ability to critically reflect on our choices, to hear what the crowd thinks, but to ultimately choose for ourselves.

It is through our ability for reason and self-determination that we find what is right for ourselves, develop our individuality, fulfill our highest potential, and in turn become happier people. But if the pressure of public opinion becomes too great, with too little ability to shield our lives from that pressure, that inner-voice of self-reflection can become squelched in a potentially mindless conformity toward social conventions. We become like automatons of society. We risk losing ourselves in the process, not becoming our highest individual self, but rather a replicable, expendable part of an undifferentiated mass.

Mill rails against a general trend he sees toward mass conformity under the pressure of public opinion, of a general disappearance of individuals who are willing, or even have developed the inner capacities to be able to buck custom and convention and do what they feel is right for their own lives. This is not to say that Mill bashes deference to custom or fails to sees its value. The existence of customs, he says, is evidence of free decisions made by one's forebears that turned out to work fairly well for them. To that extent, one should show some degree of respect to custom, and at least fairly consider that customary ways might at times be worth adopting for oneself. But as Mill observes, customary ways of living do not necessarily fit all people at all times: "A man cannot get a coat or a pair of boots to fit him unless they are either made to his measure, or he has a whole warehouseful to choose from: and is it easier to fit him with a life than with a coat, or are human beings more like one another in their whole physical and spiritual conformation than in the shape of their feet?"[31]

A free and happy society would be one that, while perhaps teaching the ways of prevailing conventions, is also open-minded about new ways of doing things, is self-reflective on the value of altering customs for new circumstances, and actively encourages individuals to do what is right for their own lives and to question the authority of custom. But instead, the general trend that Mill sees is an attempt by society through the collective power of hostile social pressures, "to fetter the development, and, if possible, prevent the formation, of any individuality not in harmony with its ways, and compels all characters to fashion themselves upon the model of its own."[32]

Mill, however, is not a rebel without a cause. He does not value eccentricity for its own sake, unless society has become so massively conformed in its ways that the mere display of eccentricity in any capacity would at least have the value of demonstrating to others that individuals *can* break with convention. For Mill, full liberty means that at a certain age of adulthood, one has developed the emotional and intellectual capacities to make choices for oneself, including to evaluate prevailing customs, and decide which might be worth adopting and which should be ignored. This goes for the relatively trivial, such as one's taste in music, or for the much more personally impactful, such as the career choice or general life-path one follows. If on the other hand, one does something or "likes" something only because it is customary and everyone else is doing it or liking it, the person "makes no choice" at all.[33] One is rather told by society what to do and copies the order, like an imitating ape, without really choosing based on a deliberation of whether it is the right choice for oneself.

Over time, through becoming habituated by social pressures to follow custom in all matters of life, from what one does day to day to what one even allows oneself to think, Mill argues that the ability to exercise the inherent mental and emotional capacities that are needed to make personal choices for oneself weaken and atrophy, just like physical muscles that are left to wither without continual exercise. These capacities eventually become too weak to effectively take control of one's own path in life, to critically reflect on public opinion, and choose a direction for oneself, in relation to a range of concerns. Rather one learns to habitually echo the opinion and choices of the crowd, mindlessly going where the crowd goes, out of fear of social rejection.

But the conventions we become habituated to follow may only be of instrumental value for gaining social approval and a good reputation. As we become pressured to go along with the crowd we may lose that which would be *intrinsically* valuable to us, losing our deeper selves in the process. This is what Mill seems to mean by saying that the masses in their social tyranny have the power to enslave one's soul. One's soul, or psyche, becomes chained by society, constantly brought down into conformity, shaped into an ideal that is not one's own, until eventually there is no strength of character left. He says:

> Thus the mind itself is bowed to the yoke: even in what people do for pleasure, conformity is the first thing thought of; they like in crowds; they exercise choice only among things commonly done: peculiarity of taste, eccentricity of conduct, are shunned equally with crimes: until by dint of not following their own nature they have no nature to follow: their human capacities are withered and starved: they become incapable of any strong wishes or native pleasures, and are generally without either opinions or feelings of home growth, or properly their own.[34]

It is not that people choose to follow custom "in preference to what suits their own inclination. It does not occur to them to have any inclination, except for what is customary."[35] Following the orders of society becomes habitual trained behavior from a young age and essentially becomes automatic. The person habituated into conformity thereby becomes an empty vessel, an automaton programmed by society's conventions. But Mill says, "Human nature is not a machine to be built after a model, and set to do exactly the work prescribed for it, but a tree, which requires to grow and develop itself on all sides, according to the tendency of the inward forces which make it a living thing."[36] To really be free and happy, we must therefore learn to break with custom where we see fit, to not be automatically directed by public opinion—that which society approves—but to rather be guided by our own internal spontaneously experienced nature, and to consistently exercise our capacity to make rational choices of our own choosing that foster our own individual potential in its own inner-directed shape. Otherwise, the inner freedom of the individual is left lacking, and one is not truly free even if one is relatively free from the physical coercion of the state.

To feel a sense of belonging and approval, we may be willing to escape ourselves, to abandon our individual desires, to like not what we like, but what others expect us to like, to not be what we want to be, but what others expect us to be, to cease being an individual. Conformity allows us to feel part of a crowd, accepted, just like everyone else, and thereby brings us the feeling of connection that as social animals we so desperately seek, even if only a semblance of connection. But it comes at a cost to our freedom, to our ability to make choices of our own determination, based on an individual judgment of what is good for ourselves and the right thing do. We become so used to simply following the order of the crowd, becoming afraid of stepping out of line with public opinion, that we become habituated toward being, practically speaking, automated.

The digitally connected crowd, via social media, smart devices, and search engines, may greatly amplify this power of social conformity. Through the ever-increasing gaze of a pervasive audience online, we may become overly pressured, even coerced toward collective opinion, as social media's mechanism of likes, dislikes, friends, and followers constantly subjects us to the crowd's judgment along with that gaze. There is therefore a risk that our developing technological apparatus, if it continues along some of the current and possible trajectories that I will warn against in this book, presents a growing threat to individuality, one that builds upon lines from the past, but ramped up exponentially with the exponential growth of technology.

NOTES

1. Plato, "Book II," in *The Republic*, trans. Benjamin Jowett, The Internet Classics Archive, accessed July, 23, 2018, http://classics.mit.edu/Plato/republic.3.ii.html.

2. Plato, "Book II."

3. Sigmund Freud, *Civilization and Its Discontents*, trans. James Strachey (New York: W. W. Norton & Company, 1961), 68–69.

4. Freud, *Civilization and Its Discontents*, 49.

5. Alexis Kleinman, "Porn Sites Get More Visitors Each Month Than Netflix, Amazon And Twitter Combined," *HuffPost*, December 6, 2017, http://www.huffingtonpost.com/entry/internet-porn-stats_n_3187682.html.

6. "Most Popular Porn Searches – What Porn Do People Search For?," *Daily News Gazette*, last modified January 9, 2017, http://dailynewsgazette.com/2017/01/09/most-popular-porn-searches-what-porn-do-people-search-for.

7. Joe Karaganis and Lennart Renkema, "Copy Culture in the US and Germany," The American Assembly Columbia University, accessed November 6, 2018, http://piracy.americanassembly.org/wp-content/uploads/2013/01/Copy-Culture.pdf.

8. "Why Does the RIAA Hate Torrent Sites So Much?" *Music Business Worldwide*, December 6, 2014, http://www.musicbusinessworldwide.com/why-does-the-riaa-hate-torrent-sites-so-much/.

9. Anita Sarkeesian, "One Week of Harassment on Twitter," *Feminist Frequency*, accessed November 6, 2018, http://femfreq.tumblr.com/post/109319269825/one-week-of-harassment-on-twitter.

10. Jake Gammon, "Over a Quarter of Americans have Made Malicious Online Comments," *YouGov*, October 20, 2014, https://today.yougov.com/topics/politics/articles-reports/2014/10/20/over-quarter-americans-admit-malicious-online-comm.

11. Gammon, "Over a Quarter."

12. Maeve Duggan, "Online Harassment 2017," *Pew Research Center*, July 11, 2017, https://www.pewresearch.org/internet/2017/07/11/online-harassment-2017/.

13. Edward Godkin, "The Rights of the Citizen, IV—To His Own Reputation," *Scribner's Magazine* 8, no. 1 (1890): 59.

14. Holman W. Jenkins Jr., "Google and the Search for the Future." *The Wall Street Journal*, August, 14, 2010. https://www.wsj.com/articles/SB10001424052748704901104575423294099527212.

15. David Kirkpatrick, *The Facebook Effect: The Inside Story of the Company that is Connecting the World* (New York: Simon and Schuster, 2010), 200.

16. Kirkpatrick, *The Facebook Effect*, 200.

17. Kirkpatrick, *The Facebook Effect*, 210–11.

18. David Lyon, *The Culture of Surveillance: Watching as a Way of Life* (John Wiley & Sons, 2018).

19. J. Clement, "Number of Facebook Users Worldwide: 2008–2018," *Statista*, April 30, 2020, https://www.statista.com/statistics/264810/number-of-monthly-active-facebook-users-worldwide/.

20. "Trends in Consumer Mobility Report," Bank of America Corporation, accessed November 6, 2018, https://promo.bankofamerica.com/mobilityreport/assets/images/2015-Trends-in-Consumer-Mobility-Report_FINAL.pdf.

21. Amanda Lenhart, "Cell Phones and American Adults," *Pew Research Center*, September 2, 2010, http://www.pewinternet.org/2010/09/02/cell-phones-and-american-adults/.

22. "Global Mobile Consumer Survey: US Edition," Deloitte, accessed November 6, 2018, https://www2.deloitte.com/us/en/pages/technology-media-and-telecommunications/articles/global-mobile-consumer-survey-us-edition.html.

23. "The Generation Z Study of Tech Intimates," CommScope, accessed November 6, 2018, https://www.commscope.com/Insights/uploads/2017/09/Generation-Z-Report.pdf.

24. Mary Meeker and Liang Wu, "Internet Trends D11 Conference," SlideShare.net, accessed November 6, 2018, https://www.slideshare.net/kleinerperkins/kpcb-internet-trends-2013/52-Mobile_Users_Reach_to_Phone.

25. Rose Eveleth, "How Many Photographs of You Are Out There In the World," *The Atlantic*, November 2, 2015, http://www.theatlantic.com/technology/archive/2015/11/how-many-photographs-of-you-are-out-there-in-the-world/413389/.

26. Eveleth, "How Many Photographs."

27. Jim Edwards, "Planet Selfie: We're Now Posting a Staggering 1.8 Billion Photos Every Day," *Business Insider*, May 28, 2014, https://www.businessinsider.com/were-now-posting-a-staggering-18-billion-photos-to-social-media-every-day-2014-5.

28. "How Big is Snapchat?," *CEWE Photoworld*, accessed November 6, 2018, https://cewe-photoworld.com/how-big-is-snapchat/.

29. Mark Robertson, "500 Hours Of Video Uploaded To Youtube Every Minute [Forecast]," *Tubularinsights*, November 13, 2015, http://tubularinsights.com/hours-minute-uploaded-youtube/.

30. John Stuart Mill, *On Liberty* (Ontario: Batoche Books, 2001), 9, accessed November 6, 2018, https://eet.pixel-online.org/files/etranslation/original/Mill,%20On%20Liberty.pdf.

31. Mill, *On Liberty*, 63.
32. Mill, *On Liberty*, 9.
33. Mill, *On Liberty*, 9.
34. Mill, *On Liberty*, 57.
35. Mill, *On Liberty*, 57.
36. Mill, *On Liberty*, 55.

Chapter 2

Social Media as an Escape from Freedom

The twentieth-century psychologist and existential philosopher Erich Fromm writes that "One can only understand the power of the fear to be different, the fear to be only a few steps away from the herd, if one understands the depths of the need not to be separated."[1] We will now briefly examine some historical background to help situate this fear of being different, of being separate from the group, as it manifests itself today through social media.

For over a million years, humans evolved living together in small packs of hunters and gatherers. Their interdependence was so great that being rejected from a group might mean death or a severe deprivation of basic needs.[2] From this evolutionary perspective, our species' upbringing has bestowed us with an instinctual need for belonging.[3] If one is threatened with rejection from others, pushed away into isolation, it is therefore extremely painful. Like the physical pains of hunger, the emotional pain of rejection and loneliness signals to us that we are being deprived of something we basically need.[4] Since we are deeply motivated to avoid rejection, we are therefore constantly driven to act in ways that will gain us group approval.[5] If we find ourselves caught doing something that angers or upsets others we care about, it triggers for us the powerful and painful feeling of *shame*.

In the earliest stages of human societies, in tribal living, individuals were pressured into group conformity through the constant threat of shame, and the terrible risk of being cast out of the group. Under such primitive social conditions, there was hardly any individuality or individual freedom. Rather, a person's life was dictated by rituals and religious obligations prescribed for practically all aspects of life. Tribal life, in the macro-sense, was entirely predictable, with expectations from the tribe that each member will "behave in a meticulously prescribed and collectively approved way."[6]

In the European Middle Ages, as tribal society was broken, one was hardly any more free as an individual than before. Rather, people in feudal societies could scarcely even conceive of themselves as individuals. They *were* their social role whether it be a peasant, an artisan, or a knight. As the medieval feudal caste system fell, it opened up new possibilities for individual freedom. Capitalism let the individual choose his path for himself, but Fromm argues this was a bittersweet victory. For while a capitalist society let people better determine the course of their lives, it also destroyed the comfort, security, belongingness, and sense of personal identity, based upon a God-given order, that the medieval system had granted. This newfound freedom left people on the one hand free, but on the other hand isolated and alone. Fromm says what developed is a *fear* of this freedom and the corresponding individual separateness from a group.

To cope with this fear of being free a variety of psychological "mechanisms of escape" arose that allowed people to feel the semblance of belongingness, but at the cost of losing themselves in a larger social body. The first such mechanism was the Protestant Reformation. Fromm argues that the leaders of the Reformation taught that one must seek salvation in submitting oneself entirely to obeying God, casting away one's individual desires and individual choice, which were framed as deeply sinful. Alongside this abandonment of individuality, Calvinism also introduced a requirement that humans devote unceasing effort toward moral perfection according to the word of God. This drive toward constant moral perfection gradually morphed into a drive for constant economic productivity. Submission was no longer to overtly external authorities, such as the Church, but rather to that of an inner guilty *conscience* that compelled one to work unceasingly.

A state of frantic activity, of unceasing compulsive work, helped to distract from and soothe the anxiety of aloneness, as well as the fears of one's impending death, and the possibility of not receiving salvation. Fromm says such compulsive work was of an irrational character because one's fate in the afterlife was, according to Calvinism, predetermined by God. In essence, the compulsive nature of work replicated the compulsive behaviors of someone with neurotic anxiety.

By the twentieth century, people found their escape from freedom through two different prevailing mechanisms. One is a submission to an authoritarian state. This was witnessed in the global rise of large totalitarian governments—Nazi Germany, Stalinist Russia, Fascist Italy, and so on—that were at their height during the time of Fromm's writing. The psychological "success" of this totalitarian escape mechanism, Fromm says, stems from its blending of both masochistic and sadistic tendencies found in the human psyche. On the one hand, the individual masochistically obliterates his individual self, sacrificing it to the whole, losing his feeling of isolation and individual powerlessness by becoming submerged as part of this larger power. The feeling of individual isolation and powerlessness is further overcome through the letting loose of sadistic drives by the pain, death, and destruction dictatorships allow to be inflicted on minorities, political opponents, and other nations.[7]

The other mechanism of escape from freedom that Fromm observed in modern democratic societies like the United States is what he terms, echoing Mill, "automaton conformity":

> This particular mechanism is the solution that the majority of normal individuals find in modern society. To put it briefly, the individual ceases to be himself; he adopts entirely the kind of personality offered to him by cultural patterns; and he therefore becomes exactly as all others are and as they expect him to be. The discrepancy between "I" and the world disappears and with it the conscious fear of aloneness and powerlessness. This mechanism can be compared with the protective coloring some animals assume. They look so similar to their surroundings that they are hardly distinguishable from them. The person who gives up his individual self and becomes an automaton, identical with millions of other automatons around him, need not feel alone and anxious any more. But the price he pays, however, is high; it is the loss of his self.[8]

Fromm asserts that compared to a totalitarian society, there is certainly a possibility of nonconformity in democracies, and it is sometimes found. But there has to be a mechanism for avoiding the terrible depths of the feeling of separation. Fromm contends, "people *want* to conform to a much higher degree than they are *forced* to conform, at least in the Western democracies."[9] Automaton conformity is in a sense freely turned toward as an attempt to overcome separation. One turns away from one's own freedom.

SOCIAL MEDIA AS THE NEW MECHANISM OF ESCAPE

In the 1940s and 1950s, when Fromm was writing, he lamented the vast conformity he observed in America that pushed an individual away from pursuing a life of one's own determination. At least at that time, however, many people experienced a relatively high level of regular face-to-face group interaction. But by the end of the twentieth century, as documented by Harvard sociologist Robert Putnam in *Bowling Alone*, participation in everyday communal organizations such as unions, parent–teachers associations, Boy Scouts, and so forth—however conformist these organizations may have been—had precipitously declined along with the social bonds these organizations had generated.[10]

When asked in an interview with *People* magazine what was responsible for the sudden decades-long slide away from one another, Putnam replied:

> I think the prime suspect is television. In 1949 fewer than 5 percent of American homes had a TV. By 1959, 90 percent owned one. The number of hours Americans spend in front of the television has been rising steadily . . . Studies have shown that the more hours people spend watching television, the less they trust each other . . . Television has distanced us from our neighbors.[11]

Now, moving into the twenty-first century, with the rise of the web and social media, being glued to the omnipresent screen is no longer solely an isolating experience, at least not on the surface. Through social media and the web, we can now talk back to and through the screen, and broadcast ourselves, become our own mini-television celebrities, with the chance to go viral and attain some sort of fame, to watch and be watched by each other, and in some flickering semblance, connect to one another again through the mediation of our devices. In the disconnected society that Putnam illustrated at the dawn of the Internet age, one that in many senses remains intact despite our devices—where most of us hardly know our neighbors beyond surface-level interactions (at best), where vast portions of society works in isolated offices and cubicles (or worse), where hardly any deep bonds of community exist—it is no wonder that social media has been so quickly gravitated toward.

Our quest for connection through our devices has become constant, and compulsive. In addition to the repetitive behavior of constant phone checking, there are also the microrepetitive behaviors of incessantly tapping, pinching, swiping, and otherwise touching our devices. If checking the phone is like a cigarette break, then touching the phone is like repeatedly drawing the cigarette to one's lips. One study found that the average person touches their device's display (tapping, pinching, swiping) over 2,600 times a day, or a million times a year. The top 10 percent heaviest users were found to touch their phone over 5,400 times a day.[12] Our constant reaching for the phone can be seen as a reaching for connection in a disconnected world, a physical manifestation of our need for belonging. But the compulsive nature of our ICT use is a sign that we are not getting our fill of the deeper belonging that we need to be happy.

If there is something troubling about the compulsive use of technology so common today, we don't, however, entirely have ourselves to blame. Our addictive behavior with our phones is no accident. Silicon Valley is well aware of our psychology, that we feel a deep need for belonging, and that even a semblance of social validation, of feeling "connected," can be exploited to drive us toward more "engaged" use of apps, which drives up their revenue through increased user-data collection and increased user-exposure to paid advertisements. Sean Parker, the founding President of Facebook has confessed:

> The thought process that went into building these applications, Facebook being the first of them . . . was all about: 'How do we consume as much of your time and conscious attention as possible?' And that means that we need to sort of give you a little dopamine hit every once in a while, because someone liked or commented on a photo or a post or whatever. And that's going to get you to contribute more content, and that's going to get you . . . more likes and comments. It's a social-validation feedback loop . . . exactly the kind of thing that a hacker like myself would come up with, because you're exploiting a vulnerability in human psychology. The inventors, creators—it's me, it's Mark [Zuckerberg], it's Kevin Systrom on Instagram, it's all of these people—understood this consciously. And we did it anyway.[13]

Dopamine is one of the main neurochemicals responsible for motivation and reward. Some Silicon Valley developers have been quite upfront about the use of findings from behavioral psychology and neuroscience to induce desired behavior. Probably the most blatant company was originally called Dopamine Labs. Their website touted up front: "Connect your app to our Persuasive AI and lift your engagement and revenue up to 30% by giving your users our perfect bursts of dopamine." The headlines on their website went on to say that, "User behavior isn't luck: (it's (neuro)science). A burst of dopamine doesn't *just* feel good: it's proven to re-wire user behavior and habits." When you clicked on a link that said "Learn the Science" on their site, it took you to the Wikipedia page for Operant Conditioning.[14]

B.F. Skinner, a Harvard behavior scientist from the 1950s, is the father of operant conditioning, a system that uses external rewards and punishments to adjust behavior through positive and negative reinforcements. To test his theories, Skinner created what he called operant conditioning chambers, also known today as Skinner boxes, in which he placed trainable animals like rats and pigeons. The cages contained levers that when pressed would dispense either a positive reinforcement, a reward of food pellets for example, or would negatively reinforce the desired behavior through stopping a punishment, for example, turning off a painful electrical current running through the metal of the cage once the lever was pressed. Through these simple systems of behavior modification, he was able to train rats and pigeons to push levers repeatedly on end to receive the rewards or avoid the punishments.

Skinner also experimented with different systems of reward schedules to see at what frequency the dispensing of rewards would produce the fastest amount of lever pushing for the longest amount of time. Interestingly, of all the different schedules of reinforcement he experimented with, if the Skinner box simply dispensed a food pellet every time the rat pressed the lever, the rat pressed the lever the *least* frequently and gave up pressing the fastest. In order to manipulate the rat to repeatedly press the lever most frequently for the longest amount of time what was needed was unpredictability in terms of rewards; that is, sometimes pressing the lever produced a pellet, sometimes none, sometimes two, and so forth. This unpredictability leads an animal to push the lever over and over again to see if it will get a reward. Skinner believed that the way these animals' behavior could be manipulated in his experiments was similar to the way our human behavior could be manipulated as well to produce desired behaviors.[15]

Today, the science of operant conditioning, as noted above, is being applied directly to create manipulative or 'persuasive' technology that pushes or 'nudges' our behavior in one direction or another. Many wealthy Silicon Valley developers have been students of B.J. Fogg, director of Stanford's Persuasive Tech Lab. Professor Fogg is the founder of a field known as captology, a word he coined which stands for the study of "computers as persuasive technologies." The idea behind captology is that the lessons of behavioral psychology going back to B.F. Skinner can be drawn upon in designing software that is intentionally made to "persuade" users toward a desired outcome, a change in attitude or behavior.[16] Whether the similarity between captology and "capture" was intentional or a coincidence, capturing its users is exactly what many "persuasive" technologies have managed to achieve. Such techniques were designed by Fogg with good intentions, for example, to get students to increase their usage of learning apps. But Fogg disappointedly laments that "I look at some of my former students and I wonder if they're really trying to make the world better, or just make money." He is increasingly troubled by the applications of his theories in tech design.[17]

For an application to thrive in the online economy, where prolonged use means the collection of more valuable data and more revenue-generating ad exposure, apps must keep your attention, they must get you hooked. Lessons for inducing behavior that trace from B.F. Skinner through B.J. Fogg into most of the applications we use today come in very handy. Most notably, perhaps, are push notifications. These constant signals pop up throughout the day, grab us and push us toward using the app. They are triggers that influence our behavior.

Other mainstays of Internet architecture similarly reflect knowledge gained from psychology and neuroscience. For example, when Facebook first introduced their icons for notifications and likes, they were colored blue, for coolness and subtlety, but also largely ignored. So Facebook changed the color to red, which is a trigger color, and people got hooked. Now red notifications are common Internet architecture.[18] Or, for example, consider the pull-to-refresh mechanism, which began on Twitter and now is also common on smartphone apps. The mechanism closely resembles the pulling of a slot machine. Each time a user pulls, they are faced with a variable reward schedule. You don't know what you're going to get. It could be a bunch of likes, comments, a job offer in your e-mail inbox, or it could be a big fat nothing. Some tech insiders allege that it is common knowledge in Silicon Valley that Instagram's algorithms are designed to purposefully withhold likes so that users might be disappointed with their haul of likes and check again and again to see if they've received more, thereby purposefully heightening the addicting effects of a variable reward schedule.[19] Like the rat in the cage, or the gambler at the slot machine, we pull again and again, to try and gain this "reward"—the reward of feeling accepted and belonging.

Like a drug, the use of apps becomes a coping mechanism, in this case specifically a coping mechanism for the isolated social conditions so prevalent in the modern world, as documented by Putnam. These apps give us at least a fleeting feeling of belonging, so we use them over and over throughout each day, like a cigarette habit, to try and get a fill of what we need. But while Silicon Valley has deliberately exploited our need for belonging and the lessons from psychology and neuroscience to induce compulsive use of their products, ultimately all that their app designs can offer is a slot machine-like device to get us hooked. They can't offer the full reward that comes from using the app, the coins in the slot machine so to speak. *We* offer the reward, the feeling of belonging, the dopamine shots that come through likes, hearts, friends, followers, and so on. We wind up as a collective middleman between what the app developers want, and the individual who becomes susceptible to the design and keeps compulsively using it to gain a fleeting feeling of connectedness.

Unlike a slot machine, with social media we don't put in a quarter in order to hopefully receive a larger reward. There the input is money for the anticipated output of more money. With our ICTs, the input is rather a piece of ourselves, some digital exposure of our thoughts, words, or behaviors to the collective crowd that is watching and judging on the other end of the device. Sometimes the digital crowd gives us hearts and likes, sometimes not, and sometimes we may even receive a punishment, and be made to feel ashamed in front of the crowd. Our words and behavior, inputted into the system, are thereby nudged and reinforced toward that which gains a reward or avoids a punishment from the large and relatively anonymous audience watching and judging on the other end of our devices.

Like the rat in the Skinner box, we press our devices over and over to seek out these rewards, but we seem to be never fully satisfied, and so we keep pushing, seeking a further reward. When we post online and people like it, the process reinforces our behavior to do that again, to offer a portrait of ourselves in a crowd-pleasing way that gains us our reward of likes, hearts, and followers, these digital tokens of belonging and esteem. Meanwhile, lurking outside on the periphery is always the thing we perhaps fear the most: isolation, rejection, and shame—being cast out of the group. This may underlie the widespread modern malady of the fear of missing out (FOMO). It's a fear—an anxiety—of being cast out. So in addition to the positive reinforcement of trying to please the crowd there is the negative reinforcement of trying to avoid being shamed and rejected, to participate, but to make sure to do so in a way that pleases the group, so that we feel like we belong.

Through this Skinner box-like design, we become incentivized and motivated not only to compulsively turn to our apps in order to soothe the anxiety of aloneness and give us a sense of control over our status, but this apparatus may reinforce conformed speech and behavior in the process, through rewarding that which is liked by the crowd and pushing us far away from that which might receive a punishment of disapproval and shame. The more social media merges with the entirety of our experiences, and the more our lives are broadcast from the inside out to the collective audience connected through the web, the more we become placed digitally into a world-encompassing Skinner box where we become directed by what pleases the crowd.

The mechanism of rating and following on the Internet, of collectively scoring one another, ramps up the degree of collective judgment and pressure to levels that in many ways were never before possible thereby leading us to more deeply reflect on how others see us—this online mass that watches us—and thereby how we see ourselves. The power of these mechanisms stems from the fact that these scores, ratings and judgments, are not without deep emotional resonance. Rejection in the form of an online failure is not markedly less painful than "in real life." Rather, a low or negative score on one's photos or what one thought to be a witty post, makes one feel stupid, excluded, embarrassed, and ashamed, and a comparatively high score makes one feel cool and approved, boosting or deflating one's self-esteem.[20] A poor score can feel as a cause for shame, a reason to hide the offense. People therefore reflexively check their social media repeatedly right after they post something. If the post hasn't received any positive attention, it's usually quickly deleted. The shame makes us naturally want to hide, and on the other end our desire for approval makes us want to keep sharing digital offerings of ourselves—our thoughts, words, or actions—with the hopes for a volcanic explosion from the bottom of the screen—of hearts, thumbs-up, and a boost in the size of our friends and followers. Since we turn to our phones for connection throughout the day, we constantly find ourselves subjected to these pressures from the crowd.

CROWD CONFORMITY EFFECTS ON SOCIAL MEDIA

Social media gives us a new opportunity to craft how we appear to others in the social sphere through the creation of our online presence, or digital self.

In the real world, we craft and perform an identity as well, but in the digital world, there is a significantly larger degree of removal, and much more scrutiny given to each little element of our performed and designed self. Our digital self becomes separated from our concrete body—a media creation, projected onto a screen, that we actively craft—a digital body. But this creation is ultimately not ourselves, *per se*, but a virtual self, a virtual body, a simulation of oneself on a screen. It is as if we have a split self, real and virtual. We can look at our digital self from outside as an object and that object becomes our emissary to the global village and often, increasingly often, the first impression or image that others have of us.

One's projection onto this digital body, living today and perhaps forever on the ever-present screen, is brought before the crowd, and then is subsequently shaped by its massive and continual social pressures. We thereby craft our digital self in response to this ever-present online feedback loop from the crowd-cloud that hovers above our digital bodies. We design our digital self—this product brand we are turning ourselves into—in order to gain approval from the crowd and avoid being rejected and discarded by consumers of our personality. Through performing before this digital phantom Nero of the online crowd, with its thumbs-up, down, and shaming silence, we learn to "optimize" our online self through trial and error to gain positive feedback, and to be approved by the crowd.[21] We "optimize" our digital self by presenting as likeable, well-rounded, and approved members of a group, that have the same thoughts, feelings, opinions, interests, and behaviors as others in that group, and hide any inclinations that might prove otherwise.

One set of social media researchers declared that "Facebook constitutes a close to ideal environment for studying conformity,"[22] because it allows a large number of people to observe each other's actions while attempting to assert their status.[23] This is true of most social media platforms. Social media is structured more or less as an ongoing popularity contest. We commonly seek not only to belong but also to belong to the most people within our crowds, and to be as approved as possible. Researchers noted that "'*Being popular among friends*' was a claim that seems to have underlined many identity projects on Facebook," and they noticed a "fierce competition among Facebook users for the size of social networks they claimed to possess."[24] This all-encompassing social media quest for popularity naturally orients oneself toward conformity. Economics professor Douglas Bernheim, speaking of conformity more broadly, says people are "willing to suppress their individuality and conform to the social norm because they recognize that even small departures from the norm will seriously impair their popularity."[25]

In our quest for belonging through social media, people commonly almost seek to become one's crowd, to disappear into a group, and merge identity from one of individuality to one of a collective identity. For example, researchers found on Facebook that users almost always present photos of themselves in groups, and rarely alone, "indicating, among other things, an effort to construct a group-oriented identity."[26] Furthermore, researchers found that Facebook users "tried to avoid making explicit self descriptions . . . the appeal is as much to the likeability of [one's] crowd . . . as it is to the personal qualities of the Facebook users themselves."[27]

Elsewhere we find digital echoes close to two hundred years later of Mill's contention that "even in what people do for pleasure, conformity is the first thing thought of; they like in crowds."[28] In a study entitled "Like What You Like or What Others Like: Conformity and Peer Effects on Facebook" the researchers affirmatively concluded that users were significantly more likely to "like" someone's post only if several other strangers had already liked it, or a valued "friend" had liked it. No one wanted to be seen as the only person liking something—that their own preferences might be different or against group norms. Furthermore, if a valuable friend liked something, then by liking it too they could maybe rub off some of the other's status onto themselves through affiliation, in the never-ending quest for popularity and approval.[29]

On the other end, researchers found that Facebook users hid privately or implicitly disclosed aspects of their lives that were contrary to popular ideals.[30] In a study by the Pew Research Center, they concluded that social media might actually increase self-censorship both online and offline because "the broad awareness social media users have of their networks might make them more hesitant to speak up because they are especially tuned into the opinions of those around them." This ambient awareness may set off a spiral of silence where popular views become increasingly popular and other views become increasingly silent out of fear of rejection for an unpopular view.[31] The Internet and social media, for all its potential for free expression, increasingly becomes an avenue of self-censorship. One group of researchers specifically studying this issue concluded that self-censorship on Facebook was "common practice."[32]

As one's digital self—this online "you"—gets shaped into conformity through the crowd by "social-validation feedback loops" it becomes uniquely attached to your "in-real-life" body. And so a simultaneous exchange occurs between the two entities, our digital self and our IRL self. As we broadcast idealized portraits of our IRL self online, we then in turn adjust our IRL self so as to meet with popular approval when we are broadcast online again. At a certain point, our IRL self and digital self practically merge. It's not surprising then that the sociologist of technology, Sherry Turkle, finds a college student obsessing over online details, perfecting his digital self as "he feels pressure to perform [his digital self] all the time because that is who he is on Facebook."[33] Elsewhere, a seventeen-year-old high-schooler describes this process of matching one's IRL self to one's digital self: "we all check Instagram constantly . . . . When I post a photo on Instagram I know that just about every person I am connected to in the real life will see my photo, decide whether or not to like it, and then judge me subconsciously . . . Your Instagram defines who you are."[34] We thereby risk becoming defined by an image or "brand" of ourselves that we sell to a crowd, becoming alienated, in a sense a product of that crowd marketed toward them.

ALIENATION IN THE DIGITAL BODY

Karl Marx first described the concept of alienation or self-estrangement in terms of alienation of one's labor: "The alienation of the worker in his product means not only that his labour becomes an object, an *external* existence, but that it becomes *external to him*, independent, alien to him, an independent power that confronts him; the life he gave to the object confronts him, hostile and alien."[35] In Marx's view, under such conditions, the soul inside the human is essentially sucked dry in the production of the object. Rather than work being an extension of ourselves and an unfolding of our unique talents, we become alien to ourselves, watching ourselves perform actions that are pulled forth from our bodies by an external power. We are building the object, but it is as if the object controls us from the inside. We build it and curse it at the same time. This is what is meant by self-estrangement or alienation in terms of labor. People become like empty vessels, watching their machine-like bodies in action, outside themselves, as if observable objects, commodities, robots. Workers on factory assembly-lines might feel this way, treated like machines for the objects of production, dehumanized stand-ins until technology can replace them; whereas a small artisan, freely investing her powers into her craft, the object becoming an extension of herself, would experience the opposite of alienation, but rather realization of herself and her powers through her craft.

Roughly a century later, Fromm drew upon this Marxist framework of alienation and applied it to the conditions of the more modern workforce. Here Fromm argued that alienation was made manifest in the type of social character that became prevalent in the West around this time. He referred to this character type as a "marketing orientation," which grew in conjunction with the development of the "personality market." What characterizes the personality market in any field is that one is valued less for one's skills and more for having a "pleasant personality" that is accepted by others. One does not gain material success predominantly by skills, rather "the 'personality factor' . . . plays a decisive role. Success depends largely on how well a person sells himself on the market, how well he gets his personality across, how nice a 'package' he is; whether he is 'cheerful,' 'sound,' 'aggressive,' 'reliable,' 'ambitious.'"[36]

The personality market extends the process of alienation where not only is one's labor alienated, but one's sense of identity is alienated as well. One becomes a "personality package" of whatever types of people are fashionable and "in demand" as prescribed by forces outside the individual's control such as through advertising and Hollywood. One's personality, the qualities that make up that individual's identity, become a commodity and the individual becomes also the seller of that commodity. He sells not only his skill-set but also the type of person he projects himself to be.

Through selling this personality, Fromm argues that a person becomes estranged from himself. He is disconnected from his own inner-potential, his innate powers as a person "because what matters is not his self-realization in the process of using them but his success in the process of selling them. Both his powers and what they create become estranged, something different from himself, something for others to judge and to use."[37] Rather than saying, I am what I do in the process of my activity, in the direct unfolding of my talent and potential, I detach myself and become an image created on a piece of paper, and I sell that image, hired for being that image; one "looks at himself as he would look at an outsider: I have an image of myself."[38] But this image is not really of my own making since I am attempting to sell a popular product and am therefore pushed by the forces of the "personality market." I develop personal qualities, "which can best be sold."[39]

As I begin to view myself, "as a package and from the outside,"[40] this image of myself that I view and sell becomes who I am since I am then pressured to maintain that identity that has won me the reward. In the process of selling my personality, there becomes no stable self. My sense of identity comes not through a process of self-realization, but "constituted by the sum total of roles I can play: 'I am as you desire me.'"[41] I develop personal qualities based on whatever qualities are in demand on the personality market.

As my sense of identity becomes oriented toward packaging and selling an image, my sense of self-worth becomes dependent on my worth to others in the personality market; "Since modern man experiences himself both as the seller and as the commodity to be sold on the market, his self-esteem depends on conditions beyond his control. If he is "successful," he is valuable; if he is not, he is worthless."[42] In this process of selling myself, I then become beholden to this valued image. My personality is replaced with an alien personality developed by powers external to me; in Fromm's words, "I alienate myself from my own human experience and project this experience onto something or somebody outside, and then try to get in touch with my own human being, by being in touch with the object to which I have projected my humanity."[43]

On social media, we project our human experience onto an object outside ourselves more profoundly than ever. We literally look at it on a screen and become attached to the object in a way that now shapes us. Through the Internet and social media, we sell ourselves as commodities to the crowd on the other end of the screen and attempt to perform in ways that meet the demands of the audience. We check in compulsively over and over again to make sure that the crowd is still with us and that we are performing well, getting good ratings. Our innate desire to be part of the crowd only reinforces this pseudo-self, this digital image which we attempt to squeeze into.

As we check over and over, we do not judge our worth so much in terms of capital anymore, the price we fetch, but in terms of our social capital, the likes and followers we fetch. As Fromm says of the personality market: "This situation makes [me] utterly dependent on the way others look at [me] and forces [me] to keep up the role in which [I] once had become successful. If I and my powers are separated from each other then, indeed, is my self constituted by the price I fetch."[44] Similarly, through social media and the Internet, who we are becomes separated from ourselves, an image that stands over and defines us, our sense of value or esteem becomes dependent on valuation in this online personality market. Our digital selves are given clear indications of value through numbers like follower counts usually stamped right next to our faces and a myriad of social metrics reported to us for nearly every piece of our lives that are exposed to the crowd. Our sense of self-worth may become based on our ability to receive positive feedback online, feeling good when those numbers are up, but bad when they crash down. We therefore attempt to chase those numbers, to boost the ratings in the reality show that permeates our lives, and become the personality that is most popular and in demand. But in the process, we become something other than who we really are. We become *saddled* with an identity, which is really only a popularly approved image or impression, not the actual unfolding of our inner-potential, of words and behavior without calculation.

Through social media, I begin to view myself as a thing, a thing which I attempt to make desirable and "in demand" to others, and the higher my likes and followers, the more desirable a thing. In the end, I become alienated and estranged not only from myself but also I become alienated from my fellow person as well. They may also be reduced to things, to their images, to be used and judged. Others may become like objects to be added to my collection of "friends" and "followers," various trophies to be displayed on my virtual shelf. As Fromm says of the personality market: "The difference between people is reduced to a merely quantitative difference of being more or less successful, attractive, hence valuable."[45] Similarly, I am likely to judge the worth of my "friends" and "followers" based on their status online, their number of likes, comments, or followers.

Today, it is commonplace to hear people speak about "branding" themselves online. As we become brands, we build ourselves up as commodities to be sold on the personality market. But unlike in Fromm's time, the personality market now extends beyond the labor sphere to practically *all* aspects of our lives, all social spheres, whether for work, dating, or friends. In almost every type of human relationship, we are made to feel that success now means marketing one's digital self, this personal brand, to the online crowd. These images of ourselves are increasingly the first impression that people now have of us in the different relationships that make up our lives. But through becoming a brand, we risk becoming commodities to be judged and used by others, with our sense of worth based upon current ratings.

The person as a brand becomes like a corporation with one's online audience the shareholders. The digitally incorporated individual may increasingly become not really the individual at all, but rather a product designed for the crowd and sold to the crowd for the reward of social capital. In a sense, we are literally branded by the crowd, marked with an identity that stems not from within, but from the dictates of a force outside of our control, a self that has become lost in its attempt to become a valuable item to others, constantly reinforced through the compulsive nature of checking one's status online in the ever-fluctuating personality marketplace. In this way, through our attempts to brand ourselves, the supposed precondition of "success" in the modern world, we risk becoming defined by our online brand, internalizing and in a sense becoming our branded digital self.

As an especially interesting or ironic twist, we are told again and again by influencers or other gurus of online branding to be "authentic" in our self-branding. But an authentic person is, we might say, not a brand. An authentic person is one with one's powers, and acts in a way to unfold and realize one's potential, guided by this inwardly unfolding process that one wills into existence. By contrast, through turning ourselves into brands, we take our powers and place it on a digital object outside ourselves, and try to realize who we are and feel our self-worth through that image that is made to be marketable to the crowd.

The more this identity is performed and displayed on permanent record in front of an indefinitely large online audience, the more opportunities there are for us to be seen as not living up to this identity, and suffering an embarrassing mishap. The pressure of society demands that we continue to perform these roles. After all, a brand must be consistent and reliable as any brand one might purchase in a store. It's not clear that we can easily abandon our branded self and start over with some sort of new self-experimentation when the self we've crafted online has a permanently recallable presence. In either case, if we've become habitually reinforced to perform the identity that gains us likes and validation, we risk getting stuck in these roles even if we could change them because we don't want to lose the positive reinforcement we've received, and we are scared of being shamed or cast out in front of everyone online.

This performance of the self is nothing new in and of itself. The sociologist Erving Goffman in his 1956 study of face-to-face interactions, *The Presentation of Self in Everyday Life*, explicitly drew upon a framework of theater to describe the interactions he observed in daily life. But these types of ceremonial performances of the self were accompanied by a "backstage" where people were out of character.[46] However, through social media and smart devices carried at all times, we increasingly become always online, without a backstage, always "on," and therefore increasingly pressured to perform images of ourselves sold as valued brands to audiences for good ratings. Even when we feel we are "being ourselves," we may be performing a popular character crafted for an audience online, never just *being* ourselves, but rather calculating a projection of ourselves for ratings, a projection which we increasingly merge with, even if the character we perform may be designed to appear "liberated" or "Bohemian."

To sum up, from a Marxian perspective, the alienated laborer becomes like a machine, an empty vessel playing a physical role on an assembly line. From a Frommian perspective, we might say that the alienated person on social media becomes like a personality machine, emptied out and programmed by society, watching oneself do as society signals one to do. The former is a cog in an economic machine, the latter a cog in a social machine. The necessity to brand ourselves as a condition of economic and social "success" in the modern world encourages us to view ourselves as things, our identities projected into the hands of the crowd, shaped, and reflected back upon us. We watch ourselves on a screen, judge ourselves based on how others judge us on the screen, and act out the desired roles as directed accordingly. We lose ourselves to the crowd in the process. This in turn leads to a sort of nihilism or meaninglessness. As an automaton of society nothing really matters to *me*, what is important is what matters to *them*, but this could be anything. By embodying the values of the crowd and its public opinion in my brand, I become an embodiment of "they."

NOTES

1. Erich Fromm, *The Art of Loving* (Toronto, New York, London: Bantam Books, 1967), 11.

2. C. Nathan DeWall, Timothy Deckman, Richard S. Pond Jr, and Ian Bonser, "Belongingness as a Core Personality Trait: How Social Exclusion Influences Social Functioning and Personality Expression," *Journal of Personality* 79, no. 6 (2011): 1281–314.

3. Roy F. Baumeister and Mark R. Leary, "The Need to Belong: Desire for Interpersonal Attachments as a Fundamental Human Motivation," *Psychological Bulletin* 117, no. 3 (1995): 497–529.

4. Rob Margetta, "The Profound Power of Loneliness," National Science Foundation, February 3, 2016, https://www.nsf.gov/discoveries/disc_summ.jsp?cntn_id=137534.

5. Baumeister and Leary, "The Need to Belong."

6. David Riesman, *The Lonely Crowd* (New Haven & London: Yale University Press, 1971), 25.

7. Erich Fromm, *Escape from Freedom* (New York: Avon, 1969).

8. Fromm, *Escape from Freedom*, 209–10.

9. Erich Fromm, *The Sane Society* (New York & Toronto: Rinehart & Company, Inc., 1955), 11.

10. Robert D. Putnam, *Bowling Alone: The Collapse and Revival of American Community* (New York: Simon & Schuster, 2000).

11. Nancy Day, "Our Separate Ways," *People*, last modified September 25, 1995, http://people.com/archive/our-separate-ways-vol-45-no-13/.

12. Michael Winnick, "Putting a Finger on Our Phone Obsession Mobile Touches: A Study On Humans and their Tech," *dscout*, June 16, 2016, https://blog.dscout.com/mobile-touches.

13. Mike Allen, "Sean Parker Unloads on Facebook 'God Only Knows What it's Doing to Our Children's Brains,'" *Axios*, November 9, 2017, https://www.axios.com/sean-parker-unloads-on-facebook-god-only-knows-what-its-doing-to-our-childrens-brains-1513306792-f855e7b4-4e99-4d60-8d51-2775559c2671.html.

14. Dopamine Labs, accessed November 16, 2018, https://web.archive.org/web/20180224003954/https://usedopamine.com/.

15. Saul McLeod, "Skinner – Operant Conditioning," *SimplyPsychology*, accessed November 16, 2018, https://www.simplypsychology.org/operant-conditioning.html.

16. B. J. Fogg, Gregory Cueller, and David Danielson, "Motivating, Influencing, and Persuading Users: An Introduction to Captology," in *The Human-Computer Interaction Handbook*, ed. Andrew Sears (Boca Raton: CRC Press, 2007), 159–72.

17. Ian Leslie, "The Scientists Who Make Apps Addictive," *1843*, October/November 2016, https://www.1843magazine.com/features/the-scientists-who-make-apps-addictive.

18. Paul Lewis, "'Our Minds Can Be Hijacked': The Tech Insiders Who Fear a Smartphone Dystopia," *The Guardian*, October 6, 2017, https://www.theguardian.com/technology/2017/oct/05/smartphone-addiction-silicon-valley-dystopia.

19. Eric Andrew-Gee, "Your Smartphone is Making You Stupid, Antisocial, and Unhealthy. So Why Can't You Put It Down?," *The Globe and Mail*, last modified January 6, 2018, https://www.theglobeandmail.com/technology/your-smartphone-is-making-you-stupid/article37511900/.

20. Patti M. Valkenburg, Jochen Peter, and Alexander P. Schouten, "Friend Networking Sites and Their Relationship to Adolescents' Well-being and Social Self-esteem," *CyberPsychology & Behavior* 9, no. 5 (2006): 589.

21. Valkenburg et al., "Friend Networking," 586.

22. Johan Egebark and Mathias Ekström, "Like What You Like or Like What Others Like? Conformity and Peer Effects on Facebook," *IFN Working Paper*, no. 886 (2011): 14, http://www.ifn.se/wfiles/wp/wp886.pdf.
23. Egebark and Ekström, "Like What You Like or Like," 14.
24. Shanyang Zhao, Sherri Grasmuck, and Jason Martin, "Identity Construction on Facebook: Digital Empowerment in Anchored Relationships," *Computers in Human Behavior* 24, no. 5 (2008): 1826–27.
25. B. Douglas Bernheim, "A Theory of Conformity," *Journal of Political Economy* 102, no. 5 (1994): 864.
26. Zhao, Grasmuck, and Martin, "Identity Construction," 1827.
27. Zhao, Grasmuck, and Martin, "Identity Construction," 1831.
28. Mill, *On Liberty*, 57.
29. Egebark and Ekström, "Like What You Like or Like," 17.
30. Zhao, Grasmuck, and Martin, "Identity Construction," 1829–30.
31. Keith Hampton et al., "Social Media and 'Spiral of Silence'," *Pew Research Center*, August 26, 2014, http://www.pewinternet.org/2014/08/26/social-media-and-the-spiral-of-silence/.
32. Sauvik Das and Adam Kramer, "Self-censorship on Facebook," in *Seventh International AAAI Conference on Weblogs and Social Media* (2013): 125.
33. Sherry Turkle, *Alone Together: Why We Expect More from Technology and Less from Each Other* (New York: Basic Books, 2012), 185.
34. Eric, "Finstagram: The Instagram Revolution," *Medium*, February 10, 2015, https://medium.com/bits-pixels/finstagram-the-instagram-revolution-737999d40014.
35. Karl Marx, *Early Political Writings* (Cambridge: Cambridge University Press, 1994), 72.
36. Erich Fromm, *Man For Himself: An Inquiry Into the Psychology of Ethics* (New York: Holy, Rinehart and Winston, 1947), 69.
37. Fromm, *Man For Himself*, 72–73.
38. Erich Fromm, "Dealing with the Unconscious in Psychotherapeutic Practice: 3 Lectures 1959," *International Forum of Psychoanalysis* 9, nos. 3–4 (2000): 173.
39. Fromm, *Man For Himself*, 77.
40. Fromm, "Dealing with the Unconscious," 173.
41. Fromm, *Man For Himself*, 73.
42. Fromm, *Man For Himself*, 72.
43. Fromm, "Dealing with the Unconscious," 170.
44. Fromm, *Man For Himself*, 73.
45. Fromm, *Man For Himself*, 73.
46. Erving Goffman, *The Presentation of Self in Everyday Life* (London: Harmondsworth, 1978).

Chapter 3

Meaninglessness in the Present Age

How do we free ourselves from the sort of automaton conformity and alienation described in chapters 1 and 2? The founding existentialist philosopher Søren Kierkegaard argues that in order to break free, to become our authentic selves, as well as to deeply bond with others in community, we must first be gripped by passion. To follow one's passion, he says, means to commit oneself to "an idea for which I am willing to live and die."[1]

Our personal calling in life, what we feel truly passionate about, what defines who we are apart from the crowd, arises in a sense irrationally. Or rather than irrational, we might say that passion is trans-rational. One feels that there is something beyond oneself, in which one has a role to play and is summoned toward. We might not fully understand it, but be moved by it nevertheless. Through this calling one is, as Hubert Dreyfus puts it, "*given* an individual identity that opens up an individual world . . . These special commitments are experienced as gripping our whole being. Political and religious movements can grip us in this way, as can romantic relationships and, for certain people, such vocations as science or art."[2] Dreyfus explains further that "When we respond to such a summons with what Kierkegaard calls infinite passion, that is, when we respond by accepting an *unconditional commitment*, this commitment determines what will be the significant issue for us for the rest of our life."[3] In this sense, there is an authentic self that is summoned, waiting to be made manifest in reality. It is through following one's calling, through passionately committing to it on an ongoing basis, that one realizes one's self as a result.

Passionate commitment to one's calling is a difficult task, but it is also a labor of love that brings one fulfillment and meaning in life. On top of being difficult, following one's calling is also risky. As Dreyfus says, "such a commitment makes one vulnerable. One's cause may fail. One's lover may leave." However, he explains, "Only a risky unconditioned commitment and the strong identity it produces can give an individual a world organized by that individual's unique qualitative distinctions."[4]

Because passionately committing to your calling is a difficult and risky lifelong task, the strength, determination, and bravery needed to follow your passion only strengthens your individuality, and makes you refuse to not be yourself, to act as if just any sort of life is equally good for you, to act as if the customary life prescribed by public opinion—the social norms, fashions, and customs—is the right one for you. By being true to your passion, you then stand in contradiction to another as a strong separate individual, steadfast in determination to be yourself as you hear your calling. By following your calling, you create a life for yourself that is uniquely yours, an irreplaceable identity that is uniquely yours, and not prepackaged as part of a mass body.

By implementing one's unique task, one's calling, one can then say, "this is my life and who I am, this is what I believe in strongly, what is right for me, and what I stand for." This is how we escape the nihilism and meaninglessness of a life directed externally by society rather than through one's passions. You put your foot down for what really matters for you, and this concretizes value in the world. By being passionately devoted to one's calling, one breaks through nihilism by establishing, as Kierkegaard says, "an ethical stance despite the whole world."[5]

When we look back at the most inspiring individuals in history we see this link between passionate dedication and the formation of meaning in life. Kierkegaard was a poet-philosopher, that was what his life was about. He had an unending dedication to bringing out what was inside of him, this inner potential, to manifest it in reality, and in turn to realize himself in the world. Only he could say what he was passionate about, who his true self was, because only he could hear his calling.

To be clear, to follow one's calling is not to search for oneself, at least directly. That is not the aim. Rather, the existential analyst Viktor Frankl argues that in order to realize ourselves, we must actually *transcend* ourselves, dedicating ourselves to this higher calling, this thing of value outside ourselves. The aim that one must be directed toward fulfilling is this thing of value, not oneself. Frankl says:

> Self-actualization is not a possible aim at all; for the simple reason that the more a man would strive for it, the more he would miss it. For only to the extent to which man commits himself to the fulfillment of his life's meaning, to this extent he also actualizes himself. In other words, self-actualization cannot be attained if it is made an end in itself, but only as a side-effect of self-transcendence.[6]

To transcend oneself, and through that realize one's inner potential, we must dedicate ourselves to that which is calling us. It is only by having something that one is willing to live and die for that we create a meaningful life because then the value is determined by that which stems from within. It is the opposite of the nihilism that says I go wherever the crowd goes, whatever is trending, one way is as good as the other if the crowd gives a thumbs up. That leads instead to a fundamental meaningless. One's story then becomes simply written by the arbitrariness of public opinion.

THE ENDLESS BUZZ OF DISTRACTION

In order to find one's calling, Kierkegaard insists we must go *inwards* to hear it, to silence the noise of the external world and the chatter of public opinion.[7] Frankl expounds upon this explaining that "the meaning of our existence is not invented by ourselves, but rather detected."[8] To detect this inner-calling, the meaning of our lives, requires both an embrace of solitude combined with the concentration needed to go deeply inwards into that solitude. But our always-on, always-connected devices may interfere with these necessary conditions for finding one's calling, the meaning of our lives, pulling us away from this necessary inwardness. Even just carrying our devices all the time constantly orients us toward externalities, readying us to be pulled into the concerns and opinions of others at any moment with the signal of a chime.

In terms of the mental concentration needed in order to go inwards, an increasing amount of scientific experiments have shown that our phones distract us, decrease our ability to concentrate on tasks, creating what some researchers have called a "brain drain." In a pair of studies, researchers suggested that the mere presence of a smartphone may reduce available cognitive capacity, that is the ability to fully concentrate on a specific task, as well as general fluid intelligence, which has to do with a person's ability to solve new problems. In the studies, which involved over 520 undergraduates, they asked the students to solve a series of cognitive tests. One group was asked to leave their phone in another room, the second was allowed to leave it in their bag or pocket, and the third group was allowed to place their phone on their desk. All participants were instructed to turn their phone on silence with the ringer and vibrate off.

What was found was that the mere presence of one's phone appeared to reduce one's cognitive capacities. Those who had their phone in another room performed the best on the tests. Those with their phone on their desk performed the worst. Those with their phone in a bag or in their pocket performed in the middle. The more salient the presence of one's phone, the worse one performed on these cognitive measures.⁹ Commenting on these and other similar studies, Nicholas Carr writes:

> Smartphones have become so entangled with our existence that, even when we're not peering or pawing at them, they tug at our attention, diverting precious cognitive resources. Just suppressing the desire to check our phone, which we do routinely and subconsciously throughout the day, can debilitate our thinking. The fact that most of us now habitually keep our phones "nearby and in sight," the researchers noted, only magnifies the mental toll.[10]

We need concentration in order to exercise the inwardness needed to hear our calling, a capacity that may be degraded by the habitual and constant distraction of our ever-connected devices. Crucially, for inwardness, we also need solitude. Some cultures ritualistically cultivate an appreciation and embrace of solitude. But there is a loss of solitude in modern technological society that may be contributing to a loss of individuality through a diminishment of the contemplative inner-space needed to find one's calling.

Today, behind our screens, physical isolation is common, but solitude, a concentrated being alone with oneself which one embraces rather than runs from, is becoming scarce. We increasingly find it almost excruciating to be alone with ourselves for even a short period of time. In one shocking study, researchers asked participants to sit alone in a room for fifteen minutes with only their thoughts to entertain themselves. The only external stimulus in the room was a button they could push which would self-administer an electric shock. Before being left in the room, the participants had all explicitly said they would *pay* to avoid an electric shock. Yet being left alone in a room with only their thoughts for fifteen minutes, 67 percent of the men and 25 percent of the women shocked themselves at least once. The researchers concluded that "simply being alone with their own thoughts for 15 minutes was apparently so aversive that it drove many participants to self-administer an electric shock that they had earlier said they would pay to avoid."[11]

Without an earlier comparison, we cannot know if these results would have been any different in the past, but if our always-connected culture has diminished our ability to concentrate, it is reasonable to think that this would also diminish our ability to be in solitude and experience inwardness. But without inwardness we cannot hear our calling, only the endless buzz of distraction away from ourselves, and toward the opinion of the crowd. If we cannot find ourselves inwardly, if we are always oriented externally, going where the others go, we cannot break free from the alienation of automaton conformity.

In our technological society, we may be pushed away from the tough individual commitment necessary to fulfill our calling, which we can only find through continually going inward, and trying to grasp, however murky it may be, what is a life well lived for us. We are instead deluged with the buzz of the crowd, and our lives become directed by its noise, and its pressures for us. Rather than committing to what calls us, and taking an ethical stance despite the world, we risk fluctuating in the wind with whatever is most approved by the crowd. But Kierkegaard says the resolutely passionate individual "would rather be something small, if still faithful to himself, than all sorts of things in contradiction to himself."[12] The authentic individual would rather have no likes, and be oneself, than to be trending on Twitter with a million likes, and become merely a heralded sample, interchangeable with all the rest.

COMMITMENT AND COMMUNITY

Kierkegaard famously wanted "That Individual" etched on his tombstone. Some argue that Kierkegaard over-elevates the status of the individual to a degree that comes at the expense of relationships to others and community. But this conflict between strong individual identity and community is a false dichotomy. We realize ourselves *in and with others* in forming communities. But we cannot form strong bonds with each other if we have lost our individuality in a crowd. Rather, in Kierkegaard's view, it is only *through* strengthening one's individuality that one comes to be capable of deeply uniting with others. Kierkegaard says, "Not until the single individual has established an ethical stance despite the whole world, not until then can there be any question of genuinely uniting; otherwise it gets to be a union of people who separately are weak, a union as unbeautiful and depraved as a child-marriage."[13]

If separate individuals are not strong in themselves, resolute in what they really care about, their bonds, if any, will be shallow. If I unite with others in the deep bonds of a mutually devoted real-world community, I do so because I am bound with others who in their own inner resolve have come to the same conclusions as myself about what is of value. In mutually committing to that thing of value, transcending ourselves in dedication toward it, we help to realize it in ourselves and each other. We form a team devoted to a shared cause. If I do not initially have an opinion of my own of what is valuable, I may be inspired by another's passion, who through her individual devotion has shown me something worth dying for. The passion of another then becomes my own through my own devotion.

Kierkegaard refers to the object of passion as a 'third' in a relationship, the 'idea' that strongly binds two individuals. It is not a feeling, *per se*, but rather a sensed direction, though understood only incompletely, toward a value which binds the individuals together in a shared life. Revolutionaries are united in their passionate devotion to the cause they are fighting for—freedom, justice, or peace—deep adherents of a faith are united in their passionate devotion to religion (which Kierkegaard held as the ultimate aim), and artists are united in their passionate devotion to art. Robert Perkins explains that "Persons ideally relate to each other through the idea. In this way there is both social unity and individuality, for each has his own task, the full development of his relation to the third, and through the third the relation to each other."[14] It is therefore not only through passion that individuals become themselves but also through passion that individuals unite into a strong community. Kierkegaard has us view an authentic community as being like an orchestra. Each is devoted to a shared object, the piece of music, but each is personally responsible for fulfilling one's individual task in relation to the whole, and plays with a singular passion.[15] Each has a personal *responsibility* for the success or failure of the whole.

Kierkegaard uses an example of revolutionary ages of the past to help illustrate how meaningful relationships form through passionate commitment. Being in a revolutionary situation, where concrete actions are actually happening on the ground, one is together, in the simultaneity of the situation, with real people, in real time, doing real things that help form shared opinions and worldviews born out of direct first-hand experience. In a revolution people cannot detach themselves from their opinions. Even if one does not have an opinion of one's own at a certain moment, but simply adopts that of the majority or minority, in a movement where one is committed to action in the real world, one becomes actually responsible for the outcome of the pursuit of actions stemming from that opinion. The opinion of others therefore becomes one's own since a person rises or falls with others in its pursuit. Through real-world commitment and action people stand in supportive solidarity with leaders, and therefore strengthen others in their resolve, and genuinely unite around the idea worth fighting for. An individual leader is often the one who deciphers the thing of value, the idea toward which a community is bonded in striving to realize, but it is ultimately the idea that stands above the community as the true guide, not the leader.

We can think of the civil rights movement of the 1950s and 1960s as a good illustration of how community forms out of passionate individuals mutually devoted to a cause. The cause of freedom, justice, and equality was something that people were willing to live and die for, and many people *did* suffer and die for the cause. Individual leaders emerged who committed themselves to an ethical stance despite what the majority thought at the time of their ideas. Despite the whole world these civil rights leaders were committed to justice, and they were willing to risk themselves for their stance. In the process, they realized their powers and through this formed deeply united communities. Here we have a template for what it means to be part of an authentic community. It involves personal passion, shared devotion, mutual assistance, giving, sacrifice, risk, and resolve. Self-actualization then occurs as a side-effect of the realization of an object of value—this "third" or "idea" in a relationship—that stands as a deep ideal hovering above the group and giving support from below.

To be part of a community people must mutually devote themselves to a cause, and so one is giving of oneself to the community through the mutual commitment to the realization of that idea of shared value. This squares with the earliest notions of what makes for a community. The Italian philosopher Roberto Esposito has conducted an etymological study of the Latin word *"communitas"* and finds that what was originally understood is that "The subjects of community are united by an 'obligation,' in the sense that we say 'I owe you something,' but not 'you owe me something.'"[16] In a community, one seeks to help one another fulfill a shared calling. One does not lose oneself in the crowd simply looking at what the other is doing and attempting to blend in. Quite on the contrary, if others are not oriented toward the idea or third in a relationship, one who is able to decipher this value, however incomplete, may stand apart from the crowd and attempt to orient others toward the third. That individual may then become a leader of a community, and through one's leadership give of oneself to the community to help bring them to this higher value. It is through this loving of others, this giving, that one attempts to fulfill the demands of one's passionate calling.

BELONGINGNESS AND DIGITAL DISCONNECTION

One might be tempted to think that if I blend into a hyperconnected digital crowd, I'm at least gaining belonging to some sort of community. But whatever sense of community is being developed through our technologies is arguably only a simulacrum of a real community. Through social media, we do form some sort of media-connected entity. But there is no simultaneity of real people in the same place in real time who are committed to being there, who take a risk to be there. No feet on the ground. No movement. No community of dedication to a shared object of devotion—Kierkegaard's "third."

Rather than direct involvement in a community, through our experience of the world mediated by a screen, Howard Tuttle says, "everything tends to become a spectator sport for us—we watch or 'reflect' on the spectacles of life around us, be they athletic or political, judicious, or religious; we take them all as news events that we can look at 'objectively' and abstractly and, above all, passively and impersonally."[17] Rather than getting off the computer, and dedicating one's life to a cause, it's easier to just sit back and observe the world passing, going through the motions, and never really passionately committing to a calling in a lifelong way, to live and die for that cause. Enthusiasm swells for a moment over some issue, there's a lot of excitement, and then people fall back into the ease and comfort of an administered modern society. The mass media, Dreyfus explains, "promotes ubiquitous commentators who deliberately detach themselves from the local practices out of which specific issues grow and in terms of which these issues must be resolved through some sort of committed action."[18] We instead scroll through an endless newsfeed, we have an opinion and a comment on everything, even if we hardly know anything about what we are commenting on or really do anything about it. Social media turns us into the epitome of the chattering class that Kierkegaard thought characterizes the modern age.

Rather than community, one's "friends" and followers on social media become more a network of people from whom we mostly make an exchange of social capital, mutually boosting each other's popularity status, through the reciprocity of liking one another's content. It's a system of exchange in a network of partners to which one does not really feel obligated, to whom many feel readily "ghostable" at a touch of a button. Rather than feeling a sense of obligation to this digital collection of people that we carry in our pockets, and a shared devotion to a common cause *above* the group, toward which we transcend together, we are oriented toward viewing our followers as something which we *take* from for ourselves, which gives us the attention, validation, and likes that we crave—that gives us a simulated sense of belonging.

In our modern society, where we generally lack deep communal bonds, we turn to the Internet and social media, as a coping mechanism in order gain a feeling of belongingness and connection. It is as if from one cubicle to another, one bedroom to another, we reach out from our individual silos through our devices and attempt to overcome the isolated society we live in. But empirical evidence suggests that overall Internet connection is not giving us the sense of belonging that we need, that we would find in a community in the deeper non-social media sense. In fact, our smart devices and social media appear to be making the problem of disconnectedness worse. For all the "connection" of the Internet, loneliness researcher John Cacioppo reports that today loneliness is on the rise.[19]

As we reach out through the web in search of a feeling of connection, we "can't get no satisfaction" because it does not generate deeply united community and even pulls us away from such community, and into our devices, where community might otherwise arise. Researchers studying Facebook and the need for relatedness conclude that Facebook (and I would bet all social media) is used as a coping device to feel more connection, but that it ultimately gives the user only

> transient positive feelings while using . . . but may not solve underlying real-life social problems that gave rise to feelings of loneliness or disconnection; ultimately, those problems may even get worse. The portrait that arises is of a

person who is addicted to a coping device that does not approach problem-resolution directly but, rather, approaches a pleasant distraction from problems.[20]

The more we use our tech to feel connected, the more it appears to only make the problem of disconnection worse. It is as if we dig a deeper hole burrowing further into our devices. Notably, face-to-face interactions have rapidly decreased overall among younger generations in recent years, and technology is likely to blame. Decades-long research on generational differences by Jean Twenge found that since smartphones were released in 2007 there have been unprecedented and dramatic declines in the amount high schoolers are hanging out with friends, dating, and even having sex.[21] Twenge finds that "The number of teens who get together with their friends every day has been cut in half in just fifteen years, with especially steep declines recently . . . . College students in 2016 (vs. the late 1980s) spent four fewer hours a week socializing with their friends and three fewer hours a week partying—so seven hours a week less on in-person social interaction."[22] This is happening all the while as teens have a lot more free time than past generations since they are working outside of school much less; "So what are they doing with all that time? They are on their phone, in their room, alone and often distressed."[23] Twenge argues that former face-to-face interactions are simply being replaced with screen time. Kevin, a teenager quoted by Twenge sums it up: "My generation lost interest in socializing in person—they don't have physical get-togethers, they just text together, and they can just stay at home."[24]

As sharply and dramatically as face-to-face interactions have begun to decline since the smartphone was released, there is an equally dramatic increase in teenagers who report feeling lonely and left out. The results suggest that the more time teens spend on screens, the less happy they are.[25] Our avatar connections simply do not appear to adequately fulfill our need for belonging through building tightly bonded communities.

Not only is time spent with others "in-real-life" decreasing, but the quality of face-to-face interactions appears to be degraded as well by our compulsive use of technology.[26] Experiments have provided evidence that the presence of mobile communication has negative effects on "closeness, connection, and conversation quality."[27] Undistracted face-to-face conversation is key for building real-life social bonds, perhaps most importantly for building empathy with one another. Sherry Turkle defines empathy as the "psychological capacity to put yourself in the place of another person and imagine what they are going through."[28] One study showed that young people's scores on tests designed to measure empathy levels has sharply dropped in recent years, particularly in the new millennium.[29] There is reason to believe that our increasing use of ICTs is responsible for this decline.

In another revealing study out of UCLA, researchers found that when sixth graders were sent to a tech-free summer camp, within only five days, their ability to discern the emotions of others through recognizing nonverbal emotional cues (facial expression, and so forth) increased in comparison with a control group that maintained typical tech use.[30] Turkle says that through our use of tech we suppress our capacity for empathy by "putting ourselves in environments where we're not looking at each other in the eye, not sticking with the other person long enough or hard enough to follow what they're feeling."[31] If ICTs are causing a widespread diminishment of people's capacity for empathy, it is likely also diminishing most people's ability to successfully form real-life communities and overcome separateness. With technological inundation commonly beginning today in toddlerhood, it is unclear if these capacities will be healthily developed among most people in the future.

With a society compulsively addicted to ICTs, losing empathy for one another, increasingly unavailable for deep conversation and quality face-to-face interactions, we desperately try and fill our need for overcoming separateness by diving deeper into the web. But this increased tech use may only further a lack of empathy, which then further increases loneliness and then furthers more tech usage as a coping mechanism. A vicious circle amounts like a cybernetic feedback loop that pulls us into its vortex. When everyone is plugged into the matrix, no one is left on the outside, and so we plug in deeper and deeper to feel a part of something, but never get to the root and find a true solution to the fundamental human problem of overcoming separateness. We are instead becoming, in the words of Sherry Turkle, "alone together."[32]

GLOBAL COMMUNITY AND THE PUBLIC

In 2017, Mark Zuckerberg posted a roughly 6,000-word open letter entitled "Building Global Community" which reads like a manifesto for his vision of the future of the company.[33] But when we look at what our devices and web connection are doing for our sense of belonging, we can see that the way Zuckerberg is using the word "community" in his goal of building "global community" is similar in practice to the way Facebook uses the word "friend." One cannot have hundreds or thousands of real friends when friendship involves some sort of deep dedication to one another, mutual giving to one another in pursuit of a good life, or an ideal above the group. We simply do not have the time. Millions or billions of people in a so-called "global community" can necessarily only remain strangers.

Only in passionate direct action committed to something we care deeply about do we break through a detached and even nihilistic spectatorship, joining together with others, feet on the ground in our cause, in the same time, in the same place, over and again, forming the tight bonds of strong community; not losing oneself in the crowd in a fit of passionate energy, but steadfast determination in which one is always responsible as an individual for one's behavior. But in a passionless society driven by a detached public opinion behind a screen, instead of a community of separately strong individuals emerging in their shared enthusiastic and even risky determination for a shared passion, what arises instead is, as Kierkegaard ominously heralds, "a monstrous abstraction, an all-encompassing something that is nothing, a mirage—and this phantom is *the public* . . . made up of unsubstantial individuals who are never united or never can be united in the simultaneity of any situation or organization and yet are claimed to be a whole."[34] Just as we risk replacing friends with networks, we risk replacing communities with publics. In the age of social media, where our lives are broadcast to an online crowd with increasing regularity, we are merging ever more closely with publics, and live in relation to publics in a much deeper way than in Kierkegaard's time when only the foundations were being laid through the popular press.

Although I will refer to "a public" and "the public" somewhat loosely and interchangeably, the two terms can be somewhat distinguished. English professor Michael Warner argues that there is both *the* public, which can be described as "a kind of social totality," we might say the common paradigm of thought and action that characterizes a society, but that within this totality there are, "an infinite number of publics."[35] A public, by Warner's definition, is essentially a group of strangers, who are held together through a current and ongoing media discourse based on the reading and circulation of texts. Warner adds that "Often, the texts themselves are not even recognized as texts—as for example with visual advertising or the chattering of a DJ—but the publics they bring into being are still discursive in the same way."[36] His definition aligns with the sense of a public described by Kierkegaard that is a group of people disconnected by time and place who yet view themselves as a whole through their united opinion based on the consumption of the same mass media.

According to Warner, what makes one a member of a public is not based on anything other than giving some amount of active attention to media that is attempting to impart a message. In this sense, a public is self-organizing. It comes into existence merely through attention to a shared public discourse. A public ceases to exist when the swirl of media that constitutes the basis of its set of shared ideas ceases to exist. It is like a tornado. It comes into existence with circulation and dissipates the moment that circulation stops. Publics are therefore not like traditional institutions; "They are virtual entities, not voluntary associations."[37]

One, in a sense, never really joins a public. There is no place that one enters into. It is a virtual entity that is in existence through surrounding oneself with a certain exchange of media. One declares, through one's voluntary attention—the following of a hashtag, for example—that one is a member of a public, a part of that entity. Because one exercises one's will in being a member of a public, it allows publics, under the right conditions, to take on a form of *agency* "even though that public has no institutional being or concrete manifestation."[38] We can therefore view the public not as a collection of individual entities, but as a collective entity in and of itself that has ontic status and can *act* in the world.

Warner describes the agency of the public as equal to that of what readers can do brought up to the level of the aggregate of readers conjoined in a public; "The attribution of agency to publics works, in most cases, because of the direct transposition from acts of private reading to the figuration of sovereign opinion. All of the verbs for public agency are verbs for private reading, transposed upward to the aggregate of readers. Readers may scrutinize, ask, reject, opine, decide, judge, and so on."[39] In the age of social media, however, readers are now equally writers which therefore strengthens the agency of the public. No longer can the public simply judge and reject, but now the public can also attack, disparage, and accuse others in writing. As a result, not only are we pressured to design an appealing self "brand" to be widely consumed, but the public's newfound expanded agency of writing allows the public to begin to write our story *for* us, to brand us. It also means that, as people share information and ideas through social media, everyone gains their own public, their own body of disconnected individuals that follow them through a circulation of a textual discourse, as our lives are turned into shareable media. One is thereby also much more deeply tied into publics as one's life goes increasingly on display for judgment before one's very own public.

Through this strengthening of both the agency of publics and the increased intertwining of our day-to-day lives with publics, social media allows the anonymous authority of public opinion to come to life in its most concrete form to date. Unlike the power of the public in the past, we can now interact as an individual with this phantom in a much more regular and direct fashion. Through the Internet and social media, publics take form as collective entities that we can speak to, which may condemn or approve us in return. Through fearing its power to shame and isolate us, and surrendering ourselves to its shared opinion, our decisions thereby become the decisions of the anonymous collective. The individual, joining the mentality of the crowd, being swept up by public opinion and its norms, becomes lost in this ghostly shared body. One then becomes something other than who one is, untrue to one's calling and, in that sense, untrue to one's self based upon one's given passions. As Kierkegaard says, the "'crowd' is the untruth."[40]

STATUS, ENVY, AND LEVELING

The process of losing one's individuality and becoming assimilated into the public takes place, Kierkegaard says, through *reflection*. We can think of the structure of video chats as a digital architectural embodiment of this sort of reflective process. When we video chat, we look into the screen and we see the other person, but then in the corner, as in a mirror, we appear constantly reflected back to ourselves as well. We can thereby monitor our image in real time as another looks and reacts to us. We observe ourselves as if an object to externally manipulate becoming detached from our inwardness. When we look into the social media mirror, we do not see ourselves reflected back either, but rather ourselves reflected back as mixed into the phantom crowd that haunts the mirror. We may then calculate or rationalize our behavior to gain the approval of this phantom, to make one's own face in the mirror blend in with the endless smiling and scowling faces staring back *with* us. The public stands, Tuttle says, "continually present as an abstract power of judgment over the individual,"[41] and so we are prone to adjust—assimilate as it were—and become absorbed into the public through this reflective process.

To be clear, just as Kierkegaard would say that passion is not in itself a good thing if it is, say, a passion for serial killing, and that the press is not a bad thing if it is being used as an arm of a concrete movement on the ground, reflection too is not in and of itself a bad thing if done within certain parameters. As Kierkegaard explains, "Reflection is not the evil, but the state of reflection, stagnation in reflection . . . ."[42] *Over-reflection* is the problem to Kierkegaard.

What can be understood by this over-reflection in relation to Internet culture is stagnation in an over-reflection on the opinion of the crowd, and perhaps an under-reflection in terms of inward critical thought. For example, today, we are increasingly afraid to even speak without over-reflecting. We increasingly prefer to send messages via our devices rather than speak face-to-face in real time perhaps because through our detached media-based communications, we can carefully craft, delete, and recraft each sentence in relation to how others might view our words rather than speaking spontaneously. Through over-reflection, we no longer act freely or spontaneously based on our actual feelings, nor do we speak and act based on critical self-reflection, but rather we calculate or rationalize our words or behavior to meet the standard of public opinion and gain public approval. We endlessly reflect on what "they" think, thereby becoming merely a reflection of the crowd.[43]

In the process we exhaust ourselves, not in an internal search, which can happen as well, but in seeking out the bullseye of collective opinion. We reflect endlessly on what this person would think, what that person would think, what everyone would think forever, and in this state of over-reflective stagnation the flame of passion, that leads to the decisiveness necessary for realizing one's calling, to give one's life meaning, is extinguished. We reflect on the crowd and stifle ourselves into inaction, exhausted with the thought of "what would they think" if I acted on those spontaneous revolutionary ideas that are out of the norm, that would cause me to act so "insensibly."

Through this over-reflective process, the anonymous power of the public overcomes these spontaneous inclinations and instead directs us to act according to "common sense," which usually means doing practically nothing at all, certainly nothing really out of the norm that might break free from the crowd. In Kierkegaard's words, the individual thereby becomes "leveled" and held in a "prison in which his own reflection holds him."[44] In a state of exhaustively seeking approval from the public, we become the same as everyone else, penned in by the same sense of normality.

But even if we do manage to break through our own over-reflection, even if we come to see that we are not being ourselves, on the verge of decisive action Kierkegaard says one still must break through the "vast penitentiary built by the reflection of [one's] associates" who become envious of the individual who actually *is* passionately realizing one's unique self.[45] In other words, on top of our own tendency toward stagnation, keeping ourselves down, the people around us try to keep us down as well, and try to block us from realizing our inner selves, "not tyrants and secret police, not the clergy and the aristocracy."[46]

Rather than admiring greatness, the present age—Kierkegaard says—*envies* it and attempts to hold the individual down from rising above the crowd:

> Characterless envy does not understand that excellence is excellence . . . but wants to degrade it, minimize it, until it actually is no longer excellence . . . . Envy in the process of *establishing* itself takes the form of *leveling*, and whereas a passionate age *accelerates, raises up and overthrows, elevates and debases*, a reflective apathetic age does the opposite, it *stifles and impedes, it levels*.[47]

By contrast, when individuals are strongly united through shared passion, and deeply bond over the "third" in a relationship, they come to *admire* one another for their achievements. The victory of another becomes something others can cheer on because it is a victory for the community—a further advancement of the cause they are mutually committed to even if only a few get the glory. For example, if one is truly passionate about music, then one admires someone like Beethoven or John Coltrane because of the gifts of music they have brought. In such a bonded community, although others want the glory too, it is not an envious desire, and one does not wish to spoil the other's victory, for that would be hurting the cause one is passionate about.

To hurt those who have through their achievement earned their leadership would be to hurt oneself. One has an obligation to give to one's community based upon what one can. Because people want to be like the excellent accomplished person and achieve what that individual has achieved, they are inspired by one another and are pushed forward to greatness while also being humbled at another's power.[48]

With the public, however, without that third that strongly unites individuals in community, there is no distinction that can be made between individuals based on a comparison of who is more aptly advancing that passionately devoted mutual cause. In that emptiness, Perkins says, "the public's only comparison is with itself, each one within the public."[49] People then carefully, and enviously, keep an eye on one another rather than really relating to one another. One's sense of worth becomes a comparison based on external trivialities according to who is more approved by popular opinion and empty status symbols like money and, increasingly today, the digital tokens of social media ratings. One finds oneself, as Kierkegaard prophetically says, "counting and counting."[50] What else is there by which to compare one another when there is no greater passionate cause uniting the relationship? Popularity, fame, likes, hearts, shares, followers, and so forth, become the end that the public orients itself toward. Instead of finding identity in passionately following one's given cause, and feeling validated through the extent to which one knows one is fulfilling one's given potential, Tuttle says, "individuals assign their identity to numbers, and find an inner support for their existence in a numerical status," and so for Kierkegaard, "the crowd is born."[51]

When our source of comparison is not based on who is most fully advancing a shared cause, but rather popular approval, we then come to envy rather than admire each other. This is in part because we know that just about *anything* can become popular. We are therefore not humbled by the great individual who becomes a role model, but rather feel that we deserve a number as big as anyone else in a game of trivial pursuits. Envy therefore runs rampant on Facebook, as many studies have suggested,[52] and on social media in general. We implicitly feel that anyone could just as easily be the next YouTube or TikTok viral star, it is only a matter of luck or practice, and so people might as well admire themselves.[53] We envy another who gets the credit that we feel we ought to deserve, and in an age of triviality, without passion, anyone feels, perhaps rightly, that they can achieve the mediocrity that is heralded with virality.

The result of numerical status being what makes something significant to the public means that we disregard the inwardness needed to find one's calling and through passionately following that calling become a leader. We instead become guided by the crowd. But true leaders, who follow their passion rather than the crowd, may not always be popular. For example, people surely mocked Gandhi's idea of nonviolent resistance, that one could effectively challenge a violent colonial behemoth through such nonviolent means. But through passionately following his calling, he set an example. He led by example rather than simply mimicking the existing popular trend. This is how cultures breakthrough from stagnation and new ideas are formed, by leaders following the lead of their heart rather than the lead of what is already popular.

By contrast, with the public, when numerical status becomes the marker of significance, rather than individuals being true to themselves, it is popularity that matters above all else. Where once leaders would rise above and gain significance as champions, in the present age, Kierkegaard says, "so and so many human beings uniformly make one individual; thus it is merely a matter of getting the proper number—and then one has significance."[54] Individual leadership thereby becomes lost in the public and instead the trending hashtag takes on the role of a single individual and is exalted. The lowest common denominator rises to the top. *Paddington 2* becomes the highest rated film of all time, above *Citizen Kane*, *Casablanca*, and *the Godfather*.[55] "Greatness" becomes equivalent to pleasing the crowd.

While we all demand a natural right to fifteen seconds of viral fame, to be elevated to the same status as all others, on the flipside, the envious public often finds great amusement in the fall or "fails" of another, especially if that person is a highly revered figure. This emotion is commonly referred to by the German word *schadenfreude*, the joy in witnessing someone else's misfortune or pain. This is a particularly dark side of human nature that can also easily slip into direct sadism. *Schadenfreude*, as ugly as it is, may result when we see others' misfortunes because their reduction in status gives us a feeling of comparative superiority thereby boosting our own self-esteem.[56]

Studies have shown that *schadenfreude* is linked closely with envy.[57] We may be particularly joyful when someone we envy falls or fails because then this painful feeling of inferiority is at least temporarily lessened or relieved.[58] If someone is disgraced or humiliated, we are therefore quick to join in the fun. We widely mock and laugh at them. The disgrace of publicly esteemed figures become national or global obsessions. The public is waiting for greatness to stumble so that it can stab it to death while it's down. This makes us all feel a little better about ourselves, especially when we see someone really powerful fall. The worse we feel about ourselves in comparison with others, the better we feel when an envied person fails.[59] Rather than mourning a cherished hero's disgrace, the public gleefully dances on the grave.

Kierkegaard himself was a direct recipient of this sort of envious treatment by the public as he became the relentless subject of derision from a popular Danish satirical weekly paper *The Corsair*, which he regarded as a gossip rag. *The Corsair* published a critical review of one of Kierkegaard's books in which Kierkegaard felt the reviewer did not properly understand or represent him. In return, Kierkegaard published two pieces of his own in which he blasted both the author of the review and *The Corsair* itself. Having generally been admired by *The Corsair*, Kierkegaard dished out an attack proclaiming that admiration from such a low-place was a terrible insult.

The retaliation Kierkegaard experienced for his "dis" of the paper was swift and heavy. For over a year, the widely read newspaper published taunting cartoons and articles about him that mocked petty externalities such as his voice, fashion (the length of his pant legs), and mannerisms. They couldn't challenge him on his own intellectual level. Publicly humiliated, the great philosopher was made a mockery among the streets of Denmark where he would go for frequent walks. Even children ran after him taunting him in the street. Although Kierkegaard later claimed that such a terrible experience had an edifying effect on him—which may be accurate as the episode was followed by a whole new period of authorship—his journal entries also seem to show that he was indeed very hurt by this abusive treatment. Tuttle claims that "the paper so caricatured and belittled him that it contributed to his mental depression and early death—the first philosophical martyr of the mass media."[60]

In previous eras, when the mass media was concentrated in the hands of the few, only well-known public figures such as Kierkegaard could become a target of a public attack, as occurred for him in the Corsair affair. Now, on social media, with all of us becoming broadcasted public figures, with the mass media *directly* in the hands of the public, what happened to Kierkegaard can happen to any ordinary person and potentially at a much greater scale as well. This is the flipside of viral celebrity: viral infamy.

The primary means of the public turning on an individual is through public shaming and humiliation. Today, on the Internet and social media, the number of online public shaming and humiliation incidents that have occurred so far are too great to recall here. They happen in ways both big and small. The most famous are those that attract millions of viewers around the world, but there are plenty of online shaming and humiliation incidents that take effect most directly on the level of a school or a town that may be devastating even if they are less well-known occurrences. While a public leading an attack on an individual may not always be driven by a leveling instinct, the larger public that sits back and watches the humiliating spectacle unfold is usually still dripping with *schadenfreude*. In chapter 4, we begin Part II—"Control"—by covering a few well-known relatively recent examples of global online public shaming incidents for the purpose of elucidating this new form of power, a hostile and potentially devastating exercise of public agency.

NOTES

1. Quoted in Robert L. Perkins, "Envy as Personal Phenomenon and as Politics," in *International Kierkegaard Commentary: Two Ages*, ed. Robert Perkins (Macon: Mercer University Press, 1984), 117.

2. Hubert Dreyfus, "Nihilism on the Information Highway: Anonymity versus Commitment in the Present Age," in *Community in the Digital Age: Philosophy and Practice*, ed. Andrew Feenberg and Darin Barney (Lanham: Rowman & Littlefield, 2004), 77.

3. Dreyfus, "Nihilism," 77.

4. Dreyfus, "Nihilism," 77.

5. Søren Kierkegaard, "Two Ages: The Age of Revolution and The Present Age. A Literary Review," in *The Essential Kierkegaard*, ed. Howard V. Hong and Edna H. Hong (Princeton: Princeton University Press, 2000), 267.

6. Viktor E. Frankl, *Man's Search for Meaning: An Introduction to Logotherapy a Revised and Enlarged Edition of From Death Camp to Existentialism* (New York: Simon and Schuster, 1962), 111.

7. Kierkegaard, "Two Ages," 265.

8. Frankl, *Man's Search*, 99.

9. Adrian F. Ward, Kristen Duke, Ayelet Gneezy, and Maarten W. Bos, "Brain Drain: The Mere Presence of One's Own Smartphone Reduces Available Cognitive Capacity," *Journal of the Association for Consumer Research* 2, no. 2 (2017): 140–54.

10. Nicholas Carr, "How Smartphones Hijack Our Minds," *The Wall Street Journal*, October 6, 2017, https://www.wsj.com/articles/how-smartphones-hijack-our-minds-1507307811.

11. Timothy D. Wilson, David A. Reinhard, Erin C. Westgate, Daniel T. Gilbert, Nicole Ellerbeck, Cheryl Hahn, Casey L. Brown, and Adi Shaked, "Just Think: The Challenges of the Disengaged Mind," *Science* 345, no. 6192 (2014): 76.

12. Kierkegaard, "Two Ages," 265.

13. Kierkegaard, "Two Ages," 267.

14. Perkins, "Envy," 116.

15. Christopher B. Barnett, *Kierkegaard, Pietism and Holiness* (London: Routledge, 2016), 145, http://www.tandfebooks.com/isbn/9781315591056.

16. Roberto Esposito, *Communitas: The Origin and Destiny of Community*, trans. Timothy Campbell (Stanford: Stanford University Press, 2010), 6.

17. Howard Nelson Tuttle, *The Crowd is Untruth: The Existential Critique of Mass Society in the thought of Kierkegaard, Nietzsche, Heidegger, and Ortega y Gasset* (New York: Lang, 1996), 32.

18. Dreyfus, "Nihilism," 71.

19. Laura Entis, "Chronic Loneliness Is a Modern-Day Epidemic," *Fortune*, June 22, 2016, http://fortune.com/2016/06/22/loneliness-is-a-modern-day-epidemic/.

20. Kennon M. Sheldon, Neetu Abad, and Christian Hinsch, "A Two-Process View of Facebook Use and Relatedness Need-satisfaction: Disconnection Drives Use, and Connection Rewards It," *Journal of Personality and Social Psychology* 100, no. 4 (2011): 773.

21. Jean M. Twenge, "Have Smartphones Destroyed a Generation?," *The Atlantic*, September 2017, https://www.theatlantic.com/magazine/archive/2017/09/has-the-smartphone-destroyed-a-generation/534198/.

22. Jean M. Twenge, "Why Teens Aren't Partying Anymore," *Wired*, December 27, 2017, https://www.wired.com/story/why-teens-arent-partying-anymore/.

23. Twenge, "Have Smartphones."

24. Twenge, "Why Teens."

25. Twenge, "Have Smartphones."

26. Emily Drago, "The Effect of Technology on Face-to-Face Communication," *Elon Journal of Undergraduate Research in Communications* 6, no. 1 (2015): 13–19.

27. Andrew K. Przybylski and Netta Weinstein, "Can You Connect With Me Now? How the Presence of Mobile Communication Technology Influences Face-to-Face Conversation Quality," *Journal of Social and Personal Relationships* 30, no. 3 (2013): 237–46.

28. Lauren C. Davis, "The Flight from Conversation," *The Atlantic*, October 7, 2015, https://www.theatlantic.com/technology/archive/2015/10/reclaiming-conversation-sherry-turkle/409273/.

29. Sara H. Konrath, Edward H. O'Brien, and Courtney Hsing, "Changes in Dispositional Empathy in American College Students Over Time: A Meta-analysis," *Personality and Social Psychology Review* 15, no. 2 (2011): 180–98.

30. Yalda T. Uhls et al., "Five Days at Outdoor Education Camp Without Screens Improves Preteen Skills with Nonverbal Emotion Cues," *Computers in Human Behavior* 39 (2014): 387–92.

31. Davis, "The Flight."

32. Turkle, *Alone Together*.

33. Mark Zuckerberg, "Building Global Community," *Facebook*, February 16, 2017, https://www.facebook.com/notes/mark-zuckerberg/building-global-community/10103508221158471/.

34. Kierkegaard, "Two Ages," 261–62.

35. Michael Warner, "Publics and Counterpublics," *Public Culture* 14, no. 1 (2002): 51. Project MUSE.

36. Warner, "Publics and Counterpublics," 51.

37. Warner, "Publics and Counterpublics," 60.

38. Warner, "Publics and Counterpublics," 62.

39. Warner, "Publics and Counterpublics," 89.

40. Quoted in Walter Kaufman, *Existentialism from Dostoevsky to Sartre* (Cleveland and New York: Meridian Books, 1965), 92.

41. Tuttle, *The Crowd is Untruth*, 35.

42. Kierkegaard, "Two Ages," 264.

43. Tuttle, *The Crowd is Untruth*, 34.

44. Kierkegaard, "Two Ages," 257.

45. Kierkegaard, "Two Ages," 257.

46. Kierkegaard, "Two Ages," 257.

47. Kierkegaard, "Two Ages," 258.

48. Perkins, "Envy," 113.

49. Perkins, "Envy," 124.
50. Kierkegaard, "Two Ages," 263.
51. Tuttle, *The Crowd is Untruth*, 34.
52. Helmut Appel, Alexander L. Gerlach, and Jan Crusius, "The Interplay between Facebook Use, Social Comparison, Envy, and Depression," *Current Opinion in Psychology* 9 (2016): 44–49.
53. Søren Kierkegaard, *The Present Age*, trans. Alexander Dru (New York and Evanston: Harper & Row, 1962), 38.
54. Kierkegaard, "Two Ages," 259.
55. Jack Shepherd, "Paddington 2 becomes Rotten Tomatoes' Best Reviewed Movie of all Time," *The Independent*, January 19, 2018, https://www.independent.co.uk/arts-entertainment/films/news/paddington-2-rotten-tomatoes-review-best-top-positive-negative-a8167351.html.
56. Richard H. Smith, *The Joy of Pain: Schadenfreude and the Dark Side of Human Nature* (Oxford: Oxford University Press, 2013), 2.
57. Smith, *The Joy of Pain*, 114.
58. Smith, *The Joy of Pain*, 110.
59. Smith, *The Joy of Pain*, 8.
60. Tuttle, *The Crowd is Untruth*, 11.

Part II

CONTROL

Chapter 4

The Spectacular Power of the Public

In 2015, the life of Dr. Walter J. Palmer, a dentist from Bloomington, Minnesota, imploded. On a big game hunt that year Palmer shot Cecil the Lion, the beloved and protected Zimbabwean treasure, whose killing sparked an international outrage. Online, the *New York Times* reported that Palmer quickly became the target of "seemingly endless shaming . . . strong enough to effectively dismantle his digital life . . . . Angry people sent a surge of traffic to Dr. Palmer's website, which was taken offline. Vitriolic reviews flooded his Yelp page. A Facebook page titled 'Shame Lion Killer Dr. Walter Palmer and River Bluff Dental' drew thousands of users. Dr. Palmer's face was scrubbed from industry websites." He was doxed online with the contact information for his home, work, and that of his family dug up and posted on the Internet.[1] His wife and daughter, who had nothing to do with the killing of Cecil, were threatened.[2] Anyone close to Palmer became essentially guilty by association and was punished as a result. A local crisis manager who was hired by Palmer, asked only to circulate an initial statement to the public, quickly ended his involvement after the digital mob came after him and flooded his Yelp page with degrading comments.[3] Protestors took camp outside his dental office screaming "Murderer! Terrorist!" signs were pinned on his office doors: "WE ARE CECIL," "#CatLivesMatter," and ominously, "ROT IN HELL."[4] This forced him to shutter his practice for weeks, affecting all of his staff, and reopening only with security guards out front.[5] A vacation home in Florida was vandalized, the words "LION Killer!" spray-painted across the garage door and severed pigs feet were strewn across the driveway.[6]

Palmer declared that he had relied on his local guides and had no idea that the lion he was hunting was protected, nor of its fame. In subsequent court hearings, Palmer was cleared of any misconduct by Zimbabwean authorities.[7] But to the public avenging Cecil's death, he was as guilty as could be right from the start. The massive worldwide online shaming that Palmer received in return was subsequently described as a "reputational annihilation."[8] As our technology begins to seamlessly blend the digital and physical worlds together, an annihilation of one's reputation, this "dismantling of one's digital life," is increasingly a dismantling of one's IRL life. I am personally *very* against big game hunting, and generally against hunting altogether, but the issue at hand is whether the public should be able to dismantle someone's life at its whim. The harm inflicted by public shaming online can be a serious punishment and is comparable to the level of harm inflicted in the public shaming punishments of medieval Europe and colonial America. We can get a better perspective of the depth of harm inflicted in online shaming sanctions, and the subsequent power of the public that can inflict that harm, by placing public shaming in that proper historical context.

PUBLIC SHAMING IN THE IRL VILLAGE

With the revival of public shaming online, the public now has a power in its possession that rivals state-level sanctions once banished from the world ostensibly on account of their cruelty. In the West, public shaming has its roots most directly in medieval Europe. Under European monarchies, public shaming and humiliation sanctions weren't the *most* gruesome punishments monarchs were capable of inflicting. The worst punishments involved obscene bodily tortures that were largely absent in shaming sanctions. But public shaming sanctions were one of the main methods by which monarchs demonstrated sovereign power over their subjects. Therefore, understanding the underlying logic of sovereign power will help us to better understand what is occurring with the dynamics of power involved in public shaming online and how this might point to the reemergence of an authoritarian force.

In *Discipline and Punish,* Michel Foucault details the methods by which sovereign power was established under monarchical rule in premodern times. The main features of sovereign power were that it was exercised: (1) arbitrarily, often being carried out at the whim of the sovereign; (2) through spectacle, by making a highly visible example out of the offender in order to teach a lesson; and (3) disproportionately, deliberately obliterating the individual to demonstrate a show of the monarch's power in front of everyone.

In the European Middle Ages, any challenge to the monarch's power was considered an "offense" because the monarch was in a sense literally offended. Since the monarch was the absolute power of the state, the sovereign in and of himself, and there was no rule of law over the monarch, then to offend him therefore *was* to violate the law. He was the body of law himself, the final arbiter of right and wrong. He was not constrained by the power of the people, and the rule of law over him, like a democratically elected president or prime minister is supposed to be. Foucault argues he rather *was* the power over the people. One was, therefore, at the mercy of the sovereign's whim arbitrarily.

For those who offended the monarch, even slightly, they would be made an example of through a highly visible spectacle of punishment on a scaffold set-up in the public square with the offender exposed before the whole village or town in his degrading weakness. These punishments included public shaming and humiliation, though in the most extreme cases, the monarch ordered the most obscene tortures on the offender's body, sometimes literally tearing the victim apart piece by piece and reducing his body to nothingness in front of an often-exuberant audience. This is what the monarch did to demonstrate that she was beyond challenge.

The sovereign, in theory, was an absolute monstrous beast, a leviathan in the Hobbesian sense, and yet at the same time Foucault argues that the monarch was mechanical, rigid, prescribed, quantified, and deliberate in carrying out his violence. The meticulous proportion that the monarch deliberately oversaw was one of extremely excessive *disproportion* designed to answer any challenge to his power with an absolute obliteration of the offender's body. This deliberately disproportionate punishment was combined with the force of spectacle described above. The aim of the spectacle of violence enacted by the monarch, Foucault says,

> is not so much to re-establish a balance as to bring into play, as its extreme point, the dissymmetry between the subject who has dared to violate the law and the all-powerful sovereign who displays his strength . . . the punishment is carried out in such a way as to give a spectacle not of measure, but of imbalance and excess; in this liturgy of punishment, there must be an emphatic affirmation of power and of its intrinsic superiority.[9]

Through this public display of brutal power the monarch teaches everyone watching a stark lesson: "The aim was to make an example," Foucault says, "not only by making people aware that the slightest offence was likely to be punished, but by arousing feelings of terror by the spectacle of power letting its anger fall upon the guilty person."[10] Without the public show, the punishment would be practically worthless. The people needed to witness the monarch's power and in fact take part in it, as a further submission to him, by appearing at the scaffold to watch and jeer the offender, as a form of reverence that further established the sovereign's power over everyone else. With severed limbs, and gasping bodies, this was the most extreme way in which the monarch kept his command, through a demonstration, and a lesson in his power for all to see.

While the public shaming and humiliation punishments that were also common in medieval Europe did not involve these brutal bodily tortures, they shared the main characteristics of sovereign power as described by Foucault: they were enacted arbitrarily, and designed to make a humiliating spectacle out of the individual through a disproportionate display of power. As public shaming sanctions were imported across the seas into colonial America, the brutal bodily punishments of the monarch were more cast aside in favor of these relatively incorporeal shaming punishments. That said, public shaming sanctions in colonial America maintained much of the characteristics of sovereign displays of power as described above.

Rituals of public shaming and humiliation were the primary punishment used for establishing and preserving the prescribed social order of the towns and villages of colonial America. There were a variety of highly ceremonial, cruel public humiliations regularly used by ruling authorities that were intended to invoke shame in offenders, and to teach them, as well as others witnessing their terrible ordeals, a vicious lesson.[11] As with the sovereign's public tortures, these were designed to make an awful spectacle out of the offending individual. Unlike today, prison incarceration was hardly used as punishment and only began to become popular starting in the nineteenth century when public shaming and humiliation was largely abolished. There is even reason to believe that many considered public shaming to be *worse* than prison, at least to some significant degree. For example, in an 1899 article published in the *British Medical Journal* a Dr. Lemaistre was cited who "asked sixty prisoners which they would choose—an hour of the pillory or three months' imprisonment, and all but two replied that they would prefer the prison."[12]

Essentially, every village and town in medieval Europe and colonial America would have had stocks and/or a pillory. They were located in the most public of places such as the market, or by the churchyard. The stocks was a basic contraption, usually just a low bench with a pair of metal bars that would hold a seated person firmly in place by his or her legs. The point of the stocks was not to inflict great physical pain on the offender, but simply to render the sentenced individual helpless for only a few hours before a mob of onlookers who would jeer and jest while many would throw things at the offender like rotten eggs, trash, and dead animals.[13]

The pillory was similar to the stocks, though perhaps more ignoble, more feared, and somewhat more physically painful. It was usually a wooden contraption with two boards that could be opened and locked together, whereby the offender would stoop down in a bent position, and stick his neck through a center hole to hold his head firmly in place, with his arms locked in adjacent holes on either side. This created a very uncomfortable position where the offender's face was thrust before the crowd, unable to be covered in shame, as we are so naturally inclined to do.

In the centers of town, the pillory was placed on a raised scaffold for all to witness an offender's humiliating spectacle. High visibility and mass publicity were the keys to its power both for humiliating the individual and for teaching a lesson to the crowd by making an example out of him. As par for the course, a mob of onlookers, perhaps driven by *schadenfreude*, and in order to appear themselves above moral disrepute, would glare disapprovingly at the offender, hurl insults, and pelt the offender's face with rotten eggs and other disgusting things. In some cases, as if this wasn't already enough, the offender would have his ears nailed to the boards of the pillory so that his face was as squarely as possible exposed to the burning, blistering crowd and their degrading projectiles. His ears would then be sliced off leaving permanent, disfiguring, degrading marks of his infamy.

With corporal punishments like the stocks and pillory, the physical pain was part of its deterring effect. The uncomfortable bodily positions of being locked into these contraptions, the items being thrown into faces by the audience, and the stings of the lash from a public whipping post, which was another popular sanction, were all part of the punishment. On occasion, things could even turn deadly at the hands of the mob letting loose with their anger on the helpless offender stuck in the pillory. But generally speaking, apart from extreme episodes, what was considered even more painful than the physical pain was the *psychological* torture of the intense shame, humiliation, and disgrace.[14]

Because the psychological torture of shame and humiliation is so effective as a form of social control, getting down into the sinews of our basic nature as social animals, in many instances, the physical component of shaming sanctions could be essentially done away with altogether. For example, one of the most popular forms of punishment was to force rulebreakers to stand on a scaffold wearing letters that designated one's offense, for example, a "B" for blasphemy, or a "D" for drunkenness.[15] Offenders could also be forced to stand in public wearing a sign that announced their crimes such as "An open and obstinate contemner of God's holy ordinances" or "public destroyer of peace."[16]

Sometimes offenders could be forced to permanently wear their letters thereby marking them for life by their misdeeds. This real-life form of punishment was immortalized in Nathaniel Hawthorne's fictional work *The Scarlet Letter*, where the main character, Hester Prynne, is publicly humiliated on a scaffold and then forced to forever wear the letter "A" in her puritanical New England town for her offense of adultery (which notably only "occurred" after her husband had disappeared and was presumed dead).

Permanent visible marks like these had the effect of permanently outcasting individuals from their communities.[17] No one struck a physical blow against Hester Prynne. She was merely humiliated and marked with a sign. But this annihilated her reputation, permanently outcasting her from society, and that is what made it so dreadful.

FROM GROUPS TO NETWORKS

Part of what made public shaming work as a form of social control in premodern villages had to do with the conditions of their living arrangements. The towns of colonial America, for example, were in general extremely small, disconnected from one another, with few transients, and little population turnover. Therefore, most people were lifelong residents, and practically everyone would have known everyone else.[18] The psychological torture of being humiliated before essentially every person one had ever known and would ever know, would have been overwhelming for any ordinary person. Extending the punishment indefinitely, they would then have to continue to live and work beside these people who would subsequently shun them.[19] With rejection and loneliness being as painful and detrimental to one's well-being as we know them to be, this would have been a terrible ordeal. At a time when people still lived together in close-knit communities with their lives deeply intertwined, being shunned would be especially devastating to both one's emotional and physical well-being.

As people moved from towns and villages to the larger cities coming into development in the nineteenth century, public shaming gradually became abolished, and was almost completely obsolete by the start of the twentieth century. Some argue that due to the *anonymity* that was engendered in modern cities through the sheer size and transient nature of the population, public shaming in a twentieth-century city simply could no longer be very effective. As sociologist Steven Nock explains, "to shame another, that person must be known and must be a member of the group applying the shame. An outsider, or stranger, cannot be shamed this way."[20]

In a modern city, unlike a village, most people would be strangers to one another; shaming would therefore not bring about the utterly devastating feeling of full-blown humiliation or rejection from all the people one cares about and relies upon that was only possible in more intimate living conditions. Furthermore, if someone had been shamed in one place they could in theory start relatively afresh somewhere new without a lifelong reputational fallout. Shaming therefore arguably had to be replaced as a central sanction even if the ostensible rationale for its abolition was in many people's minds one of humanitarian reform.[21]

But now the world is rapidly becoming much smaller once again through our information and communication technologies. As our ICTs "re-tribalize" us on a worldwide scale, we are moving into the "global village" that media scholar Marshall McLuhan prophesied decades ago.[22] Now separated groups that may have functioned rather autonomously within the anonymity of a larger social body are dissolving into a network.

A network is different than a group because a group is relatively closed off and so what happens in one group setting is largely isolated from what happens in another. That means, among other things, that a person can move from one group to another without occurrences in one group necessarily affecting outcomes in another. Different norms are therefore able to spring up in different settings with different groups. We can act differently in one group than we would with another, act differently with our friends than we would with our colleagues, our families, and so on. It also means that whatever shame and rejection an individual might face from one group didn't have to carry over to the next.

But not so in the global village. Instead, information about one's life is consistently being shared online and is thereby exposed before a large and often only loosely connected audience of hundreds or thousands of friends with each one of these people connected into a whole different set of relationships in the network. Even private group communications, direct messaging, and ephemeral posts are only a screenshot away from entering permanently into this larger network. Rather than information being contained to a group, one is indirectly networked into the entire "global community," with about 83 percent of all Twitter followers, for example, connected within only *five* steps of interconnection.[23] As a result, there is no way to effectively gate off the flow of information and become anonymous in the larger society as would have been possible in the twentieth century.

When all groups are networked together globally, it is increasingly difficult to pick up and start over again if one is thoroughly rejected by a cluster of "nodes" in the network. One's marred reputation, and the subsequent fallout, can jump from cluster to cluster like a virus spreading throughout the network. Rather than being able to start over fresh with different groups, one may instead become cut off, and disconnected from the global network if one is thoroughly rejected in any part of the network. This new reality, of the move from groups to a network, in terms of the flows of information about people, reinstates the conditions of a traditional village in important ways, but on a global scale, that is, the "global village" McLuhan prophesied.

In a traditional village, shame was the primary psychological mechanism of control because everyone knew who you were, and everyone knew each other's business. A misstep could be experienced as a disgrace before everyone one knew, loved, or ever might come to know, because the village was small, and gossip traveled fast. In the global village of the twenty-first century, with information traveling effortlessly and rapidly on digital networks, public shaming unsurprisingly reemerges as an effective mechanism of social control since once again everyone can know each other's business and everyone can witness each other in their possible disgrace for breaking the norms of a village that spans across continents.

PUBLIC SHAMING AND HUMILIATION IN THE GLOBAL VILLAGE

One of the earliest examples of a massive online public shaming and humiliation campaign occurred in South Korea in 2005, when a young woman's dog defecated in a subway car and—probably mortified—she didn't clean it up. A fellow passenger photographed the incident with a flip-phone camera (this was before smartphones) and posted it to a popular website. Practically overnight, she became known nationwide as—loosely translated—"dog poop girl." Following publication of the user-submitted photo of the incident, humiliating memes subsequently flourished across all of South Korea. She was publicly identified and personal information about her and her relatives was revealed on the Internet, aka doxing. She began to be harassed in public—IRL public. Soon the overwhelming unwanted attention upended her life and she dropped out of her university program, in essence going into hiding from the public.

Although we can all agree that she ought to have cleaned up the poop, we can also hopefully agree that the punishment she received in return for her social transgression was completely disproportionate to her offense. If this young woman were tried in an actual democratic court for her crime, she'd probably be reasonably given a fine of the South Korean equivalent of a few hundred dollars at most. She'd pay the price, literally, and go on about her life. But in the court of public opinion even the slightest offense may be overwhelmingly punished completely disproportionately to the nature of one's offense.

In 2009 Susan Boyle, an overweight middle-aged woman, sang "I Dreamed a Dream" from *Les Miserables* on the UK reality TV show *Britain's Got Talent*. When Boyle was first introduced to the studio-theater audience, she was met with eye-rolls and laughter from the panel of judges after professing her dream of being a pop star, given that she did not fit the conventions of pop-stardom in her age or appearance. Panning to catch the crowd's reaction to Boyle's seemingly preposterous wish of stardom, a sixteen-year-old girl was briefly caught on film rolling her eyes, just like every other member of the crowd, echoing the prevailing public sentiment at that moment. Undeterred by the laughter, Susan Boyle heroically sang her heart out, "shocking" the audience that such a beautiful voice could come out of her mouth. The public suddenly made a dramatic turn, instantaneously. Now, the public was Susan Boyle's greatest defender.

After the clip of Susan Boyle went viral on YouTube, the eye-rolling teenage girl caught on camera became the subject of a massive shaming campaign in the United Kingdom. She was dubbed "1:24 girl," which noted the time she appeared rolling her eyes in the main YouTube video. Indeed, everyone was rolling their eyes at that point. Nevertheless, an example of her had to be made for her disrespect to the public's opinion. Public terror ensued against this teenage girl, in which she was threatened and harassed both online and offline. This occurrence demonstrates that there is no indiscretion too small to warrant the wrath of the global public. Even a "wrong" facial expression, caught on camera, can become cause for massive punishment. Furthermore, what the prevailing opinion is can change almost instantaneously, in this case practically in a snap, and one can be punished for being caught having ever been on the "wrong" side of public opinion even if one was only echoing the commonly held sentiment at that time. Whatever offends the public sufficiently is the offense, and the public might not even know what offends it until it is offended.

The final example we'll survey here is the now infamous 2013 case of Justine Sacco, a then relatively unknown PR agent from New York, who made an offensive joke to her relatively small group of followers on Twitter before boarding a flight to South Africa: "Going to Africa. Hope I don't get AIDS. Just kidding. I'm white!" This joke may have worked coming out of the mouth of Cartman on South Park, where the show's authors are known political satirists, but it landed very poorly on Twitter to say the least. Sacco instantaneously became an international villain as the tweet went viral worldwide and a global horde unleashed their professed outrage against this previously ordinary stranger. As she slept on the intercontinental flight to South Africa, the hashtag #HasJustineLandedYet became a trending topic on Twitter used to monitor her movements across the globe and for many to take joy, *schadenfreude*, in the personal horror Justine would awake to when turning on her phone after the flight to find her reputation had been annihilated overnight.

Upon landing at the airport in Cape Town, just hours after making the offensive joke, another stranger in this global crowd was waiting for her at the arrival gate—smartphone in hand—snapping her photo and updating the public with her whereabouts. Workers at the hotels she was booked at threatened to go on strike if she showed up, and she was told her personal safety could not be guaranteed.[24] After the torrent of shame, humiliation, and threats that followed, Justine Sacco was fired from her job, and shunned by several immediate family members. She then proceeded to temporarily flee across the planet from New York to Ethiopia, like a fugitive on the lam.

Sacco later tried to defend herself that the joke was meant to be taken sarcastically and perhaps actually meant to *point out* racial inequities between whites and blacks in South Africa regarding HIV infections. She explains: "To me it was so insane of a comment for anyone to make I thought there was no way that anyone could possibly think it was literal . . . Living in America puts us in a bit of a bubble when it comes to what is going on in the third world. I was making fun of that bubble."[25] Regardless of her professed intentions of satire, her joke was considered outrageously insensitive and she was immediately deemed a cruel racist by the public. Without a trial, her character was digitally executed in a collective act of reputational annihilation nearly instantaneously.

To be clear, I don't personally condone her joke, but Sacco's punishment was quite a price to pay. Our new mediums of communication are greatly heightening the threat that even the smallest missteps can have enormous and long-lasting negative repercussions for an individual almost immediately. What's especially notable about Sacco's episode is the sheer demonstration of the public's power to move into coordinated global action; to instantaneously locate, identify, track, mark, and crush an offender across the planet. Our new and emerging ICTs facilitate this tracking and collective mobilization. For example, while Sacco was still midflight, unaware of what was happening, a Google search for her name brought up a flight-tracker, showing in real-time how long until she landed. Beneath her photo ran a slew of negative headlines about her in major news outlets before she was even aware of what was going on, before she had landed and turned on her phone.[26] Search engines like Google and social media make a situation like this possible and should arguably be held responsible for enabling its harms. But in public shaming incidents, Google and Twitter can only do so much to inflict punishment and generate fear. What's really to fear is the overwhelming power of the public, connected through ICTs, that allows it a sort of hyper-agency as a collective entity to turn on ordinary individuals, to inflict harm directly upon any offender of public opinion in a way that was never before possible.

THE SOVEREIGN PUBLIC

In Philip Pettit's analysis of domination in *Republicanism*, he argues that three conditions need to be fulfilled for domination by others, and therefore a loss of liberty to occur: the agent, which may be an individual, corporate, or collective entity, has "(1) the capacity to interfere (2) on an arbitrary basis (3) in certain choices that the other is in a position to make."[27] Using this framework, we can see how all three of these aspects of domination are already being realized in the emergent power of the public.

As to Pettit's first clause, the public clearly has a "capacity to interfere" in people's lives, that is to make things worse for the individual making the choice, through a coercion of the will made by the threat of global exposure, shame, and humiliation for actions against public opinion. As for the second clause, Pettit explains that an agent interferes on an arbitrary basis if the agent is in a position to choose to interfere or not "at their pleasure," and does so "without reference to the interests, or the opinions, of those affected."[28] The public is already able to post photos, audio, video, and other information about people and publicly rip them apart as it chooses, which is often done literally with pleasure. The unwanted exposure and humiliation of the person obviously does not track with his or her interests, unless forceful assimilation into the crowd is, disturbingly, viewed as a new overarching societal interest of each person; that is, that the public knows best and one is not really free until one is forced in line with the "liberation" of the public.

Finally, Pettit's third clause points to the fact that a dominating agent need only have this capacity to arbitrarily interfere for certain choices others might make, not all choices. While it may be a stretch to say that the public can arbitrarily interfere with an individual for *any* choice one might make, nevertheless, there is an indefinite range of actions for which the public can interfere, since anything that bucks social convention is subject to its interference, and there is no real telling how collective opinion may shift and change over time. It need not be the case, either, that one experiences direct interference in order for the public to infringe upon one's liberty. Pettit rightly points out that one can have a master who is possibly beneficent, and never blocks an individual from the choices one wants to make, but that person is nevertheless still dominated by the agent and at its mercy.[29]

In terms of the logic of its use of force in online shaming and humiliation, the public is beginning to act like an authoritarian sovereign power—a monarch—as described by Foucault. Even if one may agree with the ends of shaming, and perhaps share in the public's outrage, as I often do myself, the means of online public shaming are still morally problematic in the ways highlighted above; that is, with sanctions that are disproportionate, and arbitrary, in that they are unconstrained nor defined by the rule of law and due process, but rather sanctioned based upon prevailing public opinion and feeling. Nor is online public shaming necessary in order to spread awareness of shameful or outrageous occurrences since recordings of such incidents can be broadcast while still masking an individual's identity (such as through blurring faces, which is readily available). Online public shaming is rather a form of severe extra-judicial punishment. Many might even prefer some form of corporal punishment, a physical blow, or perhaps several that is over and done with, than to be globally shamed and have one's reputation permanently destroyed, an infliction of indefinitely lasting and serious harm. It seems highly problematic that the public can wield this sort of sovereign-like power over other ordinary people even if the ends may be justified.

In drawing a comparison between the digital public and a monarch, let us first note the common parlance which one often hears in describing an episode of online public outrage. It is the *Internet* that reacts or *Twitter* that reacts to whatever *it* is offended by. The network of connected individuals online is implicitly regarded as forming a sort of single *collective* entity—the public—which like the monarch, becomes its own menacing force, readily apparent, watching over, capable of striking down upon any offender tremendously in an instant.

The effect of shaming punishments, whether in premodern villages, or online in the global village today, is one of collective action and intention, magnified by the indefinite number of onlookers. While it is often the case that only a relatively small number of people may be directly carrying out a public shaming sanction on Twitter, for example, the strength of the attack comes through it being carried out in front of everyone online who eagerly watches, or feels coerced out of fear into taking part or agreeing with the sanction. Few dare speak up for the condemned or criticize the mob's actions, lest the mob turn on them, and most will at least passively go along or praise the righteousness of the crowd so as to appear in good moral repute.

Like the sovereign in the premodern village, the public in the global village rules through its visibility and its spectacle of power, enacting an overwhelming and disproportionate public spectacle of violent force to make an example out of offenders, utterly demolishing the individual at its whim for even the slightest offense. If one offends the prevailing opinion or feeling, one of the multibillion eyes of the global public can capture it on the web, where it can go viral, and be used in efforts to deliberately shame, humiliate, and annihilate one's reputation. To be caught in the web, to be carried up and shown to all is the way the public, as an interconnected mass, exercises power. The public spectacle has been reconstituted from the days of the monarch now in the form of massive shaming and humiliation on a digital scaffold, an unrelenting form of psychological torture, once again a major tool of punishment that serves to enforce order.

With online public shaming, offenders of public opinion are thrust onto the most public stage possible, a pillory in the center of the global village, raised high above the entire world in a digital cage. The Google search, the Twitter trend, has become a virtual scaffold where the offender's digital body, including pictures of one's face, is immobilized in front of the crowd, pinned, just as the physical body was in the stocks or pillory back in medieval and colonial times, unable to hide from the exposure and humiliation before the public. The offender is pelted with humiliating insults, and threats, indefinitely, until the crowd has exhausted its anger, its *schadenfreude,* and has established itself as morally superior, beyond suspect, repelling the wrath of the public from themselves, and is ready to move on to the next offender. There is almost always *someone* in the global village's pillory at any given time. Its power lies, not so much in the number of people punished, but its looming threat, the idea instilled in everyone's minds that this could happen to *anyone*. It makes an example out of the offending individual and teaches everyone looking at the spectacle of degradation a terrifying lesson.

In addition to exercising power through highly visible displays of disproportionate punishment, like the premodern monarch, whatever offends the public at any given time is a violation of its rule and the offender is immediately judged guilty and sentenced. This is part of the arbitrary nature of rule by public opinion in the legal sense. The public decides on its whim what is acceptable or not, beyond challenge, and it is ready to tear one to pieces if offended, ready to explode with rage, sometimes for a serious moral offense, but possibly for something as small as disrespectfully rolling one's eyes, for making an ill-landed sarcastic and offensive joke, for failing to clean up after oneself, or even for just being plain weird and peculiar. There is no rule of law that comes about through a deliberative process, that constrains the public, and to which the accused individual is put on trial to see if one has violated it. What offends the public is rather determined by wherever the prevailing opinion and feeling blows, and the wind can shift in an instant.

One cannot adequately defend oneself against the amorphous invisible public, against society. If the accused are able to defend themselves in any way, it is usually only *after* they have already been punished by the public, and the damage is already done. Perhaps the most important liberal ideal of justice is thereby effectively overturned: that an individual is deemed innocent until proven guilty. Rather, as soon as damning "evidence" of an offense to public opinion is uploaded to the net, devoid of its relevant context, the individual is immediately judged guilty and punished. This presumption of guilt undermines a fundamental principle of liberal jurisprudence designed to protect us from authoritarian regimes, that "it is better that ten guilty persons escape than that one innocent suffer."[30] This is the essence of the ideal of individual rights in a liberal society, that we will not simply sacrifice a person for the greater good of society, or we will at least do all we reasonably can to prevent such an outcome.

Like a monarch, the public demands a tortured public confession of the accused to establish its righteousness and its authority as the arbiter of right and wrong. Foucault argues that the pre-modern sovereign would torture an offending individual until he confessed so as to mark the truth of the sovereign's claims on the body of the offender, to prove that the individual really is what the monarch says he is, so one can see the righteousness of the monarch for oneself directly on the offender's brutalized body.[31] Similarly, the individual shamed online today can only attempt to stem the onslaught of the public, to stave off the worst of the ongoing torture, through a public confession of wrongdoing and apology. If people try to explain or defend themselves or in any way say that they are not the monster the public is making them out to be, unless they confess and apologize for their offenses, they only arouse and worsen the public's wrath.

This process is like the authoritarian colonial power as described in *The Crucible*. The protagonist either had to confess to his alleged crimes and have his confession pinned on the door of the church for all to see, or face death. With the targets of online shaming, by confessing to their accused shamefulness, in the face of public torture, their digital bodies become inscribed with the truth of the public. Their searchable name online becomes synonymous with the evidence of their misdeed; their crime pinned on the doors of the digital church of the public, the Google search, the oracle of all modern knowledge. One's digital body thereby becomes directly inscribed with the public's power. The public holds the offender up to show that she is indeed the monster just as the public declares her to be through this tortured confession. The monster *is* in fact a monster. I Googled it: see. The public's accusation is algorithmically true, its condemnation righteous, and a shameful monster cannot be redeemed. He must rather be degraded and humiliated until he is no longer a threat, and then thrown out of the global community altogether as that is the price of shame.

Through online shaming and humiliation, there is now a concrete punishment in the hands of the public that may be sentenced upon any individual who in words or actions offends the prevailing opinion. This marks a crossing of a threshold from the automaton conformity described in Part I into the development of a more authoritarian form of control which, as Fromm explains, "use[s] threats and terror to induce this conformity."[32] Even just a few high-profile incidents of instant reputational annihilation, this sanctioning force of the public, is enough to demonstrate its obliterating power and to make others submit out of fear. This is similar to the way the nuclear bomb is the most feared tool of national power, and one of the most significant geopolitical forces, even though it has only ever been dropped twice to date in one brief, but atrocious episode.

One might object that there is a considerable difference between historical public shaming and online shaming today because of the lack of physicality in the latter. But as demonstrated with scarlet letter punishments, public shaming and humiliation does not need direct physical pain in order to be an effective and widely feared punishment. Rather, the scarlet letter was one of the *most* terrible punishments inflicted on a person precisely because of the overwhelming damage it did to one's reputation and the severe effects that had on a person's life in the premodern village, where reputations stuck.

In the global village, reputations stick once again. Online public shaming and humiliation does not need to inflict any pain directly onto the offender's IRL body in order to be an effective and highly feared sanction. Online shaming rather retains what is most important about the public shaming punishments of old, the psychological torture, and lasting pain from the shunning of a destroyed reputation. It perhaps even greatly amplifies this aspect of its power because of the scale of shame and humiliation that may occur in front of the entire networked world as well as the rather permanence of its disgrace. A branded digital body hovers over an individual like a dark cloud. As Internet and legal scholar Danielle Citron Keats says: "Hester Prynne, she had to walk through the town with a scarlet A, but at the end of the day she got to take it off . . . . When you post something really damaging, reputationally damaging, about someone online it's searchable and seeable. It's almost like it's tattooed on your head and projected throughout the world. And you can't erase it."[33]

Today, offenders of the public can effectively become marked and banished not just from the village, but from the *global* village. We saw this power exercised dramatically in the shaming of Justine Sacco who overnight became a worldwide villain, with hotel workers halfway across the planet from her hometown threatening to strike if she showed up to places where she booked a room. Doors were *literally* shut around the world as the networked public descended upon her. She was in effect, banished, or ostracized, from practically the entire planet's population, becoming an untouchable, a modern-day leper from which she can never fully recover the damage or stigma. Anyone who associates with the virally outcast individual, after all, may catch the virus by association and risk their status and the wrath of the public themselves. The shamed individual becomes socially, politically, and financially toxic, and therefore discarded, a node disconnected from the global network. There is no effective end to the punishment as the Internet never forgets and rarely forgives one's offenses. Every sentence may amount to a lifelong sentence of some significant and lasting harm.

It is therefore not quite accurate to call the power of online shaming a "digital scarlet letter." The power of the public goes well beyond that. Rather, in the global village, to be branded as an offender is a *digital mark of Cain*, a mark of being outcast that can take effect on a worldwide scale, cast down by the new arbiter of right and wrong, the popular trend. This is a tremendous power now in the hands of the public that should not be underestimated in its threatening strength. Online shaming and humiliation may be a *digital* torture and execution of the offending individual, but it is still an extremely painful punishment that can greatly harm and even completely dismantle people's lives. It is a fearsome enough punishment to be able to coerce the average person into submission with the prevailing opinion.

Jon Ronson, who to date has done the most extensive reporting on online public shaming, says, "To an extent I think we on social media are so powerful now that we put the fear of God into everybody."[34] But the rule of the public, enforced through an emergent God-like awesome terror, is not based upon rules set in stone, but rather on shifting public opinion. All we can be sure of is that if we blend into the crowd as closely as we possibly can, conform and get to the center of the herd, then we increase our likelihood of being safe from the wolves picking off those on the periphery. Conformity is therefore the best defense against the public's power, but we no longer just run to find our herd, we are rather increasingly cattle-prodded into it.

NOTES

1. Christina Capecchi and Katie Rogers, "Killer of Cecil the Lion Finds Out That He Is a Target Now, of Internet Vigilantism," *The New York Times*, July 29, 2015, https://www.nytimes.com/2015/07/30/us/cecil-the-lion-walter-palmer.html.

2. Paul Walsh, "Walter Palmer Speaks: Hunter Who Killed Lion Will Resume Bloomington Dental Practice," *Star Tribune*, last modified July 29, 2018, http://www.startribune.com/walter-palmer-speaks-hunter-who-killed-lion-will-resume-dental-practice-tuesday/325185401/.

3. Capecchi and Rogers, "Killer of Cecil."

4. Capecchi and Rogers, "Killer of Cecil."

5. Reuters, "Dentist Who Killed Cecil the Lion Reopens Office," *New York Post*, August 17, 2015, https://nypost.com/2015/08/17/dentist-who-killed-cecil-the-lion-re-opens-office/?_ga=2.27115069.1478802225.1544456004-1451322740.1544456004.

6. Reuters, "'Lion Killer': Walter Palmer's Florida Vacation Home Vandalized," *The Guardian*, August 5, 2015, https://www.theguardian.com/environment/2015/aug/05/walter-palmer-florida-home-vandalized-cecil-the-lion.

7. MacDonald Dzirutwe, "Zimbabwe Will Not Charge U.S. Dentist for Killing Cecil the Lion," *Yahoo! News*, October 12, 2015, https://news.yahoo.com/zimbabwe-says-not-charge-u-dentist-killing-cecil-133842381.html.

8. All In with Chris Hayes, "All In with Chris Hayes, Transcript 07/30/15," *MSNBC*, July 30, 2015, http://www.msnbc.com/transcripts/all-in/2015-07-30.

9. Michel Foucault, *Discipline and Punish: The Birth of the Prison* (New York: Vintage, 1995), 49.

10. Foucault, *Discipline and Punish*, 57–58.

11. Adam J. Hirsch, "From Pillory to Penitentiary: The Rise of Criminal Incarceration in Early Massachusetts," *Mich. L. Rev.* 80 (1981): 1225.

12. The British Medical Journal, "The Whipping Post and the Pillory," *The British Medical Journal* 2, no. 2013 (July 29, 1899): 300.

13. Scott E. Sanders, "Scarlet Letters, Bilboes and Cable TV: Are Shame Punishments Cruel and Outdated or Are They a Viable Option for American Jurisprudence," *Washburn LJ* 37 (1997): 364.

14. Hirsch, "From Pillory to Penitentiary," 1225–26.

15. Alice Morse Earle, *Curious Punishments of Bygone Days* (Chicago: Herbert S. Stone & Company, 1896), 88, https://books.google.com/books?hl=en&lr=&id=4SnJTvXjMrkC&oi=fnd&pg=PA1&dq=curious+punishments+of+bygone+days.

16. Earle, *Curious Punishments*, 91–92.

17. Sanders, "Scarlet Letters," 365.

18. Hirsch, "From Pillory to Penitentiary," 1223.

19. Sanders, "Scarlet Letters," 361.

20. Steven L. Nock, *The Costs of Privacy: Surveillance and Reputation in America* (New York: Aldine de Gruyter, 1993), 9.

21. Cole Stryker, "The Problem With Public Shaming," *The Nation*, April 24, 2013, https://www.thenation.com/article/problem-public-shaming/.

22. Marshall McLuhan, W. Terrence Gordon, Elena Lamberti, and Dominique Scheffel-Dunand, *The Gutenberg Galaxy: The Making of Typographic Man* (Toronto: University of Toronto Press, 2011).

23. Lee Rainie and Barry Wellman, *Networked: The New Social Operating System* (Cambridge: MIT Press, 2012), 35.

24. Jon Ronson, "How One Stupid Tweet Blew Up Justine Sacco's Life," *The New York Times Magazine*, February 12, 2015, https://www.nytimes.com/2015/02/15/magazine/how-one-stupid-tweet-ruined-justine-saccos-life.html.

25. Ronson, "How One Stupid Tweet."

26. Monica Christoffels, "Best of #HasJustineLandedYet," *Storify*, accessed October 25, 2017, https://storify.com/mpchristoffels/best-of-hasjustinelandedyet.

27. Philip Pettit, *Republicanism: A Theory of Freedom and Government* (Oxford: Oxford University Press, 2002), 52.

28. Pettit, *Republicanism*, 55.

29. Pettit, *Republicanism*, 63–64.

30. William Blackstone, *Commentaries on the Laws of England in Four Books. Notes Selected from the Editions of Archibold, Christian, Coleridge, Chitty, Stewart, Kerr, and others, Barron Field's Analysis, and Additional Notes, and a Life of the Author by George Sharswood. In Two Volumes* (Philadelphia: J.B. Lippincott Co., 1893), https://oll.libertyfund.org/titles/2142.

31. Foucault, *Discipline and Punish*, 43.

32. Fromm, *The Art of Loving*, 11.

33. Retro Report, "The Outrage Machine," *Retro Report*, June 20, 2016, https://www.retroreport.org/transcript/the-outrage-machine/.

34. Gretchen Gavett, "Why Do We Publicly Shame People Out of Their Jobs?," *Harvard Business Review*, April 6, 2015, https://hbr.org/2015/04/why-do-we-publicly-shame-people-out-of-their-jobs.

Chapter 5

P2P Surveillance

With the revival of public shaming online, the public now has a tool of punishment in its arsenal that is comparable to a state-level sanction in terms of the harm it can cause to an individual. But there is nothing for the public to punish if there is no way for the public to keep an eye out for offenders of public opinion. A system of power is not complete if it does not combine punishment with a system of surveillance to monitor for compliance with its rules.

Where there is someone or something that wishes to exert its power over you, to dominate you and force compliance with its wishes or commands, surveillance will be present in some form. This is why a hallmark of oppressive government regimes has been intense surveillance apparatuses. We need to be keenly aware of surveillance in whatever forms they may manifest since where there is surveillance, there may be power and control, which should not go without scrutiny. In addition to government and corporate surveillance, a third type of surveillance that is growing in strength and influence, and of which there needs to be more scrutiny, is surveillance by the public.

New ubiquitous information and communication technologies, in particular recording-enabled smart devices and social media programs, are giving rise to a profound new power for ordinary people to monitor and track each other on a global scale. By "ordinary" people, I mean people who do not have the advanced surveillance training of government agents, for example, or the expectations of public exposure on the scale of political leaders or other celebrities. While major social media apps such as Twitter, Facebook, and Instagram can be used to keep in touch in new and even potentially liberating ways, they can also be used to keep a constant eye on one another with alarming detail. Average users have become accustomed to habitually (and often unknowingly) widely broadcasting their locations, who they are with, what they are doing, how they are feeling, what they are thinking, and other details of their lives to audiences ranging from hundreds to sometimes millions of anonymous viewers. Perhaps even more concerning, these same online tools can be utilized to post other people's privately spoken words, sensitive images of them, and accounts of their personal actions—without their consent. I will refer to this new technologically enabled ability for the many to watch the many as "peer-to-peer" (P2P) surveillance.

P2P surveillance can be broken down specifically into its *systems of surveillance* and *systems of control*, borrowing terminology used by James Rule in his study of mass surveillance systems *Private Lives and Public Surveillance*. Rule describes *systems of surveillance* as "those activities having to do with collecting and maintaining information"[1] for the purpose of "knowing when rules are being obeyed, when they are broken, and, most importantly, who is responsible for which."[2] Such rules are fairly clear-cut for a traditional surveillance system, like police surveillance, where the rules that are being monitored for compliance are the rules of law. For P2P surveillance, however, the rules are more nebulous, usually unwritten, and sometimes unknown to an offender, but they cover everything from trivial social etiquette, relating to everyday speech and behavior, to deep personal choices, such as one's choice of romantic relationships and political affiliations. They are the rules of social convention formulated by an abstracted public opinion. Notably, such "rules" are often unclear and can fluctuate at any given time and place, which points to how arbitrary their enforcement can be.

Accompanying *systems of surveillance* are *systems of control*, which James Rule describes as actions concerning "the actual management of behavior, through sanctioning or exclusion."[3] For police surveillance systems, sanctioning and exclusion are accomplished through fines and imprisonment. With P2P surveillance (which I am using loosely to refer to P2P systems of surveillance and control), the method of managing behavior is done primarily through the sanctions of sometimes severe public shaming, humiliation, and psychological terror (that we began to look at in the last chapter) via unwanted global exposure of recorded content, "meme" manipulation of such content, uninhibited anonymous commenting, explicit judgment through rating and ranking, "doxing"—the deliberate public release of personal information such as one's home address—and a deluge of threats, often death threats, all which are accompanied by a number of exclusionary effects, both online (being removed or censored from a site) and offline (e.g., losing one's job and being largely excluded from future job opportunities).

While gossip, public shaming, humiliation, threats, ruined reputations, shunning, and their effects on people's lives are not fundamentally new forms of social control, enhanced, anonymized, and connected by new ICTs, a formerly loose power of surveillance and control, by ordinary people, is becoming organized, systematic, and enacted on a scale previously unattainable. It is a reawakening on a global scale of the gossipy medieval village, from which people once fled for the anonymity of the city, but retaining the compartmental disconnection and loneliness of the urban desert.

CURRENT EXAMPLES OF P2P SURVEILLANCE

In some cases, P2P surveillance activities are carried out sporadically, for example, by a random plane passenger who in 2015 overheard a couple breaking up midflight, photographed them, and "live-tweeted" updates and transcriptions of their rancorous dialogue, in real time, to a worldwide public of thousands of strangers; or the 2010 tragedy of Rutger's university student Tyler Clementi, who was secretly videotaped by his dorm roommate, via a hidden laptop camera, having a sexual encounter with another young man in their room, and streamed live to his classmates following an announcement of the "viewing" on Twitter (an event which directly preceded Tyler committing suicide).

In addition to these sorts of "lone wolves," who may capture and instantaneously broadcast one's actions on a global scale, websites have emerged that more systematically encourage individuals to surreptitiously record, and anonymously post photos of ordinary people caught acting in an uncustomary or unconventional fashion. PeopleofWalmart.com and PassengerShaming.com, for example, ask its users to record and broadcast compromising photos of others in Walmart shopping centers, and on airplanes and in airports, respectively. In essence then, the busiest shopping centers and transportation centers now have an indefinite number of members of the public specifically out to catch any norm-breaking behavior and post it to the Internet. TheDirty.com serves as a more general cache for embarrassing photos and gossip, of clearly identified individuals, which are then indexed on the site by city. College-specific "makeout" and "passout" Twitter handles proliferated at schools across the country, to anonymously post photos of students captured making out or passing out at parties, for their whole university population—and the rest of the world—to see. While some of these sites have fizzled out, they have been replaced by new ones such as college-specific Old Row Instagram accounts to document not only fellow students making out and passing out but an indefinite range of embarrassing photos and videos.

Other sites move beyond documenting "bad behavior" and more to trying to document and control political ideologies. Canary Mission, through the help of anonymous user submissions, monitors individuals accused of antisemitism, mostly on college campuses, generating extensive searchable dossiers, complete with photos, videos, biographical information, "infamous quotes," occupation, organizational affiliations, associates, and associated social media and web links. Some of the posts appear to be of content that is merely critical of the Israeli government and its supporting organizations. Similarly, CampusReform.org posts confidential user-submitted hidden recordings of classroom lectures, student government meetings, and other campus activities on their website and YouTube for alleged evidence of liberal bias against conservativism on college campuses.

Uploading recordings of others without consent is not reserved for only specific sites or fringes of the Internet; rather, Lauren Cagle writes, "People circulate photographs of strangers widely through online networks; social media platforms such as Facebook, Instagram, Twitter, and Snapchat make trivial work of snapping a quick picture in public and sharing it."[4] Photos or videos of others uploaded on social media are often broadcast to intentionally shame or humiliate others. Other times users might just be posting images they find amusing, but which subsequently become cause for censure or exclusion of the broadcasted individual (e.g., pictures of people drinking at a party who subsequently lose job opportunities).

In all the abovementioned examples, individuals are unwillingly thrust before a mass audience with their only means of preventing this exposure being to *self-censor* or modify their behavior to conform to prevailing norms that avoid detection by the public. For example, in an interview with social media surveillance researcher Daniel Trottier, an undergraduate explained that: "For me to be caught on photo doing something stupid, I had to be doing something stupid in the first place. And if I avoid that . . . then it's a non-issue. They can't post photos of me that didn't happen."[5] But what the public deems to be "stupid" is at the whim of the public. Some norms and customs may be reasonably justifiable, but others are not, and what is considered "stupid" behavior is not clearly defined and subject to change at any moment.

As it is now, if there is a social aberration great enough, or even just something out of the norm like wild, unusual, and spontaneous dancing at a concert, people will feel free to pull out their cameras and film. People do this almost instinctively. When a norm has been broken, for better or worse, it seems to create implicit permission for the crowd to start filming and broadcasting that random action. What was originally carried out within the context of a relatively limited group in an ephemeral moment of time, is thereby made available to the entire world for potentially permanent viewing. Under the threat of P2P surveillance a spontaneous moment can mark your grave since your digital self outlives your IRL self. Even if the public celebrates someone's recorded behavior—say dancing particularly *well* at a concert—the threat of such worldwide and long-lasting exposure may still have a chilling effect and feel highly violating.

People do try to counter the possibility of unwanted public exposure by attempting to control the flow of information to different audiences using privacy-settings and multiple accounts (a "fake" Instagram account—finsta—for example), but with any digital media one cannot assure control over one's intended audience online. Daniel Trottier found, for example, that Facebook users acknowledged that "attempts to limit exposure are futile,"[6] as digital information can easily leak from an intended audience to a broader public. Even information posted on Snapchat, for example, which is designed to protect privacy by exposing posts to only a limited audience for a limited time, can be screenshot and then shared with the global village permanently. What appears online about an individual, and to whom, is increasingly out of one's control. Therefore, the more that the P2P surveillance apparatus spreads, the more one must prepare to be judged at any given time by the public.

The power of P2P surveillance enables the public to potentially dominate the individual by keeping a growing lookout for, and widely exposing, offenders against popular societal conventions, or those who break or challenge social norms. One must then constantly reflect on the globally connected public in what one says or does, the more so the reach of the public eye extends, and keep guard over oneself lest one be caught in the offensive act and face the public's wrath. Self-censorship and calculated imitation of popular customs, that penetrates deeper into one's words and actions in proportion to the scale of P2P surveillance, becomes the order of the day.

As P2P surveillance brings the eyes of the masses in to peer more constantly and penetratingly into the details of our everyday lives than ever before, it brings explicit mass judgment by the crowd upon ordinary people on a scale never previously possible either. Whether through the watching and judging among the mass audience of hundreds or thousands of one's "friends" or "followers"—one's very own public—to the greater threat of an embarrassing incident becoming a trending hashtag spiraling out of one's control, the specter of shame and rejection that can scale across the universe lingers over social media and the Internet generally, pressuring us to conform our speech and behavior to that approved by the public.

As our offline lives merge ever more closely with the online realm, it brings our ordinary day-to-day existence, and our inner-thoughts, increasingly into the eyes of the public where each person becomes potentially subject to the sort of global visibility previously reserved only for political leaders and other major public figures. What media scholar John Thompson says of the heightened level of visibility brought upon by new communication media for politicians is now becoming true for billions of ordinary people worldwide:

> Whether they like it or not, political leaders today are more visible to more people and more closely scrutinized than they ever were in the past; and at the

same time, they are more exposed to the risk that their actions and utterances, and the actions and utterances of others, may be disclosed in ways that conflict with the images they wish to project. Hence the visibility created by the media can become the source of a new and distinctive kind of fragility. However much political leaders may seek to manage their visibility, they cannot completely control it. Mediated visibility can slip out of their grasp and can, on occasion, work against them . . . Politicians must constantly be on their guard and employ a high degree of reflexivity to monitor their actions and utterances, since an indiscreet act, an ill-judged remark or an unwarranted disclosure can have disastrous consequences.[7]

In this sense, we are all becoming politicians now, except that unlike politicians, ordinary people do not really consciously choose to become public figures, and they are much more personally vulnerable to the disastrous consequences of an online reputational fallout, assuming they do not have the wealth and other resources to fallback upon which celebrities usually possess. As developments in ICTs bring about more clandestine and constantly filming cameras, the public actively expands the scope of P2P surveillance and forces this type of heightened visibility across society as well as the personal fragility that comes with it. In this sense, in addition to becoming public figures, we are becoming each other's paparazzi as well. Privacy as a means of escape from the public eye, as a right to be left alone from its overwhelming force, becomes increasingly unavailable.

THE FUTURE OF P2P SURVEILLANCE

The invasive potential of P2P surveillance only increases as recording and monitoring devices continue to proliferate with increased acceleration and become more clandestine—being embedded in regularly worn items like lapel-clip "lifelogging" cameras, augmented reality glasses and "smart" contact lenses, as well as flying quietly through the skies in sophisticated drones sold casually as toys to children (thereby allowing even presumed-to-be-private spaces such as one's own backyard to become within reach of the public eye). If augmented reality (AR) glasses become common, which is widely expected in the tech industry,[8] this means that it will become increasingly difficult to know when one is in fact being recorded and broadcast, as cameras recording may become as ubiquitous as eyes seeing.

At the time of this writing, all the major tech companies are investing in software and hardware to make wearable AR devices the new paradigm computing platform. For example, at the 2017 Facebook f8 conference, Mark Zuckerberg said of his current developments that "We all know where we want this to get eventually. We all want glasses or eventually contact lenses that look and feel normal but let us overlay all kinds of information and digital objects on top of the real world."⁹ Echoing Zuckerberg was, Michael Abrash, Oculus's chief scientist who similarly declared:

> We know what we really want: AR glasses . . . . They aren't here yet, but when they arrive they're going to be the great transformational technologies of the next 50 years . . . instead of carrying stylish smartphones everywhere, we'll be wearing stylish glasses . . . these glasses will offer AR, VR, and everything in between, and we'll wear them all day and we'll use them in every aspect of our lives.¹⁰

The explosive popularity of Pokémon GO, an early AR game in which videogame characters were projected atop the real world via smartphone screens, demonstrates vividly the enormous potential market for AR especially for whoever can land the "killer" AR device, which will likely be as described above: a pair of glasses, if at first without recording capabilities due to privacy concerns, probably eventually with such capabilities once the public is more comfortable with these devices. Of course, forecasting is only forecasting. Google likely didn't forecast their first major wearable AR device, Glass, to be such a flop. But other breakthrough technologies have experienced such fitful starts. For example, a precursor to the iPad was the Apple Newton, which was in production from 1993 to 1998. It suffered from similar limitations as Google Glass, but in time those limitations were overcome when the iPad came out a little over a decade later.

Tech companies want badly for us to have these devices. AR eyewear likely represents the holy grail for data collection and behavior modification (the chief model of Silicon Valley profitmaking), since through these devices tech companies could potentially surveil everything users experience (at least visually) and nudge users in real time at the level of one's very senses. Silicon Valley will likely push and push and try various iterations until they one day perhaps strike just the right combination of function, style, price, and advertising that allows a critical mass to form in the market so that wearing these devices becomes cool and normalized. In such a scenario, eventually people might risk becoming socially disadvantaged if they are not plugged into this new shared AR. This will be the ultimate fear of missing out. The whole world will be laughing all at once at a joke only present in AR. Without these devices, one will be on the outside, separated from the new merged digital-physical reality, in an almost separate universe entirely, and even become the butt of everyone's joke: "Those stupid luddites." To not be left out, more and more people may adopt these devices.

If AR glasses bring the ubiquitous smartphone cameras that are already holstered in most people's pockets today, out onto most people's faces and bodies tomorrow, the public's cameras will thereby become constantly drawn, aimed, ready to shoot at random or even constantly firing. A trend toward wearing cameras on one's face or body will mean that it becomes harder to detect when one is being recorded. This will greatly intensify the chilling feeling that at any moment one's speech and behavior may wind up permanently on the Internet for all to see, and will likely increase the average person's self-censorship of their words or behavior. Every conversation you have with someone may in effect be a conversation with *everyone* since behind the glasses will rest not just the user's eyes, but potentially the eyes of the entire global public. A society armed with cameras out and filming all the time may be a polite society, but it is also a society constantly on edge.

As user-generated live-streaming audio and video become more common, with live-streaming services gaining popularity, such as the Twitter-owned Periscope and Facebook Live, and as screens increasingly overlay or saturate people's field of vision through augmented and virtual reality technologies, potentially real-time collective monitoring of ordinary people by the masses risks becoming pervasive. If these trends continue unabated, we may one day be forced to operate under the assumption that practically anything said or done may not only be recorded, but also broadcast for all to see and hear, searchable on a global scale, permanently. As the P2P surveillance apparatus expands, we will likely feel increasing pressure with increasing frequency to act in accordance with prevailing customs, lest we be caught on camera for our indiscretions. Since commercial ICTs are carried into private residencies, we cannot assume protection from global exposure even in spaces traditionally marked off from the public.

The ability to more regularly bring cameras into private spaces, and in particular, the norm of widely exposing captured footage to the public, makes the potential for P2P surveillance to affect ordinary people's behavior and speech arguably more far-reaching than traditional police surveillance practices. Unlike traditional police surveillance that is relatively constrained to public spaces and can only punish transgressions of the law, the public knows practically no bounds, and all is of its concern. Only under the most historically corrupt circumstances would police surveillance agencies similarly expose embarrassing or delicate footage of ordinary individuals to the public, such as Herbert Hoover's COINTELPRO threatened to do against anti-war activists and other political dissidents they routinely wiretapped, or Soviet Union police forces like the Stasi. In other words, people may become significantly less chilled in their day-to-day speech and behavior by CCTV police cameras, and other forms of government surveillance, than by the cameras in the hands (and perhaps one day in the eyes) of the public, as the latter is relatively unconstrained in both its capture and its dissemination of information on a massive scale.

The surveillance power of these clandestine recording technologies may become further amplified as commercial facial and voice recognition technologies become more powerful and accessible. This will potentially allow for instant identification of individuals, both in real life and online, and automatically tagged and indexed online recording archives, searchable by name, for any uploaded content. Facebook's facial recognition software, creepily called 'DeepFace', can already identify individuals in photos with near 100 percent accuracy,[11] likely soon surpassing human capabilities. A Russian app called FindFace allowed anyone to instantly match and identify a photograph of a stranger, through powerful facial recognition technology, to their database of hundreds of millions of individuals pulled from the popular Russian social media site VKontakte. Theoretically, a similar feature could be used to match faces to any image on the entire Internet, thereby automatically identifying individuals in any uploaded photograph or video.[12]

In fact, at the time of writing, a company called Clearview AI is selling a service to hundreds of law enforcement agencies that does essentially just that. Clearview AI has scraped images from across the Internet from major sites such as Facebook, YouTube, and even Venmo, amassing a database of three billion "faceprints." If a user enters a photograph of a person into their software, it will return photos from across the Internet in which that person is found, including links to those sites. Although these faceprints were scraped from major Internet sites against their stated policies, that apparently hasn't stopped over 600 law enforcement agencies from recently adopting the technology. The company is currently developing a prototype of their facial recognition to be used with AR glasses. This is obviously an extremely dangerous technology in the hands of the police, but many expect this type of service to eventually be made available to the public as well, if not from Clearview AI than from a copycat company.[13]

What these technologies in the hands of the public would mean is that as the public collectively records and broadcasts individuals, any speech or action caught up in this roving P2P surveillance net may no longer remain an anonymous random passing occurrence, but could rather become immediately attached to an individual's identity and be permanently searchable online. In other words, through P2P surveillance, the public could potentially seamlessly, and automatically, develop vast crowdsourced and auto-indexed *dossiers* on people that could be retrieved by command via a keyword search of a person's name, or a match of their photo. This developing apparatus would actualize Marshall McLuhan's more dour predictions for the global village, which was arguably a potent vision of a coming dystopia despite the often perceived positive connotations of the "global village." For example, media and education professor William F. Baker explains:

> [McLuhan] told us there would someday be "one big gossip column," powered by an "electronically computerized dossier bank," that would keep an uneraseable record of our tiniest actions. This would be the background noise against which our lives would play out . . . . McLuhan did not think of the global village as a happy place at all. He saw it as a place of terror, the home we would all have to move to when electronic media had finished re-tribalizing us.[14]

Facial recognition technologies would not only make information collection seamlessly organized around a person's digital self, but it would make digital information recall seamless upon viewing a person in real life. Just as police officers may identify a subject, and call up any collected information on a person, an average person could do so instantaneously with any stranger one meets. As a small demonstration of this potential, an early Google Glass app called NameTag allowed individuals to identify strangers simply by looking at them, and to automatically pull up social networking information, and even match that person against a sex offender registry.[15]

With the combination of facial recognition and smart devices, Joseph Atick, one of the inventors of facial recognition, says that "We are basically allowing our fellow citizens to surveil us."[16] As he puts it, our technology is converging to create a "perfect storm" that

> creates a worrisome environment because it opens the door for potentially achieving the unthinkable: the linking of online and offline identities. Basically we now have a proliferation of cameras operating in the real world (offline), along with the proliferation of identity-tagged images on the web (online) and a new generation of powerful face recognition algorithms capable of linking the two. For example, a person photographed by a mobile phone can be identified without their knowledge through face recognition using identity-tagged images harvested over the web. Add to this the powerful data mining capabilities provided by the ever more sophisticated web search engines and we now have the ability to surreptitiously construct a detailed profile of someone we snap with our iPhone walking down the street.[17]

Through these technologies, one's digital self and one's IRL self may practically merge. What is captured by the world wide web of P2P surveillance offline may become automatically attached to one's digital self online, and what is attached to one's digital self online thereby becomes automatically attached to one's IRL self offline. As a result, there is no offline, just a blended digital-physical environment that we constantly exist in. Luciano Floridi calls this trend, generally speaking, "onlife."[18] In such a case, the performance of the self in everyday life could become an ongoing performance since any passing occurrence caught on film, in any setting, "private" or not, risks becoming a permanent feature of one's digital-physical blended character. We thereby lose the "backstage," in Goffman's language. Onlife must be "on" and performing all the time as we carry around the detritus of our pasts as digital baggage overhanging our digitally merged selves.

In yet more distant possibilities of P2P surveillance, where cyborgism is likely fairly common (if not standard), it may not be unusual for people to regularly tap directly into each other's eyes and even to read each other's thoughts. In this case, the boundaries between individuals may almost completely dissolve. While such developments are extremely speculative, and if they are to occur, probably decades off into the future, they are not as "sci-fi" as they may sound. The technology to tap directly into someone's eyes essentially already exists through camera-equipped and virtual reality glasses. This possibility is heightened by the "smart" contact lenses that are also in development. The possibility of camera-equipped bionic eyes (which already exist in rudimentary form) and implants would merely smooth that transition.

Meanwhile, mind-reading technology may become common in the future as well. Today Facebook asks "what's on your mind," tomorrow it may not need to ask. Facebook confirmed in 2017 that they have a "secretive division" working on mind-reading technology with the goal to allow people to type directly from their brains at 100 words-per-minute. The project is being overseen by Regina Dugen, head of Facebook's experimental technologies division, creepily called "Building 8." She used to lead DARPA, the U.S. military's advanced technology wing. Of the technology, which would essentially allow direct telepathy, she states, "It sounds impossible but it's closer than you think."[19] Other prominent developers working on similar mind-reading technology include Elon Musk with his brain-computer interface company Neuralink.

As these privacy-eroding technologies rapidly advance, we need to be thinking about the potential consequences of what Facebook calls an "ultimately transparent" society. Remember, these changes don't happen all at once. Privacy gets eroded step by step.[20] It is now common for young people to have their locations constantly on display on a map for all their "friends" via Snapchat's Map feature or to be perpetually tracked by their parents, even in college, via Live360. The type of transparency and diminishment of privacy that has already become standard for young people today would have been horrifying to many previous generations. There may be benefits to such connectedness, but youth today may also become numb to the tremendous erosion of privacy they already experience, and they might not know what they've lost. If we reach some Borg-like, hive-mind future where individuality essentially ceases to exist, its inhabitants will know no better, but their lives may be considerably diminished nonetheless. Future developments in

ICTs and their public adoption are of course uncertain, and the more extreme applications are less likely, but the current plausible trajectories are alarming.

A group of social media researchers led by Ben Marder have begun to conduct experiments that demonstrate how the chilling effects of social media can extend offline into one's "real life." They speculate that "the omnipresence of personal recording devices, facial recognition and [social media] may lead us with little resistance towards an Orwellian society based on peer-to-peer surveillance."[21] In James Rule's aforementioned study of mass surveillance in the late 1960s, he noted the limitations of the surveillance systems of his time that kept them from being "total" surveillance regimes like that depicted in Orwell's *1984*, specifically citing limitations in: (1) size, (2) centralization of files, (3) speed of information-flow and decision-making, and (4) points of contact with those under surveillance.[22] Although much has changed since his time, Rule's framework remains a useful way to conceptualize the degree to which mass surveillance systems are approaching a level of "totality," much as the fictional construct of Orwell's Big Brother remains relevant as well for a similar purpose. Using Rule's analysis as a litmus test, we can see that P2P surveillance already equals, surpasses, or may soon surpass technological limitations that would prevent it from becoming a "total" surveillance apparatus; that is, that would allow for enough gaps in coverage so that an individual is never felt to be under constant control and could, for better or worse, escape scrutiny for past or present deeds.

Because of the vast storage power of the net there is (1) no *size* limit to how many people can be tracked and monitored, and practically no limits to how much information can be stored on each person, as digital memory continues to become exponentially cheaper and more powerful. Every single person can readily have an electronic dossier automatically generated online, and there is an indefinite amount of information that can be recalled with an online search. There is practically no limit to how much information can be readily coped with, as the use of automatic indexing and instantaneous search allows the system to avoid becoming overwhelmed with data. Algorithms prove the ultimate bureaucratic clerk for filing and recalling data in an information warehouse that would make totalitarian dictatorships of the past weep in awe.

Information on individuals is also (2) highly *centralized*, as search indexes like Google allow the web to function as a universal surveillance server, accessible to anyone, anywhere, to view and add to collected information on individuals, thereby making it increasingly impossible to escape one's past. Most people in developed countries have direct access to search and can therefore potentially modify the central global database from their pockets.

(3) Speed of information-flow and decision-making is already extremely efficient through the virality of the net, as demonstrated in Sacco's tweet that

led to a successful global citizen-enacted manhunt within a matter of hours. This efficiency will only increase as people become more deeply intertwined with their ICTs, becoming increasingly worn on the body and eyes, thereby allowing for people to receive continuous alerts and updates even more immediately. Google alerts can already be activated to send a notification as information on a person becomes available online, allowing for automated monitoring and tracking of selected targets. Furthermore, the subtlety of decision-making may reach the Orwellian level of allowing the public to effectively predetermine people's actions, as privacy experts foresee sophisticated predictive algorithms being made available to the public.[23]

As for (4) the points of contact with those under surveillance, P2P surveillance can incorporate information on people essentially any place where there are others with cameras connected to the net. This means there are already billions of roaming points of contact around the globe, and the system could allow an even greater ability to locate and punish deviant individuals as facial recognition may become more commonly accessible in "smart" devices. There are already few places on the planet where one can fully escape the net of P2P surveillance, even as the public is only just becoming conscious of this new power. Currently, Google's Project Loon and Facebook's Aquila are being rolled out to beam down wi-fi from the skies to the world's most remote locations, so the global village infrastructure will soon be nearly complete.

THE CROWDSOURCED PANOPTICON

In a 2017 *Wired* magazine tech-advice column, a question is posed: "When someone melts down in public, can I record it? (please?)" The answer given is that in order to watch out for one another's safety and well-being: "We need to keep our cameras up, arrayed in a kind of crowdsourced Panopticon."[24] While I understand the sentiment, that through constantly keeping our "cameras up" we can catch potential abuses of innocent people in public, it is still the case that the Panopticon is an architectural design for a prison. Like most prisons, the Panopticon is usually seen as something to escape rather than something to purposefully construct around ourselves.

The Panopticon, originally designed by the utilitarian philosopher Jeremy Bentham, is a simple architectural design, a technology, that Bentham thought would most efficiently ensure mass conformity and control through visibility. Michel Foucault, who famously analyzes the Panopticon and how its core design principles facilitate power in modern society, explains that it is a method of creating "power through transparency" and "subjection by illumination."[25] The core of the Panopticon's design consists of a roundhouse with prison cells encircling all sides, visibly open, light shining upon them, and stacked on top of each other to form circular walls. In the center is a watchtower which is cleverly installed with a combination of venetian blinds and mirrors so that inmates in their cells, all at an equal distance from the tower, can never be sure if they are being watched by the guard. The inmates, exposed, know that the guard is there and *could* be watching, but the guard remains *anonymous*. The architecture generates, in Bentham's words, "the sentiment of a sort of omnipresence,"[26] an omnipresent gaze. What's essential then to the Panopticon's intended design is that all subjects in the monitored space are transparent and the monitoring authority is invisible so that one never knows when one is being watched. It is an apparatus of *"seeing without being seen."*[27]

With the subjects in the Panopticon made constantly visible and the authority invisible, the intended result is that the subjects in their cells soon appropriate the established field of behavior on their own, always making sure to conduct themselves according to the rules of the institution, since they may be under surveillance at any given time and their indiscretions perceived immediately. While in the Panopticon one might not *actually* be monitored at any given moment, the constant visibility generated by the design creates a permanent state of tension, and a power relation between the institutional authority and the subject under watch that operates without interruption and automatically. Foucault memorably tells us that "visibility is a trap"[28] because it is through visibility that one first comes under control. Through the state of constant uncertainty over whether one is being watched, the prisoner ultimately internalizes the gaze of the guard, and in a sense becomes a guard over himself, constantly monitoring, judging, and correcting his own behavior, and eventually thoughts, and attitudes. Foucault says that through this arrangement, the prisoner "becomes the principle of his own subjection."[29]

With P2P surveillance, physical architecture is no longer needed to create the surveillance arrangement that Bentham imagined with the Panopticon. Rather, digital technologies create a wi-fi architecture that generates invisible walls anywhere the Internet is present. In a sense all of society becomes an institution monitoring itself, with a potential surveillance capacity that surpasses the Panopticon, as P2P surveillance is enacted on an indefinitely large scale, and monitors potentially all aspects of speech and behavior. It is the principle of the Panopticon broken free of physical architecture, coalescing with our move out of the walls of institutions, and into the free-floating net. It is a paranoiac delusion made reality as anyone may potentially be watching at any time—at least as soon as one steps foot out the front door (though not necessarily limited to that)—from one's boss, pastor, parents, children, spouse, and friends, to people one has not yet met, in places where one has not yet been.

Once media is captured, broadcast, archived, and indexed by name, time and space collapse. One must then function as if everyone is with you all the time, or is just over your shoulder ready to peer in—even people who are not yet born, who would only consume the media—your record—in the distant future. P2P surveillance is therefore like an ever-dangling hot mic to your future grandchildren. Not only does time and space collapse, but the walls that separate social spheres collapse as well. Norms which used to govern behavior solely in one context, but not in another, which allowed a person to speak in tongues with snakes on a Sunday and file clerical entries on a Monday, blur together into one homogenous soup of expectations. Conformity to a potentially global convention of a global village rips away the idiosyncrasy of insular communities of individuals who understand one another, but would be greatly misunderstood by outsiders. P2P surveillance therefore has a doubly chilling effect; neither individuals nor their communities are left alone.

As the net of P2P surveillance spreads, it allows the gaze of the world inside one's life just as Bentham believed "the doors of all public establishments ought to be, thrown wide open to the body of the curious at large—the great *open committee* of the tribunal of the world."[30] The public—that "tribunal of the world"—is today climbing into the central guard tower atop the world wide web to watch, judge, and punish. Through this apparatus, the public then instills individuals to become their own watch-guards over themselves, cautiously calculating and self-censoring like constant politicians. One therefore internalizes the gaze of the public, and monitors oneself to assure compliance with the "rules" of public opinion. The crowdsourced Panopticon we are building up around ourselves with our devices is a prison of our own operation. We are becoming the principles of our own subjection *en masse*.

The mechanism of P2P surveillance allows for the coming of a radically transparent society that so many tech luminaries have exalted in their insistence that "privacy is dead." But this dream is not new. Rather Foucault traces it back to the goal of the French Revolution, to realize the "dream of a transparent society . . . [where] opinion of all reign over each."[31] Through this mode of power—of a transparent society—Foucault says that a new sort of justice would reign, and the principle of that justice would be opinion, "not so much to punish wrongdoers as to prevent even the possibility of wrongdoing, by immersing people in a field of total visibility where the opinion, observation and discourse of others would restrain them from harmful acts."[32] This reign of opinion, Foucault explains, "represents a mode of operation through which power will be exercised by virtue of the mere fact of things being known and people seen in a sort of immediate, collective, and anonymous gaze. A form of power whose main instance is that of opinion will refuse to tolerate areas of darkness."[33]

In this sense, the crowdsourced Panopticon is perhaps the realization of this dream of a transparent society and the reign of public opinion. Through P2P surveillance, all "areas of darkness" are illuminated by "a sort of immediate, collective, and anonymous gaze" of the public generated via the glowing screens of our ICTs. Through being "immersed" in this "field of total visibility," we thereby internalize the opinion and discourse of the public, and restrain ourselves from any "harmful acts" that would be out of line with public opinion. In that sense even the "possibility of wrongdoing" is prevented since we become constantly on guard over ourselves not to offend the public or act in any way that the public might disapprove, ridicule, or humiliate us with evidence of later.

In an interview, Foucault is asked if there is any point for the prisoners to take over the central watchtower of the Panopticon. Foucault answers: "Oh yes, provided that isn't the final purpose of the operation. Do you think it would be much better to have the prisoners operating the Panoptic apparatus and sitting in the central tower, instead of the guards?"[34] Today, the public is entering that tower and becoming yet another guard. Tearing down the Panopticon altogether appears far from the course of things.

NOTES

1. James B. Rule, *Private Lives and Public Surveillance: Social Control in the Computer Age* (New York: Schocken Books, 1974), 23.

2. Rule, *Private Lives*, 22.

3. Rule, *Private Lives*, 23.

4. Lauren E. Cagle, "Surveilling Strangers: The Disciplinary Biopower of Digital Genre Assemblages," *Computers and Composition* 52 (2019): 69.

5. Daniel Trottier, "Interpersonal Surveillance on Social Media," *Canadian Journal of Communication* 37, no. 2 (2012): 328.

6. Trottier, "Interpersonal Surveillance," 329.

7. John B. Thompson, "The New Visibility," *Theory, Culture & Society* 22, no. 6 (2005): 42.

8. Alex Heath, "Facebook Says the First Technology to Replace Smartphones will be Controlled with Our Brains," *Business Insider*, April 21, 2017, http://www.businessinsider.com/facebook-smart-glasses-will-be-controlled-with-our-brains-2017-4.

9. Steve Kovach, "Mark Zuckerberg Wants to Eliminate All Screens From Your Life with Special Glasses," *Business Insider*, April 18, 2017, https://www.businessinsider.com/mark-zuckerberg-wants-to-replace-all-screens-2017-4.

10. Steven Levy, "The Race for AR Glasses Starts Now," *Wired*, December 16, 2017, https://www.wired.com/story/future-of-augmented-reality-2018/.

11. Yaniv Taigman, Ming Yang, Marc' Aurelio Ranzato, and Lior Wolf, "Deepface: Closing the Gap to Human-Level Performance in Face Verification," In *Proceedings of the IEEE Conference on Computer Vision and Pattern Recognition* (2014): 1701–8.

12. Jonathan Frankle, "How Russia's New Facial Recognition App Could End Anonymity," *The Atlantic*, May 23, 2016, http://www.theatlantic.com/technology/archive/2016/05/find-face/483962/.

13. Kashmir Hill, "The Secretive Company That Might End Privacy as We Know It," *The New York Times*, January 18, 2020, https://www.nytimes.com/2020/01/18/technology/clearview-privacy-facial-recognition.html.

14. William F. Baker, "'Fifty Years in the Global Village': Remembering Marshall McLuhan on His 100th Birthday," *The Nation*, August 4, 2011, https://www.thenation.com/article/fifty-years-global-village-remembering-marshall-mcluhan-his-100th-birthday/.

15. Charles Poladian, "NameTag: Facial Recognition App Checks If Your Date Is A Sex Offender But Should You Use It?," *International Business Times*, January 14, 2014, https://www.ibtimes.com/nametag-facial-recognition-app-checks-if-your-date-sex-offender-should-you-use-it-1539308.

16. Natasha Singer, "Never Forgetting a Face," *The New York Times*, May 17, 2014, https://www.nytimes.com/2014/05/18/technology/never-forgetting-a-face.html.

17. Joseph J. Atick, "Face Recognition in the Era of the Cloud and Social Media: Is it Time to Hit the Panic Button?," *Silicon Trust*, October 21, 2011, https://silicontrust.org/2011/10/21/face-recognition-in-the-era-of-the-cloud-and-social-media-is-it-time-to-hit-the-panic-button/.

18. Luciano Floridi, *The Onlife Manifesto: Being Human in a Hyperconnected Era* (SpringerOpen, 2015).

19. James Titcomb, "Mark Zuckerberg Confirms Facebook is Working on Mind-reading Technology," *The Telegraph*, April 19, 2017, https://www.telegraph.co.uk/technology/2017/04/19/mark-zuckerberg-confirms-facebook-working-mind-reading-technology/.

20. Daniel J. Solove, "Why Privacy Matters Even If You Have 'Nothing To Hide'," *The Chronicle of Higher Education*, May 15, 2011, https://www.chronicle.com/article/Why-Privacy-Matters-Even-if/127461.

21. Ben Marder, Adam Joinson, Avi Shankar, and David Houghton, "The Extended 'Chilling' Effect of Facebook: The Cold Reality of Ubiquitous Social Networking," *Computers in Human Behavior* 60 (2016): 589.

22. Rule, *Private Lives and Public Surveillance*, 38–39.

23. Woodrow Hartzog and Evan Selinger, "The Chilling Implications of Democratizing Big Data: Facebook Graph Search is Only the Beginning," *Forbes*, October 16, 2013, http://www.forbes.com/sites/privacynotice/2013/10/16/the-chilling-implications-of-democratizing-big-data-facebook-graph-search-is-only-the-beginning/#724f4a403ac6.

24. Jon Mooallem, "Mr. Know-It-All: When Someone Melts Down In Public, Can I Record It? (Please?)," *Wired*, August 11, 2017, https://www.wired.com/story/ethics-recording-public-confrontations/.

25. Michel Foucault, *Power/knowledge: Selected Interviews and Other Writings, 1972–1977* (New York: Pantheon, 1980), 154.

26. Jeremy Bentham, "Proposal for a New and Less Expensive Mode of Employing and Reforming Convicts," quoted in *Utilitarianism.com*, accessed December 18, 2018, https://www.utilitarianism.com/panopticon.html.

27. Jeremy Bentham, *The Panopticon Writings*, ed. Miran Bozovic (London and New York: Verso, 1995), 43.

28. Foucault, *Discipline and Punish*, 200.

29. Foucault, *Discipline and Punish*, 202–3.

30. Foucault, *Discipline and Punish*, 48.

31. Foucault, *Power/knowledge*, 152.

32. Foucault, *Power/knowledge*, 153.

33. Foucault, *Power/knowledge*, 154.

34. Foucault, *Power/knowledge*, 165.

Chapter 6

The Net of Normalization

Foucault argues that panoptical surveillance was one of the key elements of a new form of power—disciplinary power—that dominated modern society starting in the nineteenth century, largely replacing the brutal spectacle of premodern sovereign power. Here we will first look briefly at the main characteristics of disciplinary power as described by Foucault before applying this framework to an analysis of discipline as it functions through P2P surveillance and control.

What most characterizes disciplinary power is that it centers upon one's soul, or psyche, "a punishment that acts in depth on the heart, the thoughts, the will, the inclinations,"[1] rather than directly upon the body. Through perpetual training, discipline intertwines deeply into the minutiae of behavior with an overall aim to make a person *normal*, that is, like all the rest, and straighten out any noncompliant individual into a "well-rounded" member of society. In this sense, discipline instills or installs a program of normality into the individual that then controls one from the inside out. It normalizes.

As discipline forms one's psyche or soul into a conformed subject of power, this is then reflected outwardly in control over one's bodily behavior. Foucault puts it memorably: "the soul is the prison of the body."[2] Inwardly, we are trained into becoming docile, obedient, manipulatable individuals, and this translates outwardly into docile, obedient, manipulatable bodies that can be put to productive use in an indefinite number of prescribed tasks.

In disciplinary societies, Foucault argues that power is enacted simultaneously at macro- and micro-levels. At the macro-level, there are the general forms of society demarcated by law, while at the micro-level, inside the day-to-day institutions we pass through such as schools and workplaces, our psyches are disciplined to meet these general forms. Discipline allows for a technique of power and social control to penetrate much more deeply into each individual than law ever could on its own, allowing for a tight control and organization imposed over all of society. Foucault explains: "In appearance, the disciplines constitute nothing more than an infra-law. They seem to extend the general forms defined by law to the infinitesimal level of individual lives; or they appear as methods of training that enable individuals to become integrated into these general demands."[3]

Discipline accomplishes this micro-level extension of power through "a whole micro-penalty of time (lateness, absences, interruptions of tasks), of activity (inattention, negligence, lack of zeal), of behavior (impoliteness, disobedience), of speech (idle chatter, insolence), of the body (incorrect attitudes, irregular gestures, lack of cleanliness), of sexuality (impurity, indecency)."[4] Foucault terms this system of micro-penalties as "normalizing judgment." With discipline, not only is every aspect of a person's life in institutions surveilled, but one is also then judged for whether one's speech and behavior can be considered normal, or abnormal. If judged abnormal, one must be corrected into normality, or be cast out of society.

There is potentially nothing too minute to escape this web of normalizing judgment. In modern work environments, for example, one might be subject to strict electronic monitoring of the most fine-grained activities—the amount of time one spends at the keyboard or minutes away from the screen. But this normalizing judgment extends far beyond such strictly quantifiable outputs. One's attitude can be judged abnormal, one's manner of dress, the way one walks, the way one speaks, one's facial expressions, the way one carries one's body, whether one is on time, what one eats, and so forth. Foucault scholar Gary Gutting says, "The threat of being judged abnormal constrains us moderns at every turn."[5]

Anything that is observed as being abnormal is subject to disciplinary measures to get us back into line. Hubert Dreyfus and Paul Rabinow explain that "Through the specification of the most detailed aspects of everyday behavior, almost anything could be potentially punishable. The nonconformist, even the temporary one, became the object of disciplinary attention."[6] It is this normalizing judgment that allows power to operate in a fine-grained capacity, to penetrate deeply and continuously into a person's psyche. It allows discipline to shape who we are, our very identities.

A main characteristic of disciplinary power is the enormous extent to which aspects of our lives are rated and ranked, and how these are used to establish and instill a constructed conception of a statistically normal person. One of the main functions of rating and ranking is that it allows authorities to quantify behavior based on one's performances. Under the watchful eye of institutional authorities in schools, offices, and so forth, rating and ranking allow all individuals to be placed within a distributional curve, "between good and bad marks, good and bad points."[7] This is how normalizing judgment begins to get codified, how those in positions of authority determine what is normal and abnormal behavior. These notions of normality then permeate throughout society. Through rating and ranking, statistical metrics are generated for all observable human behavior. Comparisons can then begin to be easily made between who is most apt at producing the desired output, whether it be pulling levers, passing school exams, assembling a rifle, or any other prescribed action.

Space itself can then can be easily partitioned and distributed based on rank, on how well people are performing. By distributing people based on rank, it allows for a quick, easy, continuous, and fluctuating comparison between individuals. The architecture of schools, for instance, was once designed to facilitate these comparisons. Rows of students in classrooms were often distributed based upon performance levels, upon who had the highest ratings or grades. Those who were the most "good," that is, performing the highest in comparison to other individuals, sat at the head of the class. Students sitting in each row behind then felt the sting of an increasingly shameful mark viscerally indicating one's rather shameful comparative lack in front of everyone else. The worse one's character and conduct was rated the further back one fell. This is also an example of how rising rank is in itself a reward, a circulation to the head of the class, a cause for pride, and the loss of status itself a primary punishment, a move to the back, and cause for shame in front of one's peers.

There is an ever-present threat that one may be deemed so out of line with what is considered normal behavior, with what Gutting describes as "socially (or even humanly) acceptable," that one might be removed from a social collective entirely, even if the deviant behaviors are "far from the blatant transgressions that called for the excessive violence of premodern power."[8] One need not attempt regicide, for example, to be heavily punished; one could instead just hop on one foot all day at school or in the office, and after refusing requests to walk like a normal human being, be subsequently suspended, expelled, docked, or fired for disobeying orders. We always risk falling into this realm of the shameful failures, the perverts, the insane, the criminals, and the weirdos. This is the shameful class of the "abnormal." Like the delinquent student sitting in a dunce cap facing the corner with a final warning, the abnormal must be removed, shamed, corrected, or expelled, and what's considered such abnormal behavior may be practically anything.

In the culmination of disciplinary power, hierarchical surveillance (panopticism), and normalizing judgment (described above) are combined to produce what Foucault calls a "normalizing gaze."[9] This mechanism of control is institutionalized via the process of examinations. Examinations place individuals under hierarchical surveillance and then combine this gaze with a normalizing judgment through rating/grading and ranking everyone under observation for how well they perform compared to others.

With these ongoing examinations comes a plethora of writing. A file begins to form that follows each individual around recording one's tally of good and bad marks. These judgments often go down on one's "permanent record." These written records are generated in schools, workplaces, prisons, hospitals, and so forth; that is, any institution an individual may pass through in life. Think of the annual reviews for employees, or health charts for patients and report cards for students.

Through the collation of these documents, statistical curves are then drawn up, charts generated showing clearly, in unquestionable statistical form, what is a normal range of behaviors. A norm is then clearly illustrated, and a sort of "natural law" of human behavior is observed and codified. But this "natural law" does not come about naturally. Rather, this knowledge of "normality" is derived *through* the power relation of observing subjects in society's institutions. These observations of normality then help generate a discourse among experts of what is considered normal, healthy, sane, well-rounded behavior. For example, if a student is failing or misbehaving, a conversation begins to develop over what is making this child a "delinquent" type, what is the nature of her deviant behavior, and how this individual can be corrected and made normal. With the web of records, files, and documents that now follow the individual, Foucault says: *"The examination, surrounded by all its documentary techniques, makes each individual a 'case' . . . it is the individual as he may be described, judged, measured, compared with others, in his very individuality; and it is also the individual who has to be trained or corrected, classified, normalized, excluded, etc."*[10]

By making the individual into a "case" to be compared to others, and to see how normal one is, Johanna Oksala explains that "We modify our behaviour in an endless attempt to approximate the normal, and in this process become certain kinds of subjects."[11] In other words, we conform to models of "acceptable" thought, speech, and behavior that correspond with what society considers to be the thought, speech, and behavior of healthy, normal people of different sorts. There comes to be "certain kinds of subjects," or in Fromm's sense "packaged personalities," identities bound up with what is considered normal or acceptable. By contrast, abnormal and unacceptable thought, speech, and behavior are codified and modeled into standardized unacceptable identities as well. For example, there are the sexually normal people, approved sexual identities, and then there are the "perverts." The range of approved and disapproved identities is indefinite, but one is normal if one falls clearly into a statistical normal range of behavior.

To remain normal, individuals must be sure to land at least in say the fiftieth percentile or above on various measures of their thought, speech, and behavior, and they can correct their behavior to make sure they do not fall below a shameful threshold. If so they will be either corrected or excluded. Through this process discipline then works out the kinks, straightens out the deviances, and forces conformity into sets of approved identities, in line with what is seen to be statistically normal.

In summary, some of the key elements of disciplinary power that will be especially relevant to our analysis of P2P surveillance and control are as follows:

(1) Soul/Psyche: Rather than working directly on the body, discipline works on training a person's soul or psyche, to shape an individual into a "normal" identity, which in turn becomes a form of control over one's body.
(2) Micro-penalty: Disciplinary mechanisms are enacted inside the interlocked institutions people pass throughout their lives via an array of micro-penalties to bring the fine-grained minutiae of one's speech and behavior into line.
(3) Rating and ranking: These are two of the primary mechanisms of discipline used to instill normalizing judgment.
(4) Quantification: Rating is used to quantify what is statistically normal behavior.
(5) Ranked distribution: Space is distributed according to rank in order to generate quick and easy comparisons. Additionally, rising or falling in rank itself becomes a powerful form of reward or punishment for disciplined behavior.
(6) Shameful class: Those who fail to be trained or corrected to match their behavior closely enough with others, whose quantified performances fall beneath a threshold grade or score, risk being deemed shamefully abnormal and largely excluded from society.
(7) Normalizing gaze: Hierarchical surveillance and normalizing judgment combine into ongoing examinations that establish what is considered normality and who is failing or achieving it.
(8) Case-files: Results of examinations are recorded into writing that follow each individual around indefinitely. These help chart out what is considered the contours of normal behavior and turn each person into a case to be judged and worked upon in order to chart one's progress in maintaining a state of normality.

P2P EXAMINATION

In 2013, a dating app was launched called Lulu, which allowed women to anonymously rate and comment on men they knew. Lulu was colloquially known as a "Yelp for men." Here was its main setup:

> On Lulu, women can rate men in categories—ex-boyfriend, crush, together, hooked-up, friend or relative—with a multiple-choice quiz. Women, their gender

verified by their Facebook logins, add pink hashtags to a man's profile ranging from the good (#KinkyInTheRightWays) to the bad (#NeverSleepsOver) to the ugly (#PornEducated). The hashtags are used to calculate a score generated by Lulu, ranging from 1 to 10, that appears under the man's profile picture . . . Men can add hashtags, which appear in blue, but these are not factored into their overall score.[12]

Lulu was deemed to be both a double standard toward men and relatively inhumane in its degrading rating process. It generated considerable controversy and public backlash, and ultimately collapsed under the negative pressure. But that does not mean that Lulu did not enjoy substantial popularity. Before its final loss in the overall battle of public opinion, it quickly found a substantial public—especially of a younger generation more accustomed to P2P surveillance—generating 57 million profile views just months after its launch.[13]

What we saw in Lulu was a continuous hierarchical invisible gaze from a collective anonymous public, combined with an explicit normalizing judgment marked by rating and rank, resulting in a continual P2P examination of those under surveillance. It was a kind of compulsory training of a multitude of individuals to push them into a homogenous identity. This ideal male identity, embodied in a perfect ten score, defined by the homogenous values embedded in the rating metrics, was like a program installed into each person's examined soul to turn his unpolished self into "perfect boyfriend material." Anonymously crowdsourced good and bad marks for one's performances would then serve as feedback for how well the individual replicated this ideal manhood. Low scores would be naturally humiliating, and higher scores rewarding.

Lulu thereby placed each examined and graded individual into a crowdsourced feedback loop. One would perform according to the prescribed norms of mainstream male identity, and based on positive and negative feedback, attempt to maintain a normal score, continually attempt to improve upon one's score, and avoid falling into the shameful and humiliating class of those who scored so low they were effectively "undateable." Scoring shamefully low would not necessarily involve some blatant transgression. Rather, it could just be that the person was "weird," with an unusual sense of humor for example. But once they fell down in the numbers, they could essentially be excluded from the system. They failed the examination. It was therefore vital to maintain an acceptable score that indicated normality. Lulu even provided manual-like guides for how one might improve ones's score under this ongoing examination. Poorly performing individuals could therefore adjust themselves, "optimize themselves," to perform the desired homogenized identity model "better," in order to earn a higher score. The end result was to generate a catalog of human beings, turned into models of boyfriends, variations on a single theme, a normal identity, made to order.

In late 2015, a new start-up called Peeple was set to launch, which would expand the compulsory objectification and perpetual examination premise of Lulu to crowdsourced evaluations of all people in all relationships. It was to be a general "Yelp for people." Caitlin Dewey of *The Washington Post* reported that the app had planned to make it so:

> you will be able to assign reviews and one- to five-star ratings to everyone you know: your exes, your co-workers, the old guy who lives next door. You can't opt out—once someone puts your name in the Peeple system, it's there unless you violate the site's terms of service. And you can't delete bad or biased reviews—that would defeat the whole purpose. Imagine every interaction you've ever had suddenly open to the scrutiny of the Internet public . . . . Where once you may have viewed a date or a teacher conference as a private encounter, Peeple transforms it into a radically public performance: Everything you do can be judged, publicized, recorded.[14]

Although valued at nearly eight million dollars near the time of its planned launch, enough people quickly realized the negative potential of Peeple's planned functions, and a massive viral public backlash ensued which caused the app to more or less collapse. Given the failures of Lulu and Peeple, one may be reasonably tempted to rest assured that the public will never let things go too far, that it will properly regulate itself, that excessive privacy invasions and crowdsourced abuse will be appropriately curtailed. But one may also see Lulu and Peeple as a watermark for where we currently stand as a society, and a warning of where we are going.

While many may scoff at apps like Lulu and Peeple, their essential disciplinary mechanisms are all already prevalent in the public's P2P systems of surveillance and control on the Internet and social media. We are already fairly immersed into a society where through our ICTs "everything you do can be judged, publicized, recorded," as was warned of Peeple, and where an encounter that once may have been viewed as private is instead turned into a "radically public performance." For young people in particular, this mode of existence increasingly characterizes the norm of everyday reality even in the absence of sites that enact P2P examination as brutally as Peeple threatened to do. These social disciplinary forces appear primed to only get more invasive and pervasive, intertwining into our lives more deeply and minutely, even if enacted in softer and more "humane" forms so as to not evoke widespread backlash.

Through a growing crowdsourced panopticism via smartphones and social media coupled with socially networked tools to numerically score, comment on, and profile others on various social metrics related to work, friendship, and dating, the main elements of disciplinary power are in a significant way becoming enacted by the public in a rather continuous manner. Below I draw comparisons between Foucault's description of disciplinary power outlined above and how these mechanisms are enacted via P2P surveillance and control:

(1) Soul/Psyche: Via social media profiles and search engines each individual's digital self is effectively placed in a digital cell of a crowdsourced Panopticon to be worked on separately in the multitude, discipline applied to billions individually. One's digital self becomes a projection of thoughts, interests, inclinations, and so forth, made manifest on the screen to be watched and worked upon by others through disciplinary mechanisms that create behavior-shaping feedback loops. We then may internalize our digital self, shaped by the crowd, into our own psyche, coming to conform and be responsive to the dynamics that form the digital self. As we stare entranced into our black mirrors, we are subjected to a power of what Bentham described as "mind over mind,"[15] the power of the public mind absorbing the individual mind, in a disciplinary training into social conformity.

(2) Micro-penalty: Each person's personal public of "friends" and "followers" becomes like a disciplinary workshop, a classroom that hammers publicly approved models of identity into individual personalities at a detailed level, subtly, on a day-to-day basis. This micromanagement of individuals by the public can be enacted on an indefinitely large scale. There is nothing too small or minute to escape the scrutiny of disciplinary power. Every expression recorded and broadcast, voluntarily or not, may be subject to normalizing judgment, from what one says, what one thinks, how one dresses, where one goes, where one hangs out, what one eats, and down to even the most minute facial expressions or bodily gestures which, however trivial, may still be cause for potentially massive exclusionary sanctions if out of line with public opinion. The threat of abnormality is ever present in practically any interaction and any publicly observed speech or behavior.

While power functions on an ongoing basis in most people's lives most directly at this micro-level, they are quickly linked with the public at a macro-scale through the network. One might say that the general forms of society are instilled, in part, through public opinion embodied in viral celebrities and "influencers" followed by millions. Individual modeling of opinions and identities to then approximate those of approved viral figures can occur at the micro-level in the workshops of one's personal online public. Yet there remains the looming threat that at any time one can be carried up to even the highest levels of global public exposure for judgment and sanction, by the "tribunal of the world," almost instantaneously through the network. Power operates in conjunction at macro- and micro-levels, much in the way law and discipline operate in traditional institutions.

(3) Rating and ranking: Social media's standard metrics of likes, dislikes, friends, followers, and views allows for blanket quantitative rating mechanisms for people's speech and actions on an indefinite range of behaviors and expressions. Expressions of oneself captured online are rarely free from some quantified, often highly visible, and rather permanent mark. Quantifiable ratings are the standard architecture for the Internet as a whole. An individual will then most easily be corrected into behaving in a normal fashion, in line with publicly approved identities through the fear of shameful ratings and desiring the reward of status-upgrading scores. Gaining likes, friends, followers, and a boosted status is in itself a reward, and allows the public to train individuals to replicate popularly approved speech and behaviors, to replicate a performed identity—the package of acts, gestures, thoughts, words, and performances—that gets good ratings by an approving public.

(4) Quantification: Through numerical ratings, speech and behavior is quantified, and one can then visualize what is approved or normal speech and behavior. Those who receive especially high numeric scores, such as the follower counts of viral celebrities or influencers, may represent the ideal personality packages to strive for and those who receive poor or negative crowdsourced feedback, especially viral villains, provide models of what to avoid. We witness these metrics of crowdsourced feedback over and over again throughout our day-to-day lives, attached to ourselves and others, which help ingrain in us acceptable, and unacceptable, idealized, and villainized performances of identity. One is thereby schooled by the public and can "optimize" oneself to gain normal crowdsourced ratings and feedback. Through maintaining normal scores online one then feels oneself to be normal, may be viewed by others as normal, and passes the examination. All the while one may always strive harder for a higher score, a gradation that is in effect limitless, to match a publicly ideal performance of oneself in everyday life. That which is not well-rated is usually removed from public view as much as possible, but with increasing crowdsourced panopticism, the ability to shield oneself from the public's normalizing judgment shrinks.

(5) Ranked distribution: Cyberspace is often distributed according to rank. As in a traditional classroom, the best-performing "pupils" are algorithmically moved to the head of the social media feed or search results and thus further rewarded, while the low-performing pupils fall further to the bottom of a feed and into obscurity; that is, unless one crosses a certain threshold and becomes virally shamed, in which case one becomes thrust to the top of the feed for a spectacle of punishment, like an excluded child facing the wall in a dunce cap while the class watches on in ridicule. Through ranked

distribution of cyberspace, one can quickly scroll through a feed, or a list of followers, to see one's status on the gameboard of social media popularity. With each person usually marked by clearly visible scores, and often ordered based on one's performance metrics, individuals thereby become easily comparable, and feel compelled to compete with one another for likes, followers, or other metrics of approval. They can then see where they stand, and correct their behavior by performing in approved ways—in accordance with various publics—to try and move up the charts and avoid shameful marks, to be liked by the public. Rising or falling in rank in itself becomes a powerful form of reward or punishment for disciplined behavior.

(6) Shameful class: There is practically no upward limit to how many likes or followers a person may get, but there is simultaneously a threshold beneath which one may fail and enter the shameful class. Those who fall beneath the threshold of an acceptable grade, whose behavior is unable to compare closely enough to others, are often punished through exclusion. Avoidance of the shameful individual is in a sense compelled as their quantifiably low-status risks rubbing off on others like a social contagion. This may be part of what makes the widespread experience of FOMO so incredibly anxiety provoking for the modern age. One is perhaps driven by a fear of falling into the shameful class, the excluded, and being permanently left out in a torturous isolation.

(7) Normalizing gaze: Hierarchical surveillance in the form of P2P surveillance and normalizing judgment in the form of rating, ranking, commenting, friending, following, and so forth, combine into P2P examinations that establish what sort of identity, speech, and behavior is considered normal and who is successful or failing to achieve it. Under growing systems of P2P surveillance and control, each moment of one's life becomes, increasingly, a possible performance on a global stage that is reviewed and judged by an anonymously watching digital public. There is essentially no behavior too small that it may not be sanctioned or rewarded by the public and increasingly no sphere of life that is immune from its normalizing judgments, or where the ratings and comments of the public cannot have significant consequences. This is part of the totalizing nature of the P2P examination that we subject ourselves to, feel coerced to subject ourselves to, or are directly subjected to by others.

(8) Case-files: Recorded details of people's lives and crowdsourced metrics and feedback are preserved in various online documents which serve as a perpetual accountancy of one's scores of normality, saved in a file that is intimately attached to the individual, and instantly recallable by name in a centralized searchable database like Google. Results of one's examination are recorded into writing that follows each individual around. One's "electronic dossier" turns the individual into a case, serving as a record of one's

acceptability to the public, a certificate of approval, and a license to enter society. This electronic dossier is increasingly used by the public as a form of inspection, a verification that one is an approved part of the whole and ready for installation into the social machine, and to make sure that the faulty parts can be detected and either repaired or discarded, that one is and remains continuously normal.

REPUTATION AS CONTINUAL AND COMPULSORY INSPECTION

The premise that one needs a quantifiably normal or "good" reputation online to make one "employable," "friendable," and "dateable," seems to be only in one way or another expanding, and becoming more fundamental to the essential functioning and management of society in a growing "reputation economy." As a result of these emerging social forces in play, people are rushing *en masse* to build their online "social capital" and digital reputation. Brian Chesky, founder of Airbnb says, "We are only at day one in the whole idea of global reputation. There really could one day be this reputation economy that allows us to do so many different activities that we can't even imagine right now."[16] For those who fail the public's examination, low marks may not only be shameful and humiliating, but one's online profile increasingly affects one's offline opportunities, all of which can be put in serious jeopardy by negative scores, comments, and unwanted public exposure of personal information.

In terms of one's basic livelihood, a 2017 survey conducted on behalf of CareerBuilder by The Harris Poll, found that "70 percent of employers use social media to screen candidates before hiring, up significantly from 60 percent last year and 11 percent in 2006." About an equal number screen candidates using search engines like Google, and more than half of employers found content online that caused them to not hire a candidate for an open position. But employers don't just screen candidates for negative material such as "inappropriate photographs, videos, or information," but they also reward individuals for a positive social media presence.[17] One study found, for example, that one's Facebook profile photo can affect one's chances of landing an interview by 40 percent.[18] Therefore, to be fully incorporated into the economy, there is growing pressure, and in many instances it is practically required (if one risks being passed over from an interview), that one have a publicly approved display of oneself online before the global community.

But unlike a resume or CV, how we look when Googled is often not up to us. We don't get to present ourselves, but ultimately are presented through the public's mediation. Furthermore, what we are expected to "voluntarily" present about ourselves goes far beyond a presentation of our professional lives, but is rather evidence of our personal lives beyond work—photos, videos, our thoughts, and so forth—as well as evidence of how we are judged by the public—likes, hearts, followers, and other social metrics of collective approval. Thus, terms of employment now include a publicly rated and approved snapshot of our lives as a whole, a supposed assessment of our character. Through this the social spheres blur between friends, home, and work, and the public is given a considerable amount of influence over our basic life opportunities.

Apart from just one's basic livelihood, in terms of buying a house, and other material opportunities, *The Wall Street Journal* reports that more lenders are using social media to determine a borrower's creditworthiness.[19] But it goes beyond this and into affecting one's social life as well. For example, it is well-known that people commonly Google potential and current romantic partners, in addition to other social acquaintances. This will only increase as more people embrace online dating and other forms of Internet-facilitated social meet-ups. If one wishes to not be screened by the public, or if one lets one's guard down, flubs one's ongoing performance before our reality show of life, there is potentially a disturbingly high price to pay. On the extreme end, we may be essentially cast out of society, unable to get a job, a home, or a romantic partner, when we either have no ratings or if ratings plummet.

The expectation that we must offer our private lives up for continual inspection by the public for approval is starting at an increasingly young age. For example, a recent Kaplan survey found that over a third of college admissions officers screen student applicants via social media, just like employers, searching their social media accounts for any disqualifying content or for content that demonstrates approved characteristics. Thirty-eight percent of those who screen applicants online said an applicant's social media presence had a positive impact on prospective students, while 32 percent said it had a negative impact. While the majority of admissions officers today still do not screen candidates online, the majority of admission officers, nearly 60 percent, believe screening applicants is "fair game" with only the minority, around 40 percent, believing it to be "an invasion of privacy that shouldn't be done."[20] Notably, 70 percent of high school students think screening them online for college admissions is fair game as well.[21] Formulating oneself to be an acceptable member of the public, surveilled online, appears to be the majority expectation for a new generation. With teens constantly photographing, videotaping and broadcasting each other online as a part of their day-to-day social lives, this means they must be careful to constantly perform in such a manner that will gain approval not just from their immediate peers, but by the public as whole, since evidence of their speech and behavior may wind up on the Internet at almost any given time.

What sort of criteria an individual is screened for by different audiences may vary to some degree (an employer versus a potential date, for example), but when an individual's information appears on the Internet, it is all out there before the mass audience. Therefore, one must internalize the watch of this collective public gaze and act according to widely accepted norms and customs to avoid sanctions. In effect the public can collectively assert a great deal of control over the course of an individual's life through the threat of ruining people's relationships, as well as college and career opportunities for any disobedient, unruly, offensive, or abnormal speech or behavior.

Even more pressing, as the electronic and physical worlds merge through AR devices, the public may in a sense directly take a hold of the IRL body for disciplinary measures. These devices have already been demonstrated to be able to automatically pull up information about an individual online by simply looking at them. As augmented reality then displays this information on top of a person's field of vision, in effect one's digital self becomes directly imposed on top of one's IRL self. The two selves effectively merge in the augmented eye of the beholder. Therefore, everything the public has done to mark the digital body, its ratings, its comments, and other social metrics, risks being digitally marked upon one's physical body as well. The normalizing judgment of the public takes on a much greater saliency if one is pressured or effectively coerced to be displayed with these crowdsourced judgments wherever one goes online or off. In cases of online public shaming, the digital scarlet letter would then effectively become an IRL scarlet letter and the global village would become fully realized in its essence. Without touching the corporeal body, the public apparatus threatens to paint the digital body, and in turn the physical body, with a hideous digital shadow that follows wherever one goes.

One may object that the majority of the mutual monitoring and judgment going on by ordinary people today occurs through networks such as Facebook, Twitter, and Instagram where participation is largely voluntary. One can therefore simply opt out of the services to limit one's exposure. This sentiment underlies, for example, Anders Albrechtslund's characterization that the surveillance by ordinary people on these networks best be described as "participatory" and that it is "empowering," in part because it is engaged with voluntarily.[22] But in many or most of the aforementioned examples of P2P surveillance, people did not voluntarily expose information about themselves on the Internet, or certainly not for the global audience they unintentionally reached. People also routinely find themselves posted online through their friends' accounts whether they themselves belong to or are active on a social networking site, especially for younger generations where photo sharing and a high degree of transparency is already the norm. If one cannot effectively escape P2P surveillance in one's life, which is increasingly impossible, then one cannot escape the public's examination and control.

Even in cases where one must voluntarily opt-into a service, removing oneself from this pool of public judgment is not so simple as deactivating an account, or even just becoming inactive on a social network. It is increasingly difficult to fully participate in society without these profiles, as these technologies are becoming wound into the fabric of everyday life as much as ICTs of the past once did, such as radio, television, telephone, and e-mail. Social media researcher José van Dijck says that "the social push to stay connected is insidious."[23] To drop off of social media, especially for younger generations who have never known a world without it, feels akin to purposefully outcasting oneself—with isolation being one of humankind's greatest instinctual fears. Daniel Trottier reports from his interviews with undergraduates that

> Many respondents actively disliked Facebook, going so far as to deactivate their profiles. These students invariably returned to Facebook, though their absence only strengthened their criticism of the site. Their return to a service they dislike is fueled by the perceived need to stay online. Not being on Facebook is equated with being cut off from peers and social events. Nobody directly prevented them from leaving, but there are clear costs associated with leaving.[24]

Perhaps more concerning, potential employers, romantic partners, friends, and others, have arguably begun to become suspicious of those who hide in the shadows of reality. For example, *Der Tagesspiegel*, a German magazine commenting on these concerns, went as far as to point out that mass murderers James Holmes and Anders Breivik did not have Facebook accounts.[25] In a *CNN* article entitled "Why did Colorado shooting suspect avoid social media" Dr. Pamela Rutledge of the Media Psychology Research Center notes that many looking for clues about James Holmes online began to speculate what role his lack of social media played in his turn to becoming a serial killer; she says, "It's a testimony to how normal participating in the social media world is when we look at the lack of presence as an anomaly. (We wonder,) 'What's wrong with this guy that he's not at least on Facebook?'"[26] Such suspicions may explain why already 57 percent of employers today are less likely to hire applicants they could not find online.[27]

Similar suspicions surrounding those without an online presence can be found echoed across social spheres, not just limited to those affecting one's livelihood. This transcript from a *Slate* magazine dating advice podcast captures this sentiment well:

> *[Host 1]:* Imagine if this guy didn't have a Facebook profile . . . You should be suspicious of someone who is not making your relationship known publicly on a site like Facebook.

[Host 2]: I'm fine with people not having a Facebook page if they don't want one. However, I think you're right. If you're of a certain age and you meet someone . . . , and that person doesn't have a Facebook page . . . It could be some kind of red flag.[28]

Such media discourse and headlines strengthen such suspicions and reflect an already prevalent public opinion regarding the perceived abnormality of those not on social media. For example, media studies professor Laura Portwood-Stacer finds in her research that "Both users and non-users use words like 'strange,' 'weird,' 'crazy,' 'frustrating,' and 'anti-social' to describe people who choose not to be on Facebook."[29] As expectations for public profiles increase, one's absence from a site may become in effect not really an absence at all, but implicit inclusion in a "suspicious persons" category in a global database.

With employers and potential romantic partners regularly searching people's online presence before getting involved with them, a lack of information can in effect become like a lack of a permit to access the goods of society such as jobs, and the "market" for friends and romance. This effect will be further heightened if augmented reality and facial recognition become commonplace thereby allowing one to identify individuals and bring up information simply by looking at them. In such an environment, being without a publicly observable online display will viscerally mark the individual out with a question mark, and may in itself be cause for exclusion, to get away from a suspicious and potentially dangerous bogeyman in one's midst. All this makes the nature of P2P surveillance much less empowering to the extent that it is becoming like a continual mandatory licensing exam for being part of society, that demands conformity with publicly approved identities or personality packages, with the possible price paid for individual deviations from certain preset standards—for failing the inspection—being a loss of livelihood, a love life, friends, even family—and the general consuming pain of shame, rejection, and isolation that is so deeply hurtful that it regularly leads people to take their own lives.

In China, the state is using some of the very mechanisms of P2P surveillance and control to implement a nationwide "social credit" system generating a mandatory trustworthiness score for each citizen that will determine one's level of access to society from college admissions to one's placement on dating websites. China's social credit system is considered by many to be totalitarian in its implications because through its mechanism of surveillance, reward, and punishment, it forces almost all observable aspects of an individual's life into conformity with government-sanctioned speech and behavior. For better or worse, we are developing something in the West that bears striking similarities, but operating through privately held means rather than through the state, as might be expected of a decentralized capitalist society versus a centralized communist society. This may allow for a larger diversity of publics to "choose" from to be watched by in the West, a larger variety of socially approved molds to be shaped into, but whether one opts-into the eye of the public, which is already the norm, or the public directly forces its watch upon the individual, which is a growing phenomenon, there is an increasing expectation that the public should be able to monitor and keep tabs on everybody, and scrutinize ordinary people's day-to-day lives.

The power of the digitally connected public threatens to only get much more totalizing if we do not put appropriate constraints on this power now. As Mill says: "There is a limit to the legitimate interference of collective opinion with individual independence: and to find that limit, and maintain it against encroachment, is as indispensable to a good condition of human affairs, as protection against political despotism."[30] The protection and recovery of the private sphere, one that is understood to exist apart from just the blunt designations of private and public spaces, will be one way to protect against this growing overreach of the public.

NOTES

1. Foucault, *Discipline and Punish*, 16.
2. Foucault, *Discipline and Punish*, 30.
3. Foucault, *Discipline and Punish*, 222.
4. Foucault, *Discipline and Punish*, 178.
5. Gary Gutting, *Foucault: A Very Short Introduction* (Oxford: Oxford University Press, 2005), 84.
6. Hubert L. Dreyfus and Paul Rabinow, *Michel Foucault: Beyond Structuralism and Hermeneutics* (Chicago: University of Chicago Press, 1983), 158.
7. Dreyfus and Rabinow, *Michel Foucault*, 180.
8. Gutting, *Foucault*, 84.
9. Foucault, *Discipline and Punish*, 184.
10. Foucault, *Discipline and Punish*, 191.
11. Johanna Oksala, *How to Read Foucault* (New York: Norton, 2008), 59.
12. Deborah Schoeneman, "What's He Really Like? Check the Lulu App," *The New York Times*, November 20, 2013, https://www.nytimes.com/2013/11/21/fashion/social-networking-App-allows-women-to-rate-men.html.
13. Steve O'Hear, "After Rebooting, Lulu Sees Its Database Of Guys App Hit 200K Users In 8 Weeks Across U.S. Campuses," *TechCrunch*, April 9, 2013, https://techcrunch.com/2013/04/09/guys-look-away/.
14. Caitlin Dewey, "Everyone You Know Will Be Able to Rate You on the Terrifying 'Yelp for People' – Whether You Want Them to or Not," *The Washington Post*, September 30, 2015, https://www.washingtonpost.com/news/the-intersect/wp

/2015/09/30/everyone-you-know-will-be-able-to-rate-you-on-the-terrifying-yelp-for-people-whether-you-want-them-to-or-not/.

15. Bentham, *The Panopticon Writings*, 31.

16. Rachel Botsman, "Welcome to the New Reputation Economy," *Wired*, August 20, 2012, https://www.wired.co.uk/article/welcome-to-the-new-reputation-economy.

17. CareerBuilder, "Number of Employers Using Social Media to Screen Candidates at All-Time High, Finds Latest CareerBuilder Study," *CareerBuilder*, June 15, 2017, http://press.careerbuilder.com/2017-06-15-Number-of-Employers-Using-Social-Media-to-Screen-Candidates-at-All-Time-High-Finds-Latest-CareerBuilder-Study.

18. Ghent University, "Employers Use Facebook (photos) to Screen Job Candidates," *ScienceDaily*, January 14, 2016, www.sciencedaily.com/releases/2016/01/160114110719.htm.

19. Stephanie Armour, "Borrowers Hit Social-Media Hurdles," *The Wall Street Journal*, January 8, 2014, https://www.wsj.com/articles/borrowers-hit-socialmedia-hurdles-1389224469.

20. Kaplan, "Kaplan Survey: Percentage of College Admissions Officers Who Visit Applicants' Social Media Pages on the Rise Again," *Kaplan*, January 13, 2020, https://www.kaptest.com/blog/press/2020/01/13/kaplan-survey-percentage-of-college-admissions-officers-who-visit-applicants-social-media-pages-on-the-rise-again/.

21. Scott Jaschik, "Social Media as 'Fair Game' in Admissions," *Inside Higher Ed*, April 23, 2018, https://www.insidehighered.com/admissions/article/2018/04/23/new-data-how-college-admissions-officers-view-social-media-applicants.

22. Anders Albrechtslund, "Online Social Networking as Participatory Surveillance," *First Monday* 13, no. 3 (2008). https://doi.org/10.5210/fm.v13i3.2142.

23. José Van Dijck, *The Culture of Connectivity: A Critical History of Social Media* (Oxford: Oxford University Press, 2013), 51.

24. Trottier, "Interpersonal Surveillance," 323.

25. The Week, "Not on Facebook? You're Probably a Psychopath," *The Week*, accessed July 1, 2016, http://www.theweek.co.uk/facebook/48363/not-on-facebook-youre-probably-a-psychopath.

26. Doug Gross, "Why did Colorado Shooting Suspect Avoid Social Media?," *CNN*, July 23, 2012, https://www.cnn.com/2012/07/23/tech/social-media/colorado-suspect-social-media/index.html.

27. CareerBuilder, "Number of Employers."

28. Farhad Manjoo and Emily Yoffe, "Revenge of the Facebook Stalker (Transcript)," *Slate*, March 6, 2012, http://www.slate.com/articles/podcasts/manners_for_the_digital_age/2012/03/transcript_facebook_stalker_should_i_tell_a_cheating_guy_s_girlfriend_that_we_hooked_up_.html.

29. Laura Portwood-Stacer, "Media refusal and conspicuous non-consumption: The performative and political dimensions of Facebook abstention," *New Media & Society* 15, no. 7 (2013): 1049.

30. Mill, *On Liberty*, 9.

Part III

RESISTANCE

Chapter 7

Freedom from the Public Eye

There is an important distinction to be made between freedom of choice, the infinite freedom of choice, of an infinite number of paths one may go down, of the infinite number of life potentialities that may be fulfilled, and *selection* from a seemingly vast combination of allowable possibilities.[1] As we are broadcast online, we are prodded to claim and conform to different identity brands and signal ourselves as part of different publics. Some identity statuses are imposed upon us. Others we can select from a growing set of options by which to self-identify. We can wear these identifications as digital badges on our digital bodies to mix and match. Our branded identities can become rather complex based on the large number of combinations one can make based on different identity statuses available.

But if each identity status is attached to a public, if what that identity *means* is created by a public that subscribes to that identity, or claims it, if there are certain opinions that must be held in order to be part of that public, then one becomes confined by one's public or the combination of one's publics. This is in addition to the greater confines of the public at large, in which each individual public is networked and must be acceptable to and fit within the basic characteristics of the public as a whole. When we form our sense of self in this way, through the selection and combination of publicly approved mass-identity statuses, we cannot claim ourselves or have mastery over ourselves. In a sense, we are no longer ourselves. Instead, we are beholden to collective identities. We are forced into a sense of self which the public demands. This is not necessarily a new phenomenon, but our new technologies intensify this pressure and leave little room for escape.

To choose to follow one's passions one may go off in a direction that has never been ventured before, not the road less traveled, but a path not yet cut, without a public, without public approval, and likely subject to strong public censure for its inherent abnormality or weirdness. If P2P surveillance and control is suppressing the possibility to cut this original path, to make it feel like it is not even a conceivable option to go down a path that doesn't already *have* a significant public behind it, then the public becomes a threat to individual liberty, and a threat to cultural progress as well. This is so even if there is a growing list of approved publics to select from within the dominant public discourse.

Through P2P surveillance all is increasingly coming under the watch and pressure of the public as a whole constraining any radical turns to new subcultures with radically new values. What is constrained in the process of public submersion via increasing P2P examination is individuality based on the following of one's own spontaneously felt passions and creative actions based on that spontaneity, with communities that form around these spontaneities, and support these new experiments in living. One does not productively fulfill one's *own* powers and *own* potential in a public that levels that individual into conformity. One can select from what is available, but one cannot choose one's own path, just permutations of what is already there, as approved by society as a whole under the watch of the expanding public eye of the global community.

In earlier times, away from the public eye, one could more readily live within the plains of society, and in one's own private space or community, explore the bounds of real-world living free from the pressures of society. In doing so individuals and tight-knit communities could perhaps ultimately find new and better ways of living that could be transmitted to a wider culture. Take the mid-twentieth century visionary artist James Hampton, for example, who worked for the federal government by day, but by midnight, in a private garage in downtown Washington, DC, transformed into "St. James." As St. James he had visions, invented a new form of religion, and over fourteen years of exquisite, dedicated, time-consuming, and painstaking labor, built a beautiful glittering altar out of trash and other discarded objects he found around his neighborhood. This was at a time when such forms of art would have been considered *highly* erratic.

Hampton's identity and corresponding way of life, his experiment in living, had no public. He went his own way, inwardly, in a private urban garage sanctuary. He *literally* formed his own private language, captured in a book of revelations he wrote, in a strange almost Semitic-looking invented script, of which translation is to this day an ongoing challenge being taken up by cryptanalysts.[2] His beautiful altar, which he called *The Throne of the Third Heaven of the Nations' Millennium General Assembly*, was only discovered after his death. He once said of the work, "That is my life. I'll finish before I die."[3] Though he probably never did quite finish it. This echoes Kierkegaard's understanding of passion, as an individual being dedicated toward an idea for which one is willing to "live and die." Similar to Kierkegaard's understanding of how strong community forms through shared passion, Hampton's ultimate goal was apparently to open a street-side ministry in which the *Throne* would be a central teaching device. Apart from this intended private religious community, his masterwork was not for the public. Now, however, it can be viewed in Washington at the Smithsonian, where it is officially considered the greatest work of American visionary art in history.

Like his work that lives on today, Hampton's life was truly "abnormal" and truly extraordinary. But, it was a heightened level of privacy that arguably was needed for such "abnormality" to flourish. I'm not saying that there are no St. James's living today or that it's impossible to eke out the privacy needed to be freely and truly eccentric, but to remain intact one may increasingly need to find new ways to remain undercover, as the cultural force of the Internet invades privacy and often subjects individuals to unwanted publicity and hostility for anything out of the norm.

If P2P surveillance had existed in Hampton's day, his abnormal day-to-day activities surrounding the building of the Throne—of gathering trash around the neighborhood for over a decade on end, buying foil off of neighborhood winos for the silver of his altar, hauling it all back mysteriously to his private garage in a burlap sack and child's wagon—would very likely have been filmed, posted online, and probably heavily ridiculed as "crazy." It would only take one nosey person with a camera for this relatively private information to potentially traverse across the city, across the nation, and perhaps the entire global network and bring massive unwanted attention to his personal and private endeavors. Images and reports of Hampton's "crazy" behavior may have quickly spread to his government employer (and everyone else), where he may have been looked upon with suspicion and perhaps even pushed out of his job.

Under such developing conditions, where little privacy remains, his eccentric side may have become inhibited by the onslaught of public pressure, and the potential for serious negative consequences. St. James, this lived superhero of a self, a reality in which his powers were freely developed and expressed, could have been vanquished. Exposure by the public might be the kryptonite of many eccentric individual superheroes going their own way, and otherwise blazing new paths that may benefit us all. When someone is behaving out of the norm, it could be because they are visionaries ahead of the rest of us, set to lead the way. But if we are quick to cast all abnormal behavior as something to be publicized and scrutinized, we risk cutting off these new rare blooms at the root.

Today, under the growing apparatus of radical transparency, one is increasingly likely to be exposed and trigger penalties by the public if one falls outside of a publicly approved category of thought, speech, and behavior, if one falls outside the bounds of the category one subscribes to, or if one cannot be categorized at all. The public becomes like a vast bureaucracy in which one must find oneself on a form, selectable from an electronic drop-down menu, or be denied entry into society. Expressions of oneself that do not already have a public attached, that cannot be readily categorized, are in danger of being gated off and pushed out of society altogether. Through the power of the public, the frontiers of experiments in living risk being closed down.

RESISTING THE NET OF NORMALITY

When we consider how to resist the net of normality, we should reflect upon Foucault's thesis that "We must cease once and for all to describe the effects of power in negative terms: it 'excludes,' it 'represses,' it 'censors,' it 'abstracts,' it 'masks,' it 'conceals.' In fact, power produces . . . ."[4] One does not really exist, Foucault claims, as a fully formed self in opposition to power, a preexisting individuality that is repressed by power. Rather, power actively works on and crafts one's psyche and identity as opposed to preventing a separately formed, intact, whole individual self from expressing itself as one truly is. Discipline creates the docile, compliant, manipulatable individuals who are turned into certain kinds of people, certain "normal" identities. Through discipline, Foucault argues, we become products of society from the inside out, a manufactured identity.

If this is correct, how do we find freedom from disciplinary power when we are so intrinsically shaped by this power to begin with? Foucault argues it won't come from merely turning to the law for protection. Freedom of speech, for example, won't protect freedom if everything that one says is essentially programmed by society and therefore inherently unfree to begin with. One must actively subvert the program that is instilled through discipline in order to effectively resist power. Sociologist Alessandro Pizzorno elaborates:

> what stands opposed to power and ends up either free or subjected (normalised) are acts, gestures, states of mind and of body. Among them is to be found the recalcitrant, resistant, unyielding material that normalising power may fail to reduce. One will know that freedom is alive . . . when contestation, unruliness, indocility, intractability are not yet abolished, when the recalcitrant is not transformed into the dutiful.[5]

On this view, freedom is the words, acts, thoughts, the dance, that stems from spontaneity, rather than calculation. We might even say, in the vein of Kierkegaard, that freedom involves passionate action free from over-reflection. Gutting explains that for Foucault, subverting programmed identity means "individual commitment to constant self-transformation . . . [which] follows from his horror of being stuck in an identity."[6] On Foucault's view, seeing oneself as fundamentally any sort of prescribed identity is a trap because it is a way in which power works upon the individual to put them into a box, a personality package, to use Fromm's terminology. Resistance to power then comes in part through resistance against socially constructed identity; that is, how we habitually calculate our behavior to match that of identities we have been disciplined into replicating.

We might say that there is freedom where one can resist the script, the program of normality, where one has not had spontaneity so beaten out of oneself through disciplinary measures, from one's life being under such a web of infinite examination, with a looming threat of worldwide punishment, that one has become robotic—an automaton. We might say that freedom is alive where there are still passionate individuals who are able to live and die for an idea despite what the whole world may think. The intensifying pressures that are brought to bear through the spread of P2P surveillance and control, on anyone who acts even slightly in an unscripted fashion, demonstrates the way in which the public is encroaching on liberty. It is the room for spontaneity, the room for unruliness, the ability for small acts of rebellion to exist without being entirely snuffed out by an oppressive overbearing force, in this case of the public, that is part of what shows freedom is alive.

Small acts of resistance to normality can have tremendous effects on people's lives and on the subsequent communities and cultures that spawn from these small rebellious gestures. Take, for example, the mystic poet and Sufi spiritual leader Rumi and how he reportedly initiated the ecstatic spinning spiritual practice of The Whirling Dervishes:

> One day as [Rumi] walked by the goldbeater's shop he heard the hammers of the apprentices pounding the rough sheets of gold into beautiful objects. With each step he repeated the name of God; and now with the sound of the hammers beating the gold, all he heard was 'Allah, Allah'. 'Allah, Allah' became every sound he heard, and he began to whirl in ecstasy in the middle of the street. He unfolded his arms like a fledgling bird, tilted his head back, and whirled, whirled, whirled to the sound of 'Allah' that came forth from the very wind he created by his movement . . . That was the beginning of the Mevlevi order of Sufis known as The Whirling Dervishes.[7]

To spin in the streets, in a public place, is highly erratic, and abnormal behavior. It is considered "crazy." But Rumi existed in a society of old, where there weren't cameras out everywhere streaming live; he wasn't immediately broadcast to the entire world or threatened to be, with every image of a spontaneous moment of joy indelibly recorded, every strange facial expression and gesture forever analyzed, vandalized, and ridiculed by an anonymous public that could view this momentary action anywhere for all time. Had there been such social conditions, perhaps even Rumi may have never twirled and the whole tradition may have never taken off. There needs to be enough room to breathe in order for the soul to spin alive.

Today, the *sama* ceremony of The Whirling Dervishes is one of the dozens of Masterpieces of the Oral and Intangible Heritage of Humanity protected by the United Nations Educational, Scientific and Cultural Organisation (UNESCO). What may have appeared a moment of craziness was actually a moment of spiritual and cultural advance. Losing the ability to lose oneself in a moment of spontaneity, or to *deliberately* act in a fashion apart from public opinion, without being captured and permanently viewed and judged by the public, is crushing not only to the individual, but to the progress of culture.

To act out of passion involves being caught up in something that one *feels*, to embrace the thread of one's personal calling, and daring to do so. That's how new subcultures are created. That's how we wound up with something like punk rock. Take a band like The Ramones for example, commonly seen to be the first band that really sparked the punk sound. They played music that was mostly a direct predecessor of late-1950s and early-1960s garage rock. But the Ramones sped it up, cranked it up, and really let loose, singing about subjects such as boredom, drug abuse, and insanity. It was *small* differences that emerged spontaneously, out of feeling, without censoring oneself, but feeling some quirk, some moment, and not overly reflecting on it, as Kierkegaard warned against, not thinking *too* much about what others think, but rather going forth with one's vision, even going over the line one dare not go, and breaking through.

Small resistances to programmatic behavior born from spontaneity can spark entire new cultures and movements, but it requires acting in a way that no one is already acting, not caring what others think, and passionately committing to one's inner movement. It requires making one's action an end in itself, carried out for the sake of following one's passionate calling, and not as a means for some external reward like fame and celebrity, of going viral. Freedom and spontaneity, the creation of a whole new way of being, can begin with just a gesture or act that is apart from the norm, not calculated to be approved by a public. That is what it means to resist the program. That is what it means to be a leader.

To be clear, not any sort of spontaneous behavior freely acted upon constitutes a step toward a higher realization. But the way one may be gripped spontaneously, inwardly by an idea, a vision, or movement, can be the catalyst for the realization of one's inner powers. James Hampton, for example, was gripped spontaneously by his visions of the altar. It took acts of rebellious resistance to the norm to realize his vision when everyone must have thought he was crazy. He likely understood the way in which his actions were extremely out of line with normality, but rather than bringing himself into line, he continuously resisted the pressures of normality every day for years, sticking passionately and *deliberately* to his vision, to bring what was inside him into reality, and as an effect of doing so, to realize himself *as* himself, as St. James. In other words, an idea may grip the individual spontaneously, but living it out takes an act of concerted, deliberate ongoing effort, in order to realize one's vision, and in turn realize oneself. This is what passionate dedication and commitment to an idea looks like, what resistance looks like.

Individual and community resistance to the power of the public becomes increasingly snuffed out if one must constantly be aware that even a momentary spontaneous diversion from normality, from conformity with a mass-approved script of speech and action, may be filmed, broadcast to the entire world, ridiculed for eternity, and lead to one being potentially cut off from society indefinitely. That's a pressure that even the freest individuals can scarcely resist, especially as we have arguably become more interdependent on society as a whole just to survive than ever before in history, rendering us rather helpless before its massive force. If the technological trends surveyed in this work continue unabated, we risk a sort of police state of the public, with its apparatus for enforcing its opinion reaching indefinitely into every nook and cranny of one's personal and social life.

Can one spin with abandon in the face of the camera and the billion eyes behind it? Can one live out one's inner-potential without a care for how it is recorded and judged online and the consequences that may have? Who is strong enough? Who dares? Who is rebellious in the face of the public? Or shall we have to go undercover? In Kierkegaard's prophecy of the present age, he argued that the truly passionate individuals will have to remain hidden, freeing themselves from the leveling effects of public opinion, that "inorganic something, an abstraction":

> Like plainclothes policemen, they will be *unrecognizable*, concealing their respective distinctions and giving support only negatively—that is, by repulsion, while the infinite uniformity of abstraction judges every individual, examines him in his isolation. This structure is the dialectical opposite to that of the judges and prophets, and just as they risked the danger of not being respected for their respective authorities, so the unrecognized run the risk of being recognized, of being seduced into acquiring status and importance as authorities, thus preventing the highest development.[8]

On this view, perhaps the most rebellious thing one could do is quit social media altogether in repulsion. But what do you do if social media won't quit you? If one is stuck on the net, then perhaps obfuscation is the answer. Cheat on the P2P examination. Set up a social media decoy and live your life otherwise away from social media. Or maybe go the opposite route and create a deliberate spectacle. Spin in the streets like Rumi. Realize that anything you do that's abnormal in front of others, especially in a public setting, will likely be recorded and broadcast almost immediately. Deliberately use the power of spectacle to revolt against the public and its normalizing gaze as loudly and clearly as possible, and own the perhaps severe consequences that may follow. These are all possible forms of rebellious resistance in the face of the public.

PRIVACY AND COMMUNITY

Privacy is most often tied to a notion of individual liberty. But this is an incomplete picture and suggests that privacy is only valuable in a strongly individualistic framework. Rather privacy is equally necessary not just for individual liberty but also for maintaining the liberty and integrity of individual communities. P2P surveillance and control presents a threat not just to individual privacy, but perhaps even more profoundly to group privacy, which often occurs, perhaps paradoxically, in publicly accessible spaces. P2P surveillance encroaches upon the sanctuary spaces that are needed for both individuals and their communities to flourish.

Creation and individual breakthrough thrives on the existence of real-world community that supports the individual who is breaking new ground, that stands in solidarity with one another, and leadership, that creates conditions of support that foster individual spontaneity through mutual understanding. It is real people, in the same place, same time, together, lastingly in solidarity that fosters cultural progress, not the disjointed, asynchronous, ghostable publics of social media.

Very localized spots, a specific place in a specific time where real people come together committed and transcending themselves toward a shared idea, are the hotbeds for cultural birth. We wouldn't have had punk rock, for example, if we never had CBGB in New York in the late-1970s, that fostered just that sort of supportive community. In a musical and cultural sanctuary like CBGB in its early years, during a brief period of flourishing before punk itself became a scripted identity to be resisted, passion was allowed to thrive because it was a place that *encouraged* people to break from the norm and did not judge people by the standards of normal society, by the standards of the public at large.

While an audience at CBGB *was* in a sense a public, it would have been distinguishable from the sort of amorphous digital collective of millions and millions of strangers that characterizes publics today via the Internet. Instead, many people would have regularly frequented the club and would have come to know one another on a personal level, and share in their passion for the musical breakthroughs occurring in that protected space. Through this sanctuary of CBGB, centered around a shared passion, an actual community formed mutually devoted to a breakthrough idea in music. By real people coming to shows and standing in support with revolutionary leaders, like The Ramones, and one another, it was a show of solidarity, a passionate commitment to advancing the progress of music. Personal, communitywide, and cultural breakthroughs were readily had as a result.

At a place like CBGB, much of what occurred would have been considered highly erratic for its time, for example, punk styles of dance, like slam-dancing. Even today, if one were to go out slam-dancing in the streets, one would likely be filmed, and others would probably call the police. But within the confines of a supportive community, these unusual expressions are understood, and embraced. The existence of a club like CBGB, then, created a space apart from the rest of the world, with an ethos of experimentation. It was technically a public space, but it maintained a serious degree of privacy, hidden away in the slums of New York from the public at large. It allowed a privacy, not for the individual per se, but for the group who collectively maintained an existence apart from the examination and pressures of the public at large. The relatively private spaces that allow for specific group norms to flourish in communities of sympathetic associates are burst open for all to see in the face of P2P surveillance, destroying the *integrity* in which idiosyncratic group norms flourish. The controlling force of P2P surveillance thereby casts a general net of normality across society as a whole, both upon individuals *and* their associated groups, and creates a compelling force toward conformity with collective opinion that threatens liberty.

One may object that before the advent of P2P surveillance, a person might have still been caught by others in situations that exposed information about oneself to others in an unwanted manner. But while it is true that people may in fact today or in the past have encountered someone in person at, for example, a club or organization that they wish to shield their lifestyle from, say one's neighbor, the risk of such an unwanted encounter is likely very low so as not to be an overwhelmingly inhibiting factor; and if one did have such an encounter, it would probably be because the neighbor was in fact sympathetic to or directly associated with the group as well, and therefore a person for whom exposure would be of minimal negative consequence. It is highly unlikely that the nosey neighbor would in fact be at that particular location, in order to specifically monitor a specific individual for that specific social transgression or "abnormality," and if the neighbor were undergoing such surveillance activities, it would take considerable deliberate effort, and could only be done to monitor for a narrow and limited range of potential transgressions, that would need to be suspected in advance before such monitoring activities could occur. Furthermore, such deliberate "real-world" stalking of an individual would in itself be seen as a social norm violation for which the neighbor could be held accountable if caught himself. By contrast, P2P surveillance allows the neighbor to easily monitor anyone, for potentially any social deviance that is exposed on the web, with as little effort as typing in someone's name, and with zero accountability for doing so. The former limitations that kept the nosey neighbor from easily overreaching therefore fall by the wayside.

One way in which we can conceptualize the type of privacy violation that occurs through such hyperexposure, is through privacy scholars Evan Selinger and Woodrow Hartzog's work on privacy and obscurity. In their view, we maintain privacy in part because we "live and flourish in huge patches of obscurity."[9] By obscurity they mean that we maintain privacy through the high transaction costs that are often associated with gaining knowledge about us. For example, in the above scenario with the nosey neighbor, in an analog world, he may have had to essentially become a stalker on an undercover stakeout in order to uncover his neighbor's hidden lifestyle and clubgoing. The very high transaction cost made that information obscure to others, and that obscurity gave the club patron a sense of privacy to pursue an unconventional lifestyle in a rather uninhibited manner among sympathetic associates. Sure people on the street might witness this person going to the club or organization, but they also likely wouldn't remember her face or who she was. It would just be a fleeting moment that would almost certainly become quickly obscure in a person's mind. But all of these levels of obscurity melt away in the face of P2P surveillance as the transaction costs for attaining information suddenly vanish. If caught on camera, and tagged online—let's say perhaps automatically with facial recognition—then what would have been obscure information becomes indelibly marked on the individual and as easy to recall as typing one's name in, or maybe even one day just thinking about the individual. In such a chilling environment, we lose the obscurity afforded to us in our current lives, and in turn we lose the privacy needed to have what privacy scholar Julie Cohen refers to as the "breathing room"[10] to develop apart from the constant pressures of the crowd.

While some degree of unwanted exposure is necessarily a consequence of living in society, with P2P surveillance that risk of exposure is becoming great enough that one's individual and social freedom is unjustifiably impinged upon by the compelling force of the public. If there is unwanted exposure of a group who wish to keep their lifestyle choices to themselves, or a select group of sympathetic individuals, then it unduly inhibits that entire community and violates, not just an individual's privacy, but a *group*'s privacy. Explaining the concept of group privacy Luciano Floridi writes that

Consider [a] case in which the close friends and relatives (the group) of a deceased person decide to hold a private funeral. Attendance is by invitation only, but this is not meant to make the funeral 'exclusive'. The desired privacy may be due to a need for intimacy, for respectful quietness, to protect grieving and reflection, or perhaps because of cultural or religious customs. Whatever the reasons, in this case it seems very counterintuitive to argue that each member of the group (each close friend or relative of the deceased) has a right to a private funeral, or that the privacy demanded is just the collection of all individual privacies. It seems more reasonable to admit that we are in the presence of a strong, social sense of group privacy. It is the whole group as a group that has a right to that specific kind of privacy.[11]

We, of course, need individual privacy, an "immunity from the judgment of others," as Jeffrey Johnson puts it,[12] so that we can feel enough breathing room apart from the crowd to try out new things which may be stifled in the presence of others. But privacy is needed for more than just the individual. Local communities of real people in real places need privacy in order to try out new things, new experiments in living as a community, without the gaze and censure of the outside world, to exist as a group apart from the pressure of the public at large. Ferdinand Schoeman writes: "Groups or associations that are less encompassing than the society also emerge, and these also have private lives in a sense. Just as there are group pressures for individuals to conform, there are social pressures on groups to conform to some social standard, and concerns about overreaching are warranted in their case too."[13]

Group privacy is the way intimacy within relationships and communities form. As people in groups spend more time with each other, they share more information about themselves which allows them to know each other better, and become closer as a result. They thereby feel less inhibited and more free around each other. They trust one another and show affection for one another as friends and those in more intimate relationships do. Charles Fried explains that "Privacy is not merely a good technique for furthering these fundamental relations; rather without privacy they are simply inconceivable. They require a context of privacy or the possibility of privacy for their existence ... privacy is the necessary atmosphere for these attitudes and actions, as oxygen is for combustion."[14]

A certain amount of intimacy, of sharing of personal information, of a lack of inhibition, may therefore take place in one group, let's say a close group of friends, which in a second group, let's say one's classmates or colleagues, such letting-loose might feel entirely inappropriate. If these two groups are forced to be merged together, then the intimacy of the group of friends is overtaken and destroyed in the presence of their professional colleagues. This is not to say that the merging of the two groups might not produce a loosening of restrictions overall, but the freedom of behavior engendered in the group of friends, or in other intimate relationships, would nevertheless feel significantly stifled by the presence of the outside group. What we do, say, and share with one group of people is different than what we would share with another. Most people will concede, for example, that if they go out clubbing with friends on a Saturday night, they *do not* want to be watched by their boss, or clients, or their parents, or children. Such a monitoring of their activities by invisible outside parties would be stifling to one's free activity. But to the vanguard of radical transparency in Silicon Valley, breaking down the boundaries between our different relationships and associations has been one of the driving forces behind their ideological makeover of society. For example, here is Mark Zuckerberg from a 2009 interview with David Kirkpatrick in *The Facebook Effect*: "'You have one identity,' he says emphatically three times in a single minute . . . 'The days of you having a different image for your work friends or co-workers and for the other people you know are probably coming to an end pretty quickly . . . . Having two identities for yourself is an example of a lack of integrity[.]'"[15]

This illustrates how the acolytes of radical transparency may conflate privacy with secrecy, in the sense of trying to hide something bad from other people, or being malicious or duplicitous in some sense; that is, lacking integrity. But when I reveal certain information to some people, to close friends, or certain groups, in certain settings, and do not disclose such information to others in other settings, I am not in most cases keeping a "dirty" secret from everyone else, or somehow being deceitful about who I am. In contrast to the view espoused above by Zuckerberg on privacy and integrity, Fried explains, "To make clear the necessity of privacy as a context for respect, love, friendship and trust is to bring out also why a threat to privacy seems to threaten our very integrity as persons. To respect, love, trust, feel affection for others and to regard ourselves as the objects of love, trust and affection is at the heart of our notion of ourselves as persons among persons[.]"[16]

Reserving different aspects of oneself for different relationships and social spheres does not equate to a lack of integrity. Rather, as James Rachels says, "the different patterns of behavior are (partly) what define the different relationships; they are an important part of what makes the different relationships what they are."[17] How we act or present ourselves with our friends, the sides of ourselves that we reveal, is appropriately different than how we'd act or what we'd reveal to our boss or clients in most circumstances. Likewise, if our parents or children were watching us with our friends at all times, or possibly watching, we'd feel inhibited by their judgments and it would intrude upon the nature of our relationship with our close friends.

In a radically transparent society of P2P surveillance, under the watch of the globally networked public, where we are unable to maintain these separate boundaries between associations, we are increasingly forced to act with one set of relations as we would act with any other since through P2P surveillance there is a growing threat that any other person might potentially watch and listen in on our otherwise private relationships. My recourse would then either be to not behave in the way I wish to among my set of friends, for example, and thereby be stifled and chilled in my freedom of expression and the level of intimacy I have among my friends, or I'm forced to behave in a way in front of my parents, boss, clients, children, and so forth, that I don't think is appropriate to those relationships.[18] Those who went to CBGB to slam dance, for example, relied on the fact that their parents were *not* watching, in order to let loose in unusual ways that "parents just don't understand."[19] There is nothing wrong or duplicitous about this, or lacking integrity. Certain sets of judgments are simply stifling and certain sets of behaviors feel inappropriate around certain people in certain settings. Rachels argues that

> [W]e need to separate our associations, at least to some extent, if we are to maintain a system of different relationships with different people. Separation allows us to behave with certain people in the way that is appropriate to the sort of relationship we have with them, without at the same time violating our sense of how it is appropriate to behave with, and in the presence of, others with whom we have a different kind of relationship. Thus, if we are to be able to control the relationships that we have with other people, we must have control over who has access to us.[20]

What's important to preserving liberty is not just to preserve the liberty of the individual, but also the liberty of different communities, who share their own set of norms of acceptable speech and behavior. In other words, privacy is crucial not just in order for the *individual* to retain a space of action apart from the judgment of the public, but privacy is also crucial in order for the *group*, a close-knit *community*, to have a space apart from the judgment of the public. We need privacy for these different groups, between these different associations, in order to maintain the boundaries that allow for idiosyncratic communities to flourish. This is not to say that communities should be sovereign and determine all the contours of their group space apart from any consideration of the public good. But the ability to put serious constraints on the flow of information outside that community, to preserve the type of privacy necessary for intimacy to flourish is necessary to maintaining the integrity of communities, even if those communities interact primarily in publicly accessible spaces like CBGB.

Radical transparency proponents might counter that in a transparent society there would be no *need* to maintain different boundaries between different relationships as they believe "more transparency should make for a more tolerant society in which people eventually accept that everybody sometimes does bad or embarrassing things."[21] In this view, we will therefore judge each other less harshly overall because in a state of ultimate transparency we will see that everyone makes mistakes. Or perhaps those things which used to be considered embarrassing will no longer be embarrassing because through widespread exposure of that which was once hidden we will see that such behavior is rather common and statistically normal in that sense. The radical exposure forced upon all will thereby, in time, supposedly have a liberating effect. We'll have happier relationships, transparency advocates might imagine, when we *can* act around our parents, children, and bosses like we do with our closest friends because radical transparency exposes all and results in more tolerance for a wider range of behaviors, and less harsh judgment.

But this "utopian" theory about how things will all pan out in the end, once privacy is practically destroyed in a radically transparent revolution, is quite a gamble. For now the effect of increased exposure seems to be more tolerance in some respects for a wider variety of statistically widespread thoughts or behavior, but also an increasingly intolerant and puritanical society of outrage for any indiscretion exposed that is outside the realm of publicly acceptable speech or behavior. Even if the public in time becomes less easily explosive, it is highly unlikely that a feeling of pervasive judgment from the public will cease in a society in which people are increasingly transparent before the public's normalizing gaze.

But let's say we actually do get to Silicon Valley's radically transparent utopia where we have little or no ability to effectively maintain control over what others can know about us, and few boundaries available for separating relationships, but where, as a result, everyone feels connected in one "global community" and everyone becomes tolerant of most behaviors. Even if this utopian vision is possible, what is the price to be paid? The price to be paid is that I am *forced* into this new vision of society. I am a *forced* to accept this notion that how I behave in front of one group of people is how I ought to behave in front of everyone all the time. I am *forced* to lose the liberty of having control over what different associates know about me, and *forced* to accept a radical restructuring of social relations. Radical transparency proponents might argue that one is not free in the many different proverbial closets of the world and the public therefore liberates by ripping off the doors. But if a radically transparent society is a freer society, as its advocates insist, then we are, in the words of Rousseau, "forced to be free."[22] It is a state of "freedom" in domination.

PRIVACY IN PUBLIC

Some may have little sympathy for some of the examples of privacy I have discussed above such as the sort of privacy engendered at a publicly accessible club like CBGB. There is *no such thing* as privacy in public, they might say. If one has entered a *public* space, then by definition nothing is private and so the public should be entitled to watch or listen in as much as anyone present in the club at that moment. But there is still today, or at least ought to be, an expectation for a considerable degree of privacy in public spaces, that an action occurring in one setting, even if public, is not intended for everyone all the time, and ought not to be exposed before everyone all the time.

We can already see how P2P surveillance is violating this sense of privacy in public and have a taste of what's to come. For example, in 2014, there was an incident at a San Francisco punk dive bar, Molotov's, where a beta Google Glass "explorer" was wearing the head-mounted augmented reality recording device in the bar drawing extreme ire from its patrons. The "explorer" was allegedly assaulted, with the device being ripped off her face, and fist fights breaking out between one of her friends and other patrons at the bar. The incident was sparked in part by what was felt to be a major privacy violation, even though it occurred in a public venue. One of those involved in the incident said in an interview that upon seeing the Glass wearer she assumed she was being recorded and that she was "not comfortable with people taking pictures of me when I'm at the bar. Facial recognition scares the shit out of me."[23] Another patron that witnessed the incident echoed these privacy concerns: "Everybody was upset that she would be recording at a bar at last call, with obviously embarrassing behavior going on around her. People were rather insulted that someone thinks it's OK to record them the entire time they're in public."[24]

While the "explorer" was allegedly only actually recording once the altercation began, one can understand how, unlike a smartphone—which is already intrusive—the nature of Glass with its camera out, pointed, and ready to shoot would make someone feel as if they are either being recorded or about to be recorded, and would find that to be chilling and potentially violating. Even a recording indicator light is not enough to allow people relief from its aimed tension. The bar fight that broke out over the incident exemplifies the severity of the privacy violation experienced even though the device was being worn in a public establishment.

This violation of privacy in public that occurs through P2P surveillance can be understood viewing privacy through the lens of Helen Nissenbaum's concept of contextual integrity.[25] Her concept articulates that our expectation of privacy is not based merely on distinctions of private versus publicly accessible spaces, but rather on the norms of information exchange that surround different relationships in different settings. Just because one may reveal a certain aspect of oneself in a particular setting, even in a publicly accessible place, does not mean that one has forfeited one's expectation for that information to remain relatively confidential within the context of to whom, where, when, and how it was revealed. This is part of what allows us to have different relationships with different people, in different spheres of life, where one can feel free to speak and act differently depending on the context. For example, if one is slam-dancing in a punk bar among friends, even if that bar is open to the public, there is a relative expectation that the aspects of oneself that are revealed in that setting, with that particular set of present relationships, will likely not be revealed elsewhere, that one is behaving in a particular way within the context of friends and community in the dive bar and not for one's family or boss. If someone is surreptitiously recording that slam-dancer in a punk bar and streaming it to the Internet where one's words and actions are viewable by anyone worldwide, perhaps both in real-time and indefinitely thereafter, that agent of P2P surveillance is thereby damaging if not destroying the contextual integrity of the norms of information exchange expected for that setting.

If we no longer expect privacy from global public scrutiny in the circumstances described above it is because we are arguably already becoming dominated by the public. When the public becomes the violator of privacy it is unreasonable for the public to simultaneously define the new expectations of privacy. It is even more egregious when the public says that one's former reasonable expectations of privacy should be replaced with what amounts to practically the highest possible degree of exposure and publicity imaginable, as that is what is capable of occurring online.

By blowing the doors wide open for the whole world to transparently see indefinitely into the future, the context of privacy otherwise engendered by the walls of an enclosed space, or the locality of a specific time and place, is violated and even destroyed. This is how privacy violations can paradoxically occur even in public spaces. As the global community strengthens its social order through P2P surveillance it increasingly pushes all action out of the relative privacy of local-settings with specific relationships and into the realm of the global community, viewable by anyone at any time, thereby endangering the contextual integrity of interactions, and coercing a way of being that is acceptable to the broader society.

While radical transparency acolytes claim that to shield different associations from view by others, and different facets of oneself from others lacks integrity, they ignore the integrity of the context of an individual's actions, and the integrity of communities, which require freedom from hostile outside social pressures to remain united and whole in its distinct form. Privacy protects different spheres of our lives from intrusion by others in a way which we would find crushing if such boundaries were violated, and it is this protection that is needed to preserve an essential part of our liberty. In order to preserve the different ways of being that an individual may participate in, that assures social freedom, including protection of one's very *own* way of being, one's *own* experiment in living, there must be the ability to shield oneself off from the social pressures and the dominating opinion of one group upon another, barriers that P2P surveillance endangers and threatens to demolish.

None of this is to say that private individuals or communities ought to have *no* accountability to the larger society for their words or behavior. As privacy scholar Anita Allen says, "although privacy is important, it is not everything. Accountability matters too."[26] To illustrate, using one of her examples, we should not as a society allow a fundamentalist group to beat children just because they consider their congregation to be a private sanctuary and therefore no one else's business what they do within its walls. At the same time she insists that part of preserving freedom is that we are not accountable to everyone for everything; "We do not have to tell our mothers everything. We can compartmentalize our friends and get new jobs."[27] Allen warns that "suffocating, harsh, non-governmental accountability can make a person wretched."[28] It is just that sort of suffocating accountability to the public that social media and the Internet increasingly generates. Before we have an unfree and wretched society, we need a new right to privacy for the digitally hybrid age, that allows us to better control the circulation of information about ourselves over the Internet, to compartmentalize our social spheres, and to maintain ownership over one's digital self.

NOTES

1. Thank you to Heike Sefrin-Weis for helping clarify this distinction.
2. Casey N. Cep, "Cracking the Code of James Hampton's Private Language," *Pacific Standard*, last modified June 14, 2017, https://psmag.com/social-justice/cracking-code-james-hamptons-private-language-96278.
3. J. H. Barbour, "The Throne of the Third Heaven of the Nations' Millennium General Assembly," *History.org*, accessed February 5, 2019, https://www.history.org/foundation/journal/spring04/throne.cfm.
4. Foucault, *Discipline and Punish*, 194.
5. Alessandro Pizzorno, "Foucault and the Liberal View of the Individual," in *Michel Foucault, Philosopher*, ed. Timothy J. Armstrong (New York: Routledge, 1992), 207.
6. Gutting, *Foucault*, 90.
7. Andrew Weil, "Turning, Turning to the Sound of 'Allah'," *The New York Times*, July 13, 1975, https://www.nytimes.com/1975/07/13/archives/turning-turning-to-the-sound-of-allah-the-whirling-dervishes.html.
8. Kierkegaard, "Two Ages," 267–68.
9. Evan Selinger and Woodrow Hartzog, "Stop Saying Privacy Is Dead," *Medium*, October 11, 2018, https://medium.com/s/story/stop-saying-privacy-is-dead-513dda573071.

10. Julie E. Cohen, "What Privacy is For," *Harv. L. Rev.* 126 (2012): 1904.

11. Luciano Floridi, "Group Privacy: A Defence and an Interpretation," in *Group Privacy: New Challenges of Data Technologies*, ed. Linnet Taylor, Luciano Floridi, Bart van der Sloot (Cham: Springer, 2017), 91.

12. Jeffery L. Johnson, "A Theory of the Nature and Value of Privacy," *Public Affairs Quarterly* 6, no. 3 (1992): 274.

13. Ferdinand Schoeman, *Privacy and Social Freedom* (Cambridge; New York, NY: Cambridge University Press, 1992), 113.

14. Charles Fried, "Privacy," *The Yale Law Journal* 77, no. 3 (1968): 477–78.

15. Kirkpatrick, *The Facebook Effect*, 199.

16. Fried, "Privacy," 477–78.

17. James Rachels, "Why Privacy is Important," *Philosophy & Public Affairs* 4, no. 4 (1975): 327.

18. Rachels, "Why Privacy," 330.

19. Pete Harris, Will Smith, and Jeff Townes, *Parents Just Don't Understand* (New York: Jive Records, 1988).

20. Rachels, "Why Privacy," 330–31.

21. Kirkpatrick, *The Facebook Effect*, 210–11.

22. Jean-Jacques Rousseau, *The Social Contract*, in the version by Jonathan Bennett presented at www.earlymoderntexts.com, accessed February 6, 2019, 9, http://www.earlymoderntexts.com/assets/pdfs/rousseau1762.pdf.

23. Anisse Gross, "What's the Problem With Google Glass?," *The New Yorker*, March 4, 2014, https://www.newyorker.com/business/currency/whats-the-problem-with-google-glass.

24. Allie Pape, "Woman Claims Attack at Molotov's Over Google Glass," *Eater San Francisco*, February 25, 2014, https://sf.eater.com/2014/2/25/6273653/woman-claims-attack-at-molotovs-over-google-glass-updated.

25. Helen Nissenbaum, "Privacy as Contextual Integrity," *Wash. L. Rev.* 79 (2004): 119.

26. Anita L. Allen, "Privacy Isn't Everything: Accountability as a Personal and Social Good," *Ala. L. Rev.* 54 (2002): 1376.

27. Allen, "Privacy Isn't Everything," 1389.

28. Allen, "Privacy Isn't Everything," 1390.

Chapter 8

Strategies of Resistance

The original construct of a right to privacy in the United States, first came to fruition through the pioneering efforts of Samuel Warren and then soon-to-be Supreme Court justice Louis Brandeis in their 1890 *Harvard Law Review* article "The Right to Privacy."[1] What spurred their privacy concerns then, like the new ones arising today, were advances in ICTs that allowed the public to peer in and intrude upon private lives and private associations in a way that was felt instinctively to be a violation. The particular invention that sparked their concern at the time was the advent of newly mobile cameras. While the earliest iterations of photography required that individuals sit still in a single place for a lengthy exposure, Warren and Brandeis noticed that the more rapid exposure needed for "the latest advances in photographic art . . . rendered it possible to take pictures surreptitiously."[2]

While the "surreptitious" nature of the clunky camera apparatuses of the late nineteenth century may sound comical compared to the contact lens cameras being patented by Google, Sony, Samsung, and others today, the mobility engendered by the new ICTs of *their* time was still enough to give rise to the very first paparazzi. Indeed, it has long been held that Samuel Warren, a prominent socialite himself, was personally motivated to champion the right to privacy when early paparazzi secretly took intrusive photographs of his daughter's wedding and published them in newspapers. Although this story is apocryphal, it is representative of the type of privacy violations that were arising at this time and which sparked the legal movement toward privacy rights.

Today, we are all increasingly being pressured or even coerced to become public figures, not just the elite socialites of the day. *We* are becoming each other's paparazzi. Warren and Brandeis anticipated where we may be heading stating that "Numerous mechanical devices threaten to make good the prediction that 'what is whispered in the closet shall be proclaimed from the house-tops.'"³ In our time, the fulfillment of that prophecy is closer than ever. Warren and Brandeis argued that government intervention through a right to protect privacy was justified because those who invaded privacy were inflicting a deep harm upon others, which they argued was a "mental pain and distress, far greater than could be inflicted by mere bodily injury."⁴ Therefore, in order to appropriately expand upon the age-old principle that "the individual should have full protection in person and property,"⁵ it would be necessary that there be a right, among other things, to exert control and limit the circulation of photographs. This was part of the right to privacy, which they referred to as a "right to be let alone." Today, we all deserve a right to be let alone from the public as we are all becoming threatened by its invasive force in a way that was simply unfeasible in technologically simpler times.

One might object here that P2P surveillance should not really be viewed as a social harm deserving of any legal mitigation since people can simply ignore public ridicule, and not associate or work for people who take part in the ridicule (even if that encompasses nearly everyone one knows). But while P2P surveillance may in fact be an ineffective form of social control for the very few (if any) Socrates-like people among us, for whom no threat of exposure, social ridicule, or reputational destruction could stand as an inhibiting force, this does not in any way diminish the severity of the harm inflicted, and its resulting control on society as a whole. For every possible rare Socrates-like person, there is probably an equally rare Stoic-like person, for whom a lengthy prison sentence would be of no significant consequence to her happiness, and thus not a significant inhibiting force either, but this in no way diminishes the level of harm and compelling strength that we assign to prison sentences. Stanley Benn explains that

> [T]here are not many like Socrates in any society; not many have the knowledge of what they are, the virtue to be content with what they know, and the courage to pretend to be nothing else. For the rest of us, the freedom we need is the freedom to be something else—to be ourselves, to do what we think best, in a small, protected sea, where the winds of opinion cannot blow us off course.⁶

Even for those rare few who, like Socrates, are so confident and assure in themselves that no amount of public exposure and judgment could sway them from their course, such will likely not be true of the communities they belong to. Someone like Rumi may have spun in the marketplace precisely to demonstrate to himself that the negative opinion of others could not come between him and his experience of divine connection. But that likely would not have been true of the Order of the Whirling Dervishes as they took off and spread. Idiosyncratic communities need group privacy in order to let loose and spin. Similarly, at a place like CBGB, there was a kind of group privacy away from the norms of society, even in a public space. One could express oneself in new ways with the comfort of knowing that one was surrounded by other sympathetic associates. But with P2P surveillance, behind the other's digital eyes lies the whole wide world potentially watching and judging for eternity. Under these chilling conditions, we risk snuffing out the next James Hampton, the next Rumi and his Order of the Whirling Dervishes, and the next Joey Ramone and the punk rock movement.

A MUTUAL TRANSPARENCY SOLUTION?

Radical transparency proponents argue that the solution to the sorts of violations addressed in this book is not an expanded right to privacy, but rather more transparency. David Brin, author of *The Transparent Society*, argues for what amounts to a mutual transparency solution for protecting a sense of privacy:

> Today, the person who most-capably defends your privacy is . . . you. But to do that, you must be able to catch peeping toms and busybodies. And you cannot do that if they are shrouded in clouds of secrecy. Try the "Restaurant Analogy." People who are nosy, leaning toward other diners in order to snoop, are caught by those other diners. Moreover, our culture deems such intrusion to be a worse sin than anything that may be overheard. Now try setting up a restaurant where customer tables are separated by paper shoji screens, giving a surface illusion of greater privacy, but where peepers can press their ears against the screen and peer through little slits with impunity. Which approach better protects privacy? Which have people overwhelmingly chosen?[7]

Along these lines, a mutual transparency solution might involve requiring that media posted online always be posted under someone's name—never anonymously—so that one can be held accountable for the information they spread about others online and their potential privacy invasions. On the face of it this would seem a *potentially* viable solution to some of the concerns regarding the public's overreach and abusive behavior. It would, to a degree, take away the digital ring of Gyges, which in turn would theoretically lead to considerable restraint when recording and broadcasting others, as well as restraint in what people say about others online. In this case, we would all become transparent to each other, but in theory, we will largely choose to respect each other's personal space lest we become known and accountable for a potential privacy violation.

But it is unclear whether this would be as viable a solution as it might seem. In 2007, South Korea—where the "dog poop girl" incident infamously occurred—introduced a policy that all major domestic websites, with user-bases over 100,000, would have to require users to register with their real names. They could still post pseudonymously, but they'd be identifiable to the government through a national identification system. This was introduced to try and curb the type of public abuse that was regularly directed toward celebrities and politicians, which in at least one case was blamed for a famous actress's suicide.[8]

But by 2012, the system had been scrapped, deemed to be very ineffective in curbing unwanted behavior and ruled as an unconstitutional infringement on free speech. Furthermore, an analysis by the Korea Communications Commission (KCC) found that, in the first year of the real-name policy's implementation, malicious comments decreased by less than 1 percent, suggesting the policy was relatively ineffective for changing negative user behavior online. The real-name identification registry had also become a target for cyber-hackers.[9] On the other hand, an analysis by Daegon Cho of Carnegie Mellon University concluded that the real-name policy led to "significant effects on reducing uninhibited behaviors (swear words and antinormative expressions), suggesting that Real Name Verification Law encouraged users' behavioral changes in the positive direction to some extent."[10] While these results are somewhat mixed, it is not clear that this sort of real-name policy would substantially reduce abusive targeting by the public. The abovementioned study by the KCC suggests it would not, and the fact that South Korea abandoned their real-name policy is evidence of its failure to adequately curb abusive behavior online.

Of course, the South Korean system still allowed pseudonymous posting and so this might explain why it wasn't very effective at curbing abusive speech. Short of illegal speech like death threats and libel, many users probably didn't care that the government knew they were a troll. A setup more analogous to Brin's "restaurant analogy" would be a real-name policy in which users would all be identifiable to each other and pseudonymous posts would not be allowed. But Facebook maintains a real-name policy for both registering and posting, and while this probably contributes to it being a considerably less abusive atmosphere than the troll-friendly Twitter, which allows full anonymity, it is still a bastion for public shaming. The important point is that if an offending target online has spoken or acted against the prevailing opinion of the public, then it is usually considered acceptable to shame and humiliate the offender, and so there is little need to do so anonymously. It is not as if the crowds in the puritanical colonial villages that hurled insults and trash at the face of the pilloried social offenders were wearing masks. In fact, they not only *wanted* to be seen taking part in the shaming—in order to show themselves to be above moral repute—they essentially demanded that everyone else take part or otherwise one may have been seen to be siding with the public offender and risk attack themselves.

Enforcing a real-name policy online may curb some of the worst incidents of abuse, like Gamergate, where the public attacking an individual is *not* on the side of prevailing opinion, and therefore must hide themselves from the larger public. That would be no small thing. But it likely wouldn't have stopped any of the other examples noted previously such as Star Wars Kid, Dog Poop Girl, 1:24 Girl, Justine Sacco, and Cecil the Lion, since those directly involved in these attacks *were* on the side of the prevailing opinion of the public. They therefore had no need to hide since they had established themselves as "righteous," and reflected the prevailing opinion. They were more-or-less positioned as morally correct even in their attacks. Those who disagreed with the shaming usually censored their disagreement much as those in the crowds around an IRL pillory of old would have done. Furthermore, the simple existence of crowds online generates a sort of anonymity, in effect, even if individuals are technically identifiable. If a post about someone on Facebook receives thousands of negative comments, it is perceived as a collective aggregate, literally a number in which the individual as an individual is practically lost. The most it would accomplish to maintain a real-name policy like Facebook's on a site like Twitter would be to inhibit some of the most abusive speech. That's perhaps a step in the right direction, but it wouldn't undo the power of online public shaming to immediately ruin people's lives, and it would come at a cost to some of the benefits of anonymous or pseudonymous speech for political dissent.

Let's say we had a modified policy that allowed users to still post text anonymously online, but any photo uploaded must be publicly traceable back to an identifiable person. This would protect many of the benefits of online anonymous speech (at the cost of increased trolling), but might mitigate to some degree the privacy violations of P2P surveillance and nonconsensual recording. This proposal is analogous to gun control proposals that call for placing serial numbers on bullets that can be traced back to those who purchased them. In either case, camera or gun, one is more likely to be held accountable for shots fired.

But even if one's uploaded photos and videos were always attributable to the shooter online, it is again unclear whether this would create any sort of deterrence against unconsented recording and broadcasting if the prevailing opinion is on the side of the shooter. For example, there was no real outcry against the people who took photos of and broadcasted South Korea's dog poop girl since they were seen as righteous members of the public. The agent of P2P surveillance is then considered to have done the right thing, to be a hero who captured the offender of public opinion, even if the photo is deeply embarrassing, humiliating, and the person broke no laws. The nonconsensual recording and broadcasting, and subsequent reputational annihilation, is seen as deserved since the individual broke the "law" of public opinion. Likewise, no serious public reprimand came to those who posted the Star Wars Kid video. Instead, the video became popularized at the highest echelons of mainstream media even as the child suffered immensely.

All this is not to say that creating more accountability for posting about others online is not *potentially* part of a solution to protecting privacy from the public's overreach in an increasingly transparent world. But it seems to me that unless individuals have significantly more control over the flow of their information to the public, so that anything one says or does in one place and time does not threaten to be permanently broadcast globally, and permanently annihilate one's reputation, then the individual threatens to be dominated by the public.

IS RESISTANCE FUTILE?

At this point in history, the basic forms of these ICTs are so deeply entrenched in society, that it would be fruitless, and perhaps harmful, to try and fully undo them. Furthermore, while I have highlighted some of the real concerns related to their use for surveillance and control of ordinary citizens, the massive collective power ICTs enable could potentially be harnessed toward an enhanced public check on state power. For example, they can help quickly and effectively organize and mobilize large groups of people for political protests, and should be noted as well as for their sousveillance capacity, of turning the omniscient gaze back on the often abusive forces of the police and military, in particular. For example, when someone films footage of a police officer murdering an unarmed African American and posts it online, it is done to hold police accountable to the very laws which they are supposed to enforce. It is not a breach of the rule of law, in this case, but rather can be seen as a way to better its enforcement. It is an extension, in other words, of the rule of law, and an attempt to make the law function as it should.

But in order to keep this new form of collective power from enabling a social overreach that threatens ordinary individuals as well as idiosyncratic communities, we must create new technological tools for people to shield themselves from the unwanted exposure of the global community, as well as to develop a cultural sensitivity that respects a desire to be let alone. It is beyond the scope of this work to go into considerable detail about possible legal, technological, and cultural shifts for blunting the impact of P2P surveillance and control, but here I will briefly look at some specific proposals.

Broadly speaking, to preserve not only the conditions of liberty for individuals and for their communities, but for the sake of cultural progress as well, we need to create zones of privacy that, as James Moor says, "allow citizens to rationally plan their lives without fear . . . [that contain] different kinds and levels of access for different individuals."[11] Not only do we need zones of privacy, we also need zones of public anonymity. Tony Doyle clarifies the distinction between privacy and anonymity: "Roughly, we can think of privacy as preserved when we might know who the person is but not what they are doing and anonymity as preserved when we might know what is being done but not who is doing it."[12] Doyle presses further that "Zones of public anonymity mean that people will feel freer to associate with whomever they want, read and watch what they choose, and express their opinions as they see fit—freedoms essential for a healthy democracy and a truly liberal society."[13]

There are several technological tools available or in development that could possibly limit the scope of P2P surveillance allowing for such zones of privacy and public anonymity. A new contraption that is gaining some popularity is Yondr, which is basically just a locking pouch that one is asked to place one's phone in during specific events such as a performance, meeting, or class, thereby creating a relatively P2P surveillance-free environment. One then maintains possession of one's phone in the locked pouch at the event, and it can be unlocked by event staff in designated phone-use locations, or by a teacher in a classroom, and so forth. Already several famous comedians and musicians, such as Chris Rock and Jack White of The White Stripes, have required audience members to place their phones into Yondr pouches upon arrival at their shows. Yondr, or other similarly functioning technologies, could be extended to other smart devices as well, such as camera glasses, in the future.

Along these lines, a campaign called "Stop the Cyborgs" sprung up in 2013 surrounding the beta launch of Google Glass, that allowed establishments to freely download "No Glass" signs with a logo that resembled the iconography of "No Smoking" signs. In addition to the logo, the signs read "Google Glass Is Banned on These Premises."[14] Individual establishments or whole sections of town banning head-mounted or other forms of intrusive commercial recording devices could form a significant collective resistance and allow for communities to operate with lessened effects of P2P surveillance.

There are difficulties, however, with banning commercial recording devices if they are attached or implanted in someone's body, which could become common in a more distant cyborg future. Under these conditions, a ban on the device would then effectively become a ban on the individual who has physically merged with the device, and this could give rise to issues of cyborg discrimination. This isn't just science fiction. The University of Toronto professor Steve Mann, the "world's first cyborg"—a photoborg to be specific—has on many occasions experienced this form of alleged discrimination. Steve Mann has a Google Glass-like device he invented called EyeTap affixed to his skull, which offers him a version of what he calls "mixed reality." EyeTap is often cited as the inspiration behind Google Glass. In one example of such alleged cyborg discrimination, Mann was violently removed from a Parisian McDonald's when he was asked by staff to remove his EyeTap device, which he was unable to do without special tools.[15]

The violent nature of the removal of Mann from the McDonald's was of course terribly wrong, but cyborg discrimination claims may not always be compelling. For example, is an establishment's ban on guns discrimination if a cyborg has a gun surgically attached? Still, there are other technologies that are available or in development that could curtail the surveillance capacities of these devices without requiring their physical removal, and that might be preferable in a potential future where cyborgs are more common. For example, a currently available device called Cyborg Unplug detects and disconnects selected devices in its range like camera glasses from their networks, to disrupt them from broadcasting media to the Internet.

As a potentially deeper P2P surveillance blocking device, Apple has patented a technology that uses infrared sensors that turn off the recording function of personal cameras in designated areas, which is being developed primarily to prevent bootleg recordings of copyrighted material such as movies. While such technology poses dangers in the hands of the police who could use them to prevent citizens filming acts of police brutality, in the hands of ordinary people they could allow zones of relative privacy and anonymity from the public such as in one's home or in a designated privacy-protected space. This could allow a photoborg like Mann to enter an establishment where recording is prohibited without risking a violation of that establishment's policies. A more low-tech solution for limiting P2P surveillance in group settings, say a community event, is to have a "greeter" at the door who requires each attendee to place provided masking tape over the cameras on their devices upon entrance.

Of course, in a society where commercial recording devices are ubiquitous, especially a possible future where wearable recording devices are common, "privacy / anonymity zones" in publicly accessible establishments, protected through devices such as Yondr, Cyborg Unplug, or other methods to prevent recording and broadcasting, risk becoming magnets for those who expressly wish to do harm without recorded evidence. One way to combat this would be for the owners of such "privacy / anonymity protected" establishments to still employ standard surveillance devices. This might deter crime while still greatly reducing the likelihood that recordings of patrons would be disseminated to the public online. Trust in the establishment and its proprietor/s would then, however, become paramount, but the proprietor would be solely accountable for recordings and therefore much less likely to share them without warrant.

In establishments where complete freedom from recording is desired, protection by designated security, or fellow community members, as well as the possibility of old-school witness testimony, would of course still be deterrents against possible wrongdoing, as they have been for thousands of years. Aside from publicly accessible establishments, private residencies, protected against recording and broadcasting, operating as do-it-yourself music venues and creative spaces, could become especially fertile ground in the future for advancing experimental culture free from P2P surveillance.

Another low-tech, but technically challenging solution for limiting P2P surveillance, is to wear one of a series of makeup and hair designs by artist Adam Harvey from his project CV Dazzle, which block facial recognition technology from being able to identify a person when worn. While these clever fashions will allow individuals to protect some degree of anonymity from the public, the extremely eccentric and futuristic designs are sure to attract a lot of attention and recording in real life and may lead to one's image being broadcast online even if one becomes unidentifiable by facial recognition. Such fashions may enable increased anonymity in public, but they certainly won't protect a right to be let alone. It is also worth noting that technologies are being developed that are able to identify individuals by their body shape and walking gait even if their face is obscured. To avoid recognition from these devices might additionally require eccentric clothing designs or other unique fashions. Evading camera-based and online identification in the future might require turning oneself into the embodiment of a real-life anime character, like something out of Comic-Con. On a side-note, the future of style, which has so far this millennium scarcely moved on from a rehashing of twentieth-century fashions (and this may be true of music and culture more broadly), may be dictated through a struggle with emerging technologies.

The above suggestions, however, are all only partial solutions. To gain a more robust protection from P2P surveillance, especially to protect a sense of privacy and anonymity in public, we need better technological and legal tools that enable ordinary people to have much greater control over the circulation of their personal information online. There are software technologies that could theoretically be developed to allow individuals to gain this enhanced control over their information. For example, popular websites such as YouTube and SoundCloud, where users upload movies and music, feature fairly robust algorithms that detect when copyrighted material has been submitted and can block its public broadcast unless the uploader verifies that he or she is the proper owner. These same sorts of digital rights management tools, algorithms combined with facial and audio recognition technologies, could be used to detect when photos, videos, audio, or even written information about an individual (say one's e-mail or home address) has been uploaded to the Internet, and could potentially block the broadcast of that content unless approved by the individual whose information is posted. When information about a person has been submitted somewhere online one could then be notified by text or e-mail and review the content for approval before allowing it to appear, just as corporations can do with their media on YouTube, for example. Such technology could then be combined with other existing technologies that automatically blur faces (as Google Street View does) in photos or videos of people who do not give permission to be broadcast. User recordings could then be uploaded as usual, but individuals would remain blurred online unless they give explicit consent to be broadcast to the public.

A system along these lines has been proposed by Yann LeCun, the VP and chief AI scientist at Facebook, but his proposed system would only notify individuals and give them the option to be blurred in photographs *after* they are already posted online.[16] But it is crucial that a person's image or other personally identifying information be blocked or blurred until consent is given and not only after such information has been posted and harm has potentially already occurred. In my proposal, if one chooses not to opt-into the facial recognition system, and submit or allow one's faceprint to be used for such purposes, then photos or videos of oneself would remain blurred indefinitely. This would help maintain appropriate flows of information rather than the default of potentially permanent global viewing available for anything recorded and broadcast online.

Through such software, one would effectively gain increased ownership over one's digital self, much in the way digital rights management tools like YouTube's Content ID have allowed corporations to gain more effective ownership of their digital information (though far from complete control). A system like this is, however, potentially an ethical minefield: (1) it may further normalize facial recognition (and possibly speaker recognition) technologies since such a system would rely on them for identifying and masking uploaded recordings of people without consent; (2) it could lead to increased corporate or government surveillance through a further spread of such technologies, and (3) it may lead to too much censorship, though no private Internet company is beholden to free speech laws and even then free speech can be legitimately overridden at times. This proposal is possibly a technological solution to a technological problem presented by P2P surveillance, but it could wind society further down a rabbit hole into a techno-oriented surveillance state of sorts steeped with facial recognition. I therefore present this idea only very tentatively and with much caution.

However, if such a proposed technological solution were adopted, it is unlikely that such a system of digital self-ownership would be maintainable without the force of the law. To this end, the Right To Be Forgotten legislation, currently established in the EU and Argentina, is a step in the right direction. The law forces search engine companies like Google to entertain requests to have links to websites de-indexed from search results of people's names so that embarrassing and damaging information that is of no considerable interest to the public does not unfairly haunt someone indefinitely.

While a good start, I consider the law to be only a modest first legal step which does not go far enough in protecting people from the control of the public. For one, an individual cannot block information from initially appearing, so by the time they have made their appeal to have the information de-indexed, major harm may have already been inflicted. Two, it does not remove information from the Internet entirely, just makes it harder to find. Three, importantly, it puts the fate of one's digital self ultimately into the hands of an opaque bureaucracy at Google or other search engine companies. Given the sometimes severe impact of one's digital self upon one's real-life opportunities, as well as one's emotional well-being, an individual should have more control over what appears about them online. One might even argue that the public should only be able to override that personal ownership of the digital self, and force information into the public domain against the wishes of an individual, in rare circumstances, much as one has ownership over one's real-life body and only in rare circumstances can the government override that ownership (forcing blood samples after a car accident, for example, to determine possible levels of intoxication). This may sound extreme, but it reflects the extent to which our digital and IRL selves are merging and so to effectively maintain control over one's person one must maintain control over one's media extensions online.

To this end copyright could potentially serve as a building-block for new digital-era legislation that allows individuals control over what information appears about them online, sort of like major media companies use digital rights management tools and copyright to exert control over the flow of *their* information online. However, I emphasize that copyright would only be a *building block* for new legislation since copyright itself would likely be far too blunt a hammer and stifling to free speech. There is a serious risk that even a less punitive offshoot of copyright could become oppressive and overly censoring, so I again present this proposal only very tentatively and with much caution. That said, copyright's mechanism of "fair use" allows for exceptions that override copyright ownership claims, and there might similarly be something like fair use developed for posting information about public figures such as politicians online.

Along those lines, we might also come up with a system in which one can opt-into becoming a "public figure" much like there is a process that one must apply to in order to have a Twitter account verified. By opting into, or perhaps applying for this status, one might have increased media posting privileges, but would have less protections from others posting about oneself online, much like a politician. The point is that one would not be forced to become a "public figure," as is essentially becoming the case for everyone today by default. One risk of such a system of opting into "public figure" status would be that those who choose to remain "private" figures could become disadvantaged or even discriminated against as privacy becomes increasingly equated with suspiciousness and hiding dirty secrets. This is already arguably becoming the case for those who choose to protect their privacy by abstaining from social media. Still, the ability to better control the circulation of information about oneself online might be worth that risk.

Elsewhere, in terms of new privacy-protecting legal tools, laws that limit an employer's right to screen candidates online before hiring them could help limit the effects of P2P surveillance and control, and could be extended to include bans on screening applicants online by college admissions officers and money lenders as well. Recent guidelines against social media job screening from the EU push in this direction, though such potential prohibitions ought to extend to search engines as well. It's not immediately clear how to effectively enforce such policies, but simply enacting the policies is a start. Finally, bans on commercially available facial recognition technology altogether, or in part, could blunt some of the more severe impacts of P2P surveillance if they could be effectively implemented.

Finding ways to enable significantly more control over the circulation of one's information online without enabling harmful and repressive censorship, as well as figuring out the intricacies of new privacy laws, are extremely difficult challenges, perhaps some of the most difficult and important challenges of our time. But it is both out of the scope of my expertise and beyond the scope of further analysis in this work to examine the legal apparatus that might provide solutions to the problems raised in this book. There are, however, others such as privacy scholar Daniel Solove in his book *The Future of Reputation*[17] who have addressed some of my concerns at length from a more legally intricate perspective that are very much worth referring to, and of course a great amount of additional legal work and scholarship on the issue needs to be done as well. There are a number of laws that relate to recording people in public and in private residencies, as well as against inflicting emotional distress that may be helpful in the fight against P2P surveillance and control that have yet to be litigated. Legal scholar Jennifer Rothman argues that the lesser-known "right to publicity" could be a powerful tool for protecting privacy in an age of publicity. She suggests that for the current laws to more adequately address developing privacy challenges online, "we may need to see . . . people who are more willing to sue about these things." Though she adds that "no one likes lawsuits."[18]

Apart from new technological and legal instruments, changes in personal social media behavior and norms surrounding sharing recordings and information online could also help limit the impact of P2P surveillance. If people become more aware that recording and broadcasting other people without their express permission can be both violating and create a vast chilling effect, then they may be more likely to change their behavior. We might, for example, try to cultivate a culture of media consent where it is considered a violation of social norms to record others without expressly asking for permission and an even greater violation to post media of others on social media or elsewhere online without express consent. This is extremely far from the norm today where recordings are regularly done at social gatherings and routinely posted online without asking for consent. This is not to generally cast aspersion on people who regularly engage in such behavior today, which is the norm. Taking photos, videos and sharing them online has become a routine and practically instinctive part of today's culture, but it is a cultural practice that I argue ought to change. Such cultural changes alone, however, would not eliminate the chilling effects of P2P surveillance since the mere presence of ubiquitous recording devices and the threat of broadcast they present is chilling in itself—much like the presence of police officers—especially if there are no readily available legal or technological protections to control the circulation of information about oneself online; but it might be a significant improvement toward blunting the privacy-violating culture of surveillance and "sharing" that is predominant today.

As another personal behavioral change, some may consider leaving social media altogether, despite the increasing social costs of abandoning the network. Laura Portwood-Stacer, borrowing language from Herbert Marcuse's sixties' anti-consumerist "great refusal," argues that "media refusal is a way of making one's everyday lifestyle into a site of resistance against the powerful, normative force of media consumer culture. For some, it's a very personal act of resistance without any consciously political motivation; for others it's an activist expression of dissent."[19] Refusing social media would put one in perhaps surprising company. Sean Parker, the founding President of Facebook, says that he has become "something of a conscientious objector" to social media[20] and Chamath Palihapitiya, the former vice president for user growth at Facebook says he now feels "tremendous guilt" for his work, claiming Facebook is "ripping apart the social fabric of how society works," and that "I don't use that shit . . . my kids . . . they're not allowed to use that shit."[21]

Leaving social media is a form of negative resistance that takes a significant measure to ensure that one does not perpetuate the effects of P2P surveillance and control and lessens the impact of the apparatus upon oneself. This will almost certainly never be a solution adopted by many, but one that would perhaps prove fairly effective for the few interested and willing to take that leap. On the other hand, Portwood-Stacer cautions:

> It may be that refusal is only available as a tactic to people who already possess a great deal of social capital, people whose social standing will endure without Facebook and people whose livelihoods don't require them to be constantly plugged in and reachable . . . Having the option to unplug is a privilege in itself, and it may be a privilege that accrues disproportionately to those who already enjoy economic, political, and other forms of privilege . . . . For these reasons, quitting is a limited tactic for those who would strategize against Facebook and other hegemons of media culture.[22]

Another way that new social norms and practices could lessen the impact of P2P surveillance would be if we largely change the way we use social media and move away from broadcasting our personal information to the public. Instead, we could move toward using social media as a community bulletin board and for helping to organize small, local, real-world communities that primarily interact face-to-face, or maybe even live together, only supplementing those connections through online communications. In this sense, social media would become a tool for the end of real-world community, rather than a replacement for real-world community itself.

Social media sites themselves could also blunt the edge of the more brutal forms of online mob harassment through the widespread use of AI software that automatically detects hate speech and abuse, some of which are currently in development. However, if these are deployed for censorship purposes, they need to be very carefully designed and monitored, and have built-in mechanisms for appeals on removed content, since AI's, while having monitoring capacities far beyond human capabilities, may also lack a fully nuanced understanding of language, at least for now, and could sweep too broadly in its automated censorship. I entertain use of such software only very tentatively, though most social media sites do not allow certain forms of abusive speech so this would perhaps only better enforce their existing policies.

In any case, blocking online abuse and trolling, while perhaps helpful, doesn't solve the problem of online shaming. People can be massively shamed and humiliated just from unwanted content being exposed to the public without any comments at all, and shaming comments can arguably occur without any explicitly abusive language. To this end, social media companies could also be more proactive in banning forums or hashtags designed to invade privacy or encourage harassment. For example, Reddit has banned several subreddits which involved posting photos of people without permission in order to humiliate and shame them.

Sometimes changes to social networking sites have come as the result of public backlash, such as when Google briefly launched and quickly discontinued their Buzz social networking service that was widely viewed as being overly invasive of users' privacy. The public can police itself on the Internet against the overreach of P2P surveillance to some degree and may be able to be more effective if the public becomes more aware of its liberty-infringing effects. Developing new social norms for the use of these emerging ICTs will begin through spreading awareness and sparking discussion of the disproportionate power these technologies can enable. If there were popular movements against P2P surveillance and control, and in favor of privacy, tech companies would need to become more sensitive to privacy protections just to stay in business, which is occurring to some degree today. But we cannot fully rely on the public itself to prevent its own overreach, nor does history suggest the public will sufficiently place such limits upon itself. Ultimately, some limitations necessary to protect the individual from domination by the public, to protect a right to privacy in the digital era, will likely require government intervention.

In this book I have focused on the responsibility that the public has for giving rise to P2P surveillance and other harms, but that does not mean tech companies are not also responsible for this ethically problematic development and its worrisome trajectories. There is even reason to believe that advancing a culture where, as Dave Eggers satirized it in *The Circle*, "sharing is caring,"[23] is partly by design. As we saw, Mark Zuckerberg and others at Facebook early on espoused a notion of "radical transparency" or "ultimate transparency" as a goal for our society, and they are in more of a position to influence such a cultural direction than perhaps anyone else. We should therefore reject the narrative Zuckerberg has pushed in recent congressional hearings that social media is just a "tool" that can be used for harm or good.[24] As philosopher Nolen Gertz explains, that seems to imply that its construction is value neutral and any harmful use is mainly to blame on its users.[25] One may argue instead that social media companies actually facilitate or even model behavior that helps give rise to the harms described in this book. Many of the core mechanisms that enable P2P surveillance and control such as liking, tagging, sharing, and following, are designed to simplify and encode user behavior in order to better facilitate highly profitable data extraction and advertiser-driven behavior manipulation.[26] Far-reaching reforms to protect user's privacy may be unlikely absent of legislation since doing so might significantly cut into data extraction and profitability.

It is worth commenting that at the time of this writing, Instagram and Facebook have been rolling out trials of their software in which the number of likes on posts are hidden from public view. Twitter is also prototyping a version of its app where likes and other metrics on posts are initially hidden and have to be clicked on to appear. These trials suggest that social media companies are growing aware of some of the problems they've helped to create that I have addressed at length in this book, and are considering how to help remedy the situation, potential changes which I tentatively support. On the other hand, it is unclear exactly what their motivations are for these proposed changes, were they to become implemented across their platforms permanently. Three employees at Facebook, who owns Instagram, have reported anonymously to CNBC that there is a hypothesis within the company that "hiding likes will increase the number of posts people make to the service, by making them feel less self-conscious when their posts don't get much engagement."[27] Such changes may therefore be motivated more by the potential for increased use of their platforms, sharing of content, and thereby increased ad-revenue, rather than increased user well-being.

Even if their motivations may be tainted, so to speak, these could still be positive changes and part of a solution. But hiding public likes alone may in the end actually exacerbate some of the problems I have discussed in this book, if such changes only further propels a culture of "sharing" and winds us deeper into radical transparency. Hiding likes will not solve the problem of P2P surveillance. Rather by making the pervasive judgments on their platform slightly less brutal than its current state, it could help prime the world for AR headsets and a ubiquitous state of surveillance by the public. Hiding likes will not solve the problem of public shaming and humiliation since such episodes rely more on hurtful comments than likes, and even comments are not necessary for public shaming and humiliation as posting embarrassing information about others is humiliating in and of itself. Furthermore, it is likely that even if like counts are hidden from public view on many platforms, when you have teems of people attempting to publicly assert their status online, as is the nature of social media, other forms of online metrics will likely take their place; if not friend and follower counts becoming even more important than they already are to people, then how many positive comments a person appears to have received for a post.

Most importantly, unless these companies get rid of the like or heart button altogether, which they are unlikely to do because such mechanisms are key to their financial interests, then as the report-cards of one's crowdsourced ratings are made available to the user, the conformity-inducing feedback loops will continue and the urge to gear one's increasingly public life toward the end of mass approval will continue relatively intact. Few can resist regularly, even compulsively, checking up on one's status in the eyes of the world, and few are immune from the emotional effects of crowdsourced feedback even if people claim to be unaffected. To this end, one might consider downloading and installing social media "Demetricator" software by artist and software developer Benjamin Grosser. This turns off the personal display of all metrics on Facebook, Twitter, or Instagram (different software for each). By hiding the metrics of social approval from oneself, demetricators may help to disrupt the addictive social media feedback loops that depend on the dopamine bursts from users receiving likes, hearts, followers, and so forth.

Overall, anything short of a halt to the enveloping radically transparent society that social media companies are speeding us toward, will not adequately address the issues I have raised in this book, as the private sphere evaporates into a pervasive public sphere, saturated with the public's normalizing gaze. Even if changes are made to limit some of the harm of these mechanisms to users and society, it is unlikely they will ever go away as long as social media maintains a surveillance capitalism model that manipulates users to share information. Advancing a culture of P2P surveillance or "sharing" is simply in their financial interest. By blunting some of the more harsh edges, by making their platforms appear more "humane," in the end we will likely only become more ensconced within these platforms, and more subjected to a society of hyper-exposure, judgment, and its resulting chilling effects that these platforms bring to billions worldwide throughout our days.

This is why we need not only to regulate these companies to protect privacy, but potentially also need new grassroots crowdfunded, publicly funded, and subscription-based nonprofit social media competitors that are not financially incentivized toward increasing a culture of surveillance, nor to maintaining prolonged and excessive user-engagement online. Such competitors, ideally oriented as tools for building real-world community rather than replacing it, will likely never take down the current social media behemoths, but they could at least provide alternate services not inherently formulated upon facilitating data sharing and extraction, and thereby helping to prop up a culture of "sharing."

Search engine firms like Google, meanwhile, are also responsible for helping to enable the harms of P2P surveillance and control because of the way their algorithms automatically sort and circulate information. While they are not to blame for ordinary people recording and posting embarrassing information about others online, they are largely responsible for making such information easily accessible to the global public against one's will. Search engine firms, as private companies, do not have to set all information "free." While first amendment considerations in the United States might not allow for something like the EU's Right To Be Forgotten, search engine firms could still universally allow the same content removal request process that is required of them in the EU. However, absent of legislation, search engine companies are also unlikely to make such changes on their own. For example, it took countless victims before Google even allowed *requests* to de-index revenge porn from search results in the United States and they have fought hard against new revenge porn legislation.

Figuring out how to implement something like the Right To Be Forgotten, in countries such as the United States where freedom of expression is highly protected, is a tremendous task for policymakers, but one that I believe could be successful perhaps if framed as an issue of ownership over one's data as an extension of control over one's property or self. But even absent legislation, it might still be in the long-term interest of search engine firms to universally implement a broad and extensive content removal request process as this may help people gain or restore trust in these companies at a time when there are increasing concerns about privacy violations online. It is better for tech companies to be attentive to the harms their technologies might introduce or exacerbate and to proactively mitigate against them in advance, rather than to find themselves in the hot seat of a televised congressional hearing, eroding public trust in their companies, and potentially providing openings for competitors who will pledge to uphold higher moral standards.

Absent legal sanctions with real teeth, however, such congressional hearings may be merely a small price to pay for the routine privacy violations underlying the operations and financial model of Silicon Valley. On that note, if there is ever to be true democratic government power over corporations, the vast lobbying hold that tech companies exert over politics needs to be cut through drastic legal reforms. Growing popular movements that express widespread disdain for politicians that accept corporate campaign contributions could help. Further exploring the powerful financial influence Silicon Valley has over government, however, is an issue beyond the scope of this work.

Finally, tech companies generally need to be held accountable for the commercial recording devices they are implementing and for doing more in advance to mitigate the potential harms these devices introduce. The current Silicon Valley objective to ubiquitously spread wearable smart devices could tremendously exacerbate P2P surveillance. The best solutions to privacy concerns related to these commercial devices likely lies at the level of increased control over the extraction and usage of personal information and data by both corporations and ordinary people. But even if one could be assured that data collected by wearable recording devices was subject to a robust system of protections and user control, ubiquity of such devices would have a significant effect on people's sense of privacy and social power dynamics simply by the constant presence of cameras out and ready to shoot. Certain devices, such as commercially available wearable recording devices deliberately designed to be used in a surreptitious manner, or certain features such as facial recognition in wearable glasses, should potentially be permanently banned. At the very least, tech companies ought to be required to do much more to protect the privacy of those who are subject to the infringements brought upon by these devices that the industry seeks to make widespread.

Here I have highlighted some ways in which P2P surveillance and control is facilitated, even modeled for by tech companies, and to their advantage in the sense that more sharing, more surveillance, more judgment, equals more package-able, profitable data. But it is ultimately the public of ordinary people that pushes the buttons. Responsibility lies on both sides. By the public acknowledging their responsibility for the growing harms of P2P surveillance and control, the public can more readily take action to mitigate these harms. That will mean not only personal changes but also holding tech companies more accountable.

In conclusion, the work on adequately and appropriately protecting individual liberty from the growing social overreach of P2P surveillance and control, through the development of new technological tools, changes in culture, education, and regulation, needs to be taking place today with greater urgency, while many of the ICTs I have described are still in their infancy, and mechanisms for safeguarding against their abuse could be implemented before they become widely available to the public. Over one hundred fifty years ago Mill warned that "If the claims of individuality are ever to be asserted, the time is now, while much is still wanting to complete the enforced assimilation. It is only in the earlier stages that any stand can be successfully made against the encroachment."[28] In the grand scheme of things we are likely still in those earlier stages today—still toward the beginning of the "present age" prophesied by Kierkegaard—but we stand at a critical juncture. Resistance is not futile.

NOTES

1. Samuel D. Warren and Louis D. Brandeis, "The Right to Privacy," *Harvard Law Review* (1890): 193–220.
2. Warren and Brandeis, "The Right to Privacy," 211.
3. Warren and Brandeis, "The Right to Privacy," 195.
4. Warren and Brandeis, "The Right to Privacy," 196.
5. Warren and Brandeis, "The Right to Privacy," 193.
6. Stanley I. Benn, "Privacy, Freedom, and Respect for Persons," in *Philosophical Dimensions of Privacy: An Anthology*, ed. Ferdinand D. Schoeman (Cambridge: Cambridge University Press, 1984), 242.
7. David Brin, "In Defense of a Transparent Society," *David Brin*, accessed February 6, 2019, http://www.davidbrin.com/nonfiction/tsdefense.html.
8. Choe Sang-Hun, "Web Rumors Tied to Korean Actress's Suicide," *The New York Times*, October 2, 2008, https://www.nytimes.com/2008/10/03/world/asia/03actress.html.

9. The Chosun Ilbo, "Real-Name Online Registration to Be Scrapped," *The Chosun Ilbo*, December 30, 2011, http://english.chosun.com/site/data/html_dir/2011/12/30/2011123001526.html.

10. Daegon Cho, "Real Name Verification Law on the Internet: A Poison or Cure for Privacy?," *Workshop on the Economics of Information Security* 16, accessed February 6, 2019, https://www.econinfosec.org/archive/weis2011/papers/Real%20Name%20Verification%20Law%20on%20the%20Internet%20-%20A%20Poison%20or%20Cu.pdf.

11. James H. Moor, "Towards a Theory of Privacy in the Information Age," *ACM SIGCAS Computers and Society* 27, no. 3 (1997): 32.

12. Tony Doyle and Judy Veranas, "Public Anonymity and the Connected World," *Ethics and Information Technology* 16, no. 3 (2014): 208.

13. Doyle and Veranas, "Public Anonymity," 210.

14. Cyrus Farivar, "'Stop the Cyborgs' Launches Public Campaign against Google Glass," *Ars Technica*, March 22, 2013, https://arstechnica.com/tech-policy/2013/03/stop-the-cyborgs-launches-public-campaign-against-google-glass/.

15. John Biggs, "Augmented Reality Explorer Steve Mann Assaulted At Parisian McDonald's," *Tech Crunch*, July 16, 2012, https://techcrunch.com/2012/07/16/augmented-reality-explorer-steve-mann-assaulted-at-parisian-mcdonalds/.

16. John Bohannon, "Unmasked," *Science* 347, no. 6221 (2015): 492.

17. Daniel J. Solove, *The Future of Reputation: Gossip, Rumor, and Privacy on the Internet* (Yale University Press, 2007).

18. Jan R. Piedad and Kim Johnson, "Everything You Say, Do In Public Could End Up On The Internet," *Texas Public Radio*, August 22, 2018, https://www.tpr.org/post/everything-you-say-do-public-could-end-internet.

19. Portwood-Stacer, "Media Refusal," 1053.

20. Allen, "Sean Parker."

21. Julia Wong, "Former Facebook Executive: Social Media is Ripping Society Apart," *The Guardian*, December 12, 2017, https://www.theguardian.com/technology/2017/dec/11/facebook-former-executive-ripping-society-apart.

22. Portwood-Stacer, "Media Refusal," 1054.

23. Dave Eggers, *The Circle* (Canada: Alfred A. Knopf, 2013).

24. The Washington Post, "Transcript of Mark Zuckerberg's Senate Hearing," *The Washington Post*, April 10, 2018, https://www.washingtonpost.com/news/the-switch/wp/2018/04/10/transcript-of-mark-zuckerbergs-senate-hearing/.

25. Rowman & Littlefield International, "Nihilism and Technology," *Medium*, August 13, 2018, https://medium.com/colloquium/nihilism-and-technology-38575190fb82.

26. Cristina Alaimo and Jannis Kallinikos, "Computing the Everyday: Social Media as Data Platforms," *The Information Society* 33, no. 4 (2017): 175–91.

27. Salvador Rodriguez, "Facebook has a Theory that Hiding 'Likes' Will Increase Post Volume, and Instagram is Testing that Theory," *CNBC*, December 6, 2019, https://www.cnbc.com/2019/12/06/instagram-hiding-likes-could-increase-post-volume.html.

28. Mill, *On Liberty*, 68–69.

Works Cited

Alaimo, Cristina and Jannis Kallinikos. "Computing the Everyday: Social Media as Data Platforms." *The Information Society* 33, no. 4 (2017): 175–91.
Albrechtslund, Anders. "Online Social Networking as Participatory Surveillance." *First Monday* 13, no. 3 (2008). https://doi.org/10.5210/fm.v13i3.2142.
Allen, Anita L. "Privacy Isn't Everything: Accountability as a Personal and Social Good." *Ala. L. Rev.* 54 (2002): 1375.
Allen, Mike. "Sean Parker Unloads on Facebook God Only Knows What it's Doing to Our Children's Brains." *Axios*, November 9, 2017. https://www.axios.com/sean-parker-unloads-on-facebook-god-only-knows-what-its-doing-to-our-childrens-brains-1513306792-f855e7b4-4e99-4d60-8d51-2775559c2671.html.
All In with Chris Hayes. "All In with Chris Hayes, Transcript 07/30/15." *MSNBC*, July 30, 2015. http://www.msnbc.com/transcripts/all-in/2015-07-30.
Appel, Helmut, Alexander L. Gerlach, and Jan Crusius. "The Interplay between Facebook Use, Social Comparison, Envy, and Depression." *Current Opinion in Psychology* 9 (2016): 44–49.
Armour, Stephanie. "Borrowers Hit Social-media Hurdles." *The Wall Street Journal*, January 8, 2014. https://www.wsj.com/articles/borrowers-hit-socialmedia-hurdles-1389224469.
Atick, Joseph J. "Face Recognition in the Era of the Cloud and Social Media: Is it Time to Hit the Panic Button?" *Silicon Trust*, October 21, 2011. https://silicontrust.org/2011/10/21/face-recognition-in-the-era-of-the-cloud-and-social-media-is-it-time-to-hit-the-panic-button/.
Baker, William F. "'Fifty Years in the Global Village': Remembering Marshall McLuhan on His 100th Birthday." *The Nation*, August 4, 2011. https://www.thenation.com/article/fifty-years-global-village-remembering-marshall-mcluhan-his-100th-birthday/.
Bank of America Corporation. "Trends in Consumer Mobility Report." Accessed November 6, 2018. https://promo.bankofamerica.com/mobilityreport/assets/images/2015-Trends-in-Consumer-Mobility-Report_FINAL.pdf.

Barbour, J. H. "The Throne of the Third Heaven of the Nations' Millennium General Assembly." *History.org*. Accessed February 5, 2019. https://www.history.org/foundation/journal/spring04/throne.cfm.

Barnett, Christopher B. *Kierkegaard, Pietism and Holiness*. London: Routledge, 2016. http://www.tandfebooks.com/isbn/9781315591056.

Baumeister, Roy F. and Mark R. Leary. "The Need to Belong: Desire for Interpersonal Attachments as a Fundamental Human Motivation." *Psychological Bulletin* 117, no. 3 (1995): 497–529.

Benn, Stanley I. "Privacy, Freedom, and Respect for Persons." In *Philosophical Dimensions of Privacy: An Anthology*, edited by Ferdinand David Schoeman. Cambridge: Cambridge University Press, 1984.

Bentham, Jeremy. *The Panopticon Writings*, edited by Miran Bozovic. London and New York: Verso, 1995.

Bentham, Jeremy. "Proposal for a New and Less Expensive Mode of Employing and Reforming Convicts." Quoted in *Utilitarianism.com*. Accessed December 18, 2018. https://www.utilitarianism.com/panopticon.html.

Bernheim, B. Douglas. "A Theory of Conformity." *Journal of Political Economy* 102, no. 5 (1994): 841–77.

Biggs, John. "Augmented Reality Explorer Steve Mann Assaulted at Parisian McDonald's." *Tech Crunch*, July 16, 2012. https://techcrunch.com/2012/07/16/augmented-reality-explorer-steve-mann-assaulted-at-parisian-mcdonalds/.

Blackstone, William. *Commentaries on the Laws of England in Four Books. Notes Selected from the Editions of Archibold, Christian, Coleridge, Chitty, Stewart, Kerr, and Others, Barron Field's Analysis, and Additional Notes, and a Life of the Author by George Sharswood. In Two Volumes*. Philadelphia: J.B. Lippincott Co., 1893. https://oll.libertyfund.org/titles/2142.

Bohannon, John. "Unmasked." *Science* 347, no. 6221 (2015): 492–94.

Botsman, Rachel. "Welcome to the New Reputation Economy." *Wired*, August 20, 2012. https://www.wired.co.uk/article/welcome-to-the-new-reputation-economy.

Brin, David. "In Defense of a Transparent Society." *David Brin*. Accessed February 6, 2019. http://www.davidbrin.com/nonfiction/tsdefense.html.

Cagle, Lauren E. "Surveilling Strangers: The Disciplinary Biopower of Digital Genre Assemblages." *Computers and Composition* 52 (2019): 67–78.

Capecchi, Christina and Katie Rogers. "Killer of Cecil the Lion Finds Out That He Is a Target Now, of Internet Vigilantism." *The New York Times*, July 29, 2015. https://www.nytimes.com/2015/07/30/us/cecil-the-lion-walter-palmer.html.

Carr, Nicholas. "How Smartphones Hijack Our Minds." *The Wall Street Journal*, October 6, 2017. https://www.wsj.com/articles/how-smartphones-hijack-our-minds-1507307811.

CareerBuilder. "Number of Employers Using Social Media to Screen Candidates at All-Time High, Finds Latest CareerBuilder Study." *CareerBuilder*, June 15, 2017. http://press.careerbuilder.com/2017-06-15-Number-of-Employers-Using-Social-Media-to-Screen-Candidates-at-All-Time-High-Finds-Latest-CareerBuilder-Study.

Cep, Casey N. "Cracking the Code of James Hampton's Private Language." *Pacific Standard*. Last modified June 14, 2017. https://psmag.com/social-justice/cracking-code-james-hamptons-private-language-96278.

CEWE Photoworld. "How Big is Snapchat?" *CEWE Photoworld*. Accessed November 6, 2018. https://cewe-photoworld.com/how-big-is-snapchat/.

Cho, Daegon. "Real Name Verification Law on the Internet: A Poison or Cure for Privacy?" *Workshop on the Economics of Information Security*. Accessed February 6, 2019. https://www.econinfosec.org/archive/weis2011/papers/Real%20Name%20Verification%20Law%20on%20the%20Internet%20-%20A%20Poison%20or%20Cu.pdf.

Christoffels, Monica. "Best of #HasJustineLandedYet." *Storify*. Accessed October 25, 2017. https://storify.com/mpchristoffels/best-of-hasjustinelandedyet.

Clement, J. "Number of Facebook Users Worldwide: 2008–2018." *Statista*, April 30, 2020. https://www.statista.com/statistics/264810/number-of-monthly-active-facebook-users-worldwide/.

Cohen, Julie E. "What Privacy is For." *Harv. L. Rev.* 126 (2012): 1904.

CommScope. "The Generation Z Study of Tech Intimates." Accessed November 6, 2018. https://www.commscope.com/Insights/uploads/2017/09/Generation-Z-Report.pdf.

Daily News Gazette. "Most Popular Porn Searches – What Porn Do People Search For?" *Daily News Gazette*, January 9, 2017. http://dailynewsgazette.com/2017/01/09/most-popular-porn-searches-what-porn-do-people-search-for/.

Das, Sauvik and Adam Kramer. "Self-censorship on Facebook." In *Seventh International AAAI Conference on Weblogs and Social Media* (2013): 120–27.

Davis, Lauren C. "The Flight from Conversation." *The Atlantic*, October 7, 2015. https://www.theatlantic.com/technology/archive/2015/10/reclaiming-conversation-sherry-turkle/409273/.

Day, Nancy. "Our Separate Ways." *People*. Last modified September 25, 1995. http://people.com/archive/our-separate-ways-vol-45-no-13/.

Deloitte. "Global Mobile Consumer Survey: US Edition." Accessed November 6, 2018. https://www2.deloitte.com/us/en/pages/technology-media-and-telecommunications/articles/global-mobile-consumer-survey-us-edition.html.

DeWall, C. Nathan, Timothy Deckman, Richard S. Pond Jr, and Ian Bonser. "Belongingness as a Core Personality Trait: How Social Exclusion Influences Social Functioning and Personality Expression." *Journal of Personality* 79, no. 6 (2011): 1281–314.

Dewey, Caitlin. "Everyone You Know Will be Able to Rate You on the Terrifying 'Yelp for People' – Whether You Want them to or Not." *The Washington Post*, September 30, 2015. https://www.washingtonpost.com/news/the-intersect/wp/2015/09/30/everyone-you-know-will-be-able-to-rate-you-on-the-terrifying-yelp-for-people-whether-you-want-them-to-or-not/.

Dopamine Labs. Accessed November 16, 2018. https://web.archive.org/web/20180224003954/https://usedopamine.com/.

Doyle, Tony and Judy Veranas. "Public Anonymity and the Connected World." *Ethics and Information Technology* 16, no. 3 (2014): 207–18.

Drago, Emily. "The Effect of Technology on Face-to-Face Communication." *Elon Journal of Undergraduate Research in Communications* 6, no. 1 (2015): 13–19.

Dreyfus, Hubert. "Nihilism on the Information Highway: Anonymity versus Commitment in the Present Age." In *Community in the Digital Age: Philosophy and Practice*, edited by Andrew Feenberg and Darin Barney, 69–82. Lanham: Rowman & Littlefield, 2004.

Dreyfus, Hubert L. and Paul Rabinow. *Michel Foucault: Beyond Structuralism and Hermeneutics*. Chicago: University of Chicago Press, 1983.

Duggan, Maeve. "Online Harassment 2017." *Pew Research Center*, July 11, 2017. https://www.pewresearch.org/internet/2017/07/11/online-harassment-2017/.

Dzirutwe, MacDonald. "Zimbabwe Will Not Charge U.S. Dentist for Killing Cecil the Lion." *Yahoo! News*, October 12, 2015. https://news.yahoo.com/zimbabwe-says-not-charge-u-dentist-killing-cecil-133842381.html.

Earle, Alice Morse. *Curious Punishments of Bygone Days*. Chicago: Herbert S. Stone & Company, 1896. Accessed December 12, 2018. https://books.google.com/books?hl=en&lr=&id=4SnJTvXjMrkC&oi=fnd&pg=PA1&dq=curious+punishments+of+bygone+days.

Edwards, Jim. "Planet Selfie: We're Now Posting A Staggering 1.8 Billion Photos Every Day." *Business Insider*, May 28, 2014. https://www.businessinsider.com/were-now-posting-a-staggering-18-billion-photos-to-social-media-every-day-2014-5.

Egebark, Johan and Mathias Ekström. "Like What You Like or Like What Others Like? Conformity and Peer Effects on Facebook." *IFN Working Paper*, no. 886 (2011). http://www.ifn.se/wfiles/wp/wp886.pdf.

Eggers, Dave. *The Circle*. Canada: Alfred A. Knopf, 2013.

Entis, Laura. "Chronic Loneliness Is a Modern-Day Epidemic." *Fortune*, June 22, 2016. http://fortune.com/2016/06/22/loneliness-is-a-modern-day-epidemic/.

Eric. "Finstagram: The Instagram Revolution." *Medium*, February 10, 2015. https://medium.com/bits-pixels/finstagram-the-instagram-revolution-737999d40014.

Esposito, Roberto. *Communitas: The Origin and Destiny of Community*. Translated by Timothy Campbell. Stanford: Stanford University Press, 2010.

Eveleth, Rose. "How Many Photographs of You Are Out There In the World." *The Atlantic*, November 2, 2015. http://www.theatlantic.com/technology/archive/2015/11/how-many-photographs-of-you-are-out-there-in-the-world/413389/.

Farivar, Cyrus. "'Stop the Cyborgs' Launches Public Campaign against Google Glass." *Ars Technica*, March 22, 2013. https://arstechnica.com/tech-policy/2013/03/stop-the-cyborgs-launches-public-campaign-against-google-glass/.

Floridi, Luciano. "Group Privacy: A Defence and an Interpretation." In *Group Privacy: New Challenges of Data Technologies*, edited by Linnet Taylor, Luciano Floridi, and Bart van der Sloot, 83–100. Cham: Springer, 2017.

Floridi, Luciano. *The Onlife Manifesto: Being Human in a Hyperconnected Era*. SpringerOpen, 2015.

Fogg, B. J., Gregory Cueller, and David Danielson. "Motivating, Influencing, and Persuading Users: An Introduction to Captology." In *The Human-Computer Interaction Handbook*, edited by Andrew Sears, 159–72. Boca Raton: CRC Press, 2007.

Foucault, Michel. *Discipline and Punish: The Birth of the Prison*. New York: Vintage, 1995.

Foucault, Michel. *Power/knowledge: Selected Interviews and Other Writings, 1972–1977*. New York: Pantheon, 1980.

Frankl, Viktor E. *Man's Search for Meaning: An Introduction to Logotherapy a Revised and Enlarged Edition of From Death Camp to Existentialism*. New York: Simon and Schuster, 1962.

Frankle, Jonathan. "How Russia's New Facial Recognition App Could End Anonymity." *The Atlantic*, May 23, 2016. http://www.theatlantic.com/technology/archive/2016/05/find-face/483962/.

Freud, Sigmund. *Civilization and Its Discontents*. Translated by James Strachey. New York: W. W. Norton & Company, 1961.

Fried, Charles. "Privacy." *The Yale Law Journal* 77, no. 3 (1968): 475–93.

Fromm, Erich. "Dealing with the Unconscious in Psychotherapeutic Practice: 3 Lectures 1959." *International Forum of Psychoanalysis* 9, nos. 3–4 (2000): 167–86.

Fromm, Erich. *Escape from Freedom*. New York: Avon, 1969.

Fromm, Erich. *Man For Himself: An Inquiry Into the Psychology of Ethics*. New York: Holy, Rinehart and Winston, 1947.

Fromm, Erich. *The Art of Loving*. Toronto, New York, London: Bantam Books, 1967.

Fromm, Erich. *The Sane Society*. New York & Toronto: Rinehart & Company, Inc., 1955.

Gammon, Jake. "Over a Quarter of Americans have Made Malicious Online Comments." *YouGov*, October 20, 2014. https://today.yougov.com/topics/politics/articles-reports/2014/10/20/over-quarter-americans-admit-malicious-online-comm.

Gavett, Gretchen. "Why Do We Publicly Shame People Out of Their Jobs?." *Harvard Business Review*, April 6, 2015. https://hbr.org/2015/04/why-do-we-publicly-shame-people-out-of-their-jobs.

Ghent University. "Employers Use Facebook (Photos) to Screen Job Candidates." *ScienceDaily*, January 14, 2016. www.sciencedaily.com/releases/2016/01/160114110719.htm.

Godkin, Edward. *The Rights of the Citizen, IV—To His Own Reputation. Scribner's Magazine* 8, no. 1, 1890.

Goffman, Erving. *The Presentation of Self in Everyday Life*. London: Harmondsworth, 1978.

Gross, Anisse. "What's the Problem With Google Glass?" *The New Yorker*, March 4, 2014. https://www.newyorker.com/business/currency/whats-the-problem-with-google-glass.

Gross, Doug. "Why did Colorado Shooting Suspect Avoid Social Media?" *CNN*, July 23, 2012. https://www.cnn.com/2012/07/23/tech/social-media/colorado-suspect-social-media/index.html.

Gutting, Gary. *Foucault: A Very Short Introduction*. Oxford: Oxford University Press, 2005.

Hampton, Keith, et al. "Social Media and 'Spiral of Silence'." *Pew Research Center*, August 26, 2014. http://www.pewinternet.org/2014/08/26/social-media-and-the-spiral-of-silence/.

Harris, Pete, Will Smith, and Jeff Townes. *Parents Just Don't Understand*. New York: Jive Records, 1988.

Hartzog, Woodrow and Evan Selinger. "The Chilling Implications of Democratizing Big Data: Facebook Graph Search is Only the Beginning." *Forbes*, October 16, 2013. http://www.forbes.com/sites/privacynotice/2013/10/16/the-chilling-implications-of-democratizing-big-data-facebook-graph-search-is-only-the-beginning/#724f4a403ac6.

Heath, Alex. "Facebook Says the First Technology to Replace Smartphones Will be Controlled with Our Brains." *Business Insider*, April 21, 2017. http://www.businessinsider.com/facebook-smart-glasses-will-be-controlled-with-our-brains-2017-4.

Hill, Kashmir. "The Secretive Company That Might End Privacy as We Know It." *The New York Times*, January 18, 2020. https://www.nytimes.com/2020/01/18/technology/clearview-privacy-facial-recognition.html.

Hirsch, Adam J. "From Pillory to Penitentiary: The Rise of Criminal Incarceration in Early Massachusetts." *Mich. L. Rev.* 80 (1981): 1179.

Holman W. Jenkins Jr. "Google and the Search for the Future." *The Wall Street Journal*, August, 14, 2010. https://www.wsj.com/articles/SB10001424052748704901104575423294099527212.

Jaschik, Scott. "Social Media as 'Fair Game' in Admissions." *Inside Higher Ed*, April 23, 2018. https://www.insidehighered.com/admissions/article/2018/04/23/new-data-how-college-admissions-officers-view-social-media-applicants.

Johnson, Jeffery L. "A Theory of the Nature and Value of Privacy." *Public Affairs Quarterly* 6, no. 3 (1992): 271–88.

Kaplan. "Kaplan Survey: Percentage of College Admissions Officers Who Visit Applicants' Social Media Pages on the Rise Again." *Kaplan*, January 13, 2020. https://www.kaptest.com/blog/press/2020/01/13/kaplan-survey-percentage-of-college-admissions-officers-who-visit-applicants-social-media-pages-on-the-rise-again/.

Karaganis, Joe and Lennart Renkema. "Copy Culture in the US and Germany." *The American Assembly Columbia University*. Accessed November 6, 2018. http://piracy.americanassembly.org/wp-content/uploads/2013/01/Copy-Culture.pdf.

Kaufman, Walter. *Existentialism from Dostoevsky to Sartre*. Cleveland and New York: Meridian Books, 1965.

Kierkegaard, Søren. "Two Ages: The Age of Revolution and The Present Age. A Literary Review." In *The Essential Kierkegaard*, edited by Howard V. Hong and Edna H. Hong, 252–68. Princeton: Princeton University Press, 2000.

Kierkegaard, Søren. *The Present Age*. Translated by Alexander Dru. New York and Evanston: Harper & Row, 1962.

Kirkpatrick, David. *The Facebook Effect: The Inside Story of the Company that Is Connecting the World*. New York: Simon and Schuster, 2010.

Kleinman, Alexis. "Porn Sites Get More Visitors Each Month Than Netflix, Amazon And Twitter Combined." *HuffPost*, December 6, 2017. http://www.huffingtonpost.com/entry/internet-porn-stats_n_3187682.html.

Konrath, Sara H., Edward H. O'Brien, and Courtney Hsing. "Changes in Dispositional Empathy in American College Students Over Time: A Meta-analysis." *Personality and Social Psychology Review* 15, no. 2 (2011): 180–98.

Kovach, Steve. "Mark Zuckerberg Wants to Eliminate all Screens from Your Life with Special Glasses." *Business Insider*, April 18, 2017. https://www.businessinsider.com/mark-zuckerberg-wants-to-replace-all-screens-2017-4.

Lenhart, Amanda. "Cell Phones and American Adults." *Pew Research Center*, September 2, 2010. http://www.pewinternet.org/2010/09/02/cell-phones-and-american-adults/.

Leslie, Ian. "The Scientists Who Make Apps Addictive." *1843*, October / November 2016. https://www.1843magazine.com/features/the-scientists-who-make-apps-addictive.

Levy, Steven. "The Race for AR Glasses Starts Now." *Wired*, December 16, 2017. https://www.wired.com/story/future-of-augmented-reality-2018/.

Lewis, Paul. "'Our Minds can be Hijacked': The Tech Insiders Who Fear a Smartphone Dystopia." *The Guardian*, October 6, 2017. https://www.theguardian.com/technology/2017/oct/05/smartphone-addiction-silicon-valley-dystopia.

Lyon, David. *The Culture of Surveillance: Watching as a Way of Life*. John Wiley & Sons, 2018.

Manjoo, Farhad and Emily Yoffe. "Revenge of the Facebook Stalker (Transcript)." *Slate*, March 6, 2012. http://www.slate.com/articles/podcasts/manners_for_the_digital_age/2012/03/transcript_facebook_stalker_should_i_tell_a_cheating_guy_s_girlfriend_that_we_hooked_up_.html.

Marder, Ben, Adam Joinson, Avi Shankar, and David Houghton. "The Extended 'Chilling' Effect of Facebook: The Cold Reality of Ubiquitous Social Networking." *Computers in Human Behavior* 60 (2016): 582–92.

Margetta, Rob. "The Profound Power of Loneliness." *National Science Foundation*, February 3, 2016. https://www.nsf.gov/discoveries/disc_summ.jsp?cntn_id=137534.

Marx, Karl. *Early Political Writings*. Cambridge: Cambridge University Press, 1994.

McLeod, Saul. "Skinner – Operant Conditioning." *SimplyPsychology*. Accessed November 16, 2018. https://www.simplypsychology.org/operant-conditioning.html.

McLuhan, Marshall, W. Terrence Gordon, Elena Lamberti, and Dominique Scheffel-Dunand. *The Gutenberg Galaxy: The Making of Typographic Man*. Toronto: University of Toronto Press, 2011.

Meeker, Mary and Liang Wu. "Internet Trends D11 Conference." Accessed November 6, 2018. https://www.slideshare.net/kleinerperkins/kpcb-internet-trends-2013/52-Mobile_Users_Reach_to_Phone.

Mill, John Stuart. *On Liberty*. Ontario: Batoche Books, 2001. Accessed November 6, 2018. https://eet.pixel-online.org/files/etranslation/original/Mill,%20On%20Liberty.pdf.

Mooallem, Jon. "Mr. Know-It-All: When Someone Melts Down In Public, Can I Record It? (Please?)." *Wired*, August 11, 2017. https://www.wired.com/story/ethics-recording-public-confrontations/.

Moor, James H. "Towards a Theory of Privacy in the Information Age." *ACM SIGCAS Computers and Society* 27, no. 3 (1997): 27–32.

Music Business Worldwide. "Why Does the RIAA Hate Torrent Sites So Much?." *Music Business Worldwide*, December 6, 2014. http://www.musicbusinessworldwide.com/why-does-the-riaa-hate-torrent-sites-so-much/.

Nissenbaum, Helen. "Privacy as Contextual Integrity." *Wash. L. Rev.* 79 (2004): 119.

Nock, Steven L. *The Costs of Privacy: Surveillance and Reputation in America*. New York: Aldine de Gruyter, 1993.

O'Hear, Steve. "After Rebooting, Lulu Sees Its Database Of Guys App Hit 200K Users In 8 Weeks Across U.S. Campuses." TechCrunch.com. Accessed January 23, 2019. https://techcrunch.com/2013/04/09/guys-look-away/.

Oksala, Johanna. *How to Read Foucault*. New York: Norton, 2008.

Pape, Allie. "Woman Claims Attack at Molotov's Over Google Glass." *Eater San Francisco*, February 25, 2014. https://sf.eater.com/2014/2/25/6273653/woman-claims-attack-at-molotovs-over-google-glass-updated.

Perkins, Robert L. "Envy as Personal Phenomenon and as Politics." In *International Kierkegaard Commentary: Two Ages*, edited by Robert Perkins, 108–32. Macon: Mercer University Press, 1984.

Pettit, Philip. *Republicanism : A Theory of Freedom and Government*. Oxford: Oxford University Press, 2002.

Piedad, Jan R. and Kim Johnson. "Everything You Say, Do In Public Could End Up On The Internet." *Texas Public Radio*, August 22, 2018. https://www.tpr.org/post/everything-you-say-do-public-could-end-internet.

Pizzorno, Alessandro. "Foucault and the Liberal View of the Individual." In *Michel Foucault, Philosopher*, edited by Timothy J. Armstrong. New York: Routledge, 1992.

Plato. *The Republic*, trans. Benjamin Jowett. The Internet Classics Archive. Accessed July 23, 2018. http://classics.mit.edu/Plato/republic.html.

Poladian, Charles. "NameTag: Facial Recognition App Checks If Your Date Is A Sex Offender But Should You Use It?" *International Business Times*, January 14, 2014. https://www.ibtimes.com/nametag-facial-recognition-app-checks-if-your-date-sex-offender-should-you-use-it-1539308.

Portwood-Stacer, Laura. "Media Refusal and Conspicuous Non-Consumption: The Performative and Political Dimensions of Facebook Abstention." *New Media & Society* 15, no. 7 (2013): 1049.

Przybylski, Andrew K. and Netta Weinstein. "Can You Connect with Me Now? How the Presence of Mobile Communication Technology Influences Face-to-Face Conversation Quality." *Journal of Social and Personal Relationships* 30, no. 3 (2013): 237–46.

Putnam, Robert D. *Bowling Alone: The Collapse and Revival of American Community*. New York: Simon & Schuster, 2000.

Rachels, James. "Why Privacy is Important." *Philosophy & Public Affairs* 4, no. 4 (1975): 323–33.

Rainie, Lee and Barry Wellman. *Networked: The New Social Operating System*. Cambridge: MIT Press, 2012.

Retro Report. "The Outrage Machine." *Retro Report*, June 20, 2016. https://www.retroreport.org/transcript/the-outrage-machine/.

Reuters. "Dentist Who Killed Cecil the Lion Reopens Office." *New York Post*, August 17, 2015. https://nypost.com/2015/08/17/dentist-who-killed-cecil-the-lion-re-ope ns-office/?_ga=2.27115069.1478802225.1544456004-1451322740.1544456004.

Reuters. "'Lion Killer': Walter Palmer's Florida Vacation Home Vandalized." *The Guardian*, August 5, 2015. https://www.theguardian.com/environment/2015/aug/0 5/walter-palmer-florida-home-vandalized-cecil-the-lion.

Riesman, David. *The Lonely Crowd*. New Haven & London: Yale University Press, 1971.

Robertson, Mark. "500 Hours of Video Uploaded To Youtube Every Minute [Forecast]." *Tubularinsights*. Accessed November 6, 2018. http://tubularinsights .com/hours-minute-uploaded-youtube/.

Rodriguez, Salvador. "Facebook has a Theory that Hiding 'Likes' will Increase Post Volume, and Instagram is Testing That Theory." *CNBC*, December 6, 2019. https ://www.cnbc.com/2019/12/06/instagram-hiding-likes-could-increase-post-volume .html.

Ronson, Jon. "How One Stupid Tweet Blew Up Justine Sacco's Life." *The New York Times Magazine*, February 12, 2015. https://www.nytimes.com/2015/02/15/magaz ine/how-one-stupid-tweet-ruined-justine-saccos-life.html.

Rousseau, Jean-Jacques. *The Social Contract*. In the version by Jonathan Bennett presented at www.earlymoderntexts.com. Accessed February 6, 2019. http://www .earlymoderntexts.com/assets/pdfs/rousseau1762.pdf.

Rowman & Littlefield International. "Nihilism and Technology." *Medium*, August 13, 2018. https://medium.com/colloquium/nihilism-and-technology-38575190fb8 2.

Rule, James B. *Private Lives and Public Surveillance: Social Control in the Computer Age*. New York: Schocken Books, 1974.

Sanders, Scott E. "Scarlet Letters, Bilboes and Cable TV: Are Shame Punishments Cruel and Outdated or Are They a Viable Option for American Jurisprudence." *Washburn LJ* 37 (1997): 359.

Sang-Hun, Choe. "Web Rumors Tied to Korean Actress's Suicide." *The New York Times*, October 2, 2008. https://www.nytimes.com/2008/10/03/world/asia/03ac tress.html.

Sarkeesian, Anita. "One Week of Harassment on Twitter." *Feminist Frequency*. Accessed November 6, 2018. http://femfreq.tumblr.com/post/109319269825/one -week-of-harassment-on-twitter.

Schoeneman, Deborah. "What's He Really Like? Check the Lulu App." *The New York Times*, November 20, 2013. https://www.nytimes.com/2013/11/21/fashion/so cial-networking-App-allows-women-to-rate-men.html.

Schoeman, Ferdinand. *Privacy and Social Freedom*. Cambridge; New York, NY: Cambridge University Press, 1992.

Selinger, Evan and Woodrow Hartzog. "Stop Saying Privacy Is Dead." *Medium.com*. Accessed April 17, 2019. https://medium.com/s/story/stop-saying-privacy-is-dead- 513dda573071.

Sheldon, Kennon M., Neetu Abad, and Christian Hinsch. "A Two-Process View of Facebook Use and Relatedness Need-Satisfaction: Disconnection Drives Use, and

Connection Rewards It." *Journal of Personality and Social Psychology* 100, no. 4 (2011): 766–75.

Shepherd, Jack. "Paddington 2 Becomes Rotten Tomatoes' Best Reviewed Movie of All Time." *The Independent*, January 19, 2018. https://www.independent.co.uk/arts-entertainment/films/news/paddington-2-rotten-tomatoes-review-best-top-positive-negative-a8167351.html.

Singer, Natasha. "Never Forgetting a Face." *The New York Times*, May 17, 2014. https://www.nytimes.com/2014/05/18/technology/never-forgetting-a-face.html.

Smith, Richard H. *The Joy of Pain: Schadenfreude and the Dark Side of Human Nature*. Oxford: Oxford University Press, 2013.

Solove, Daniel J. *The Future of Reputation: Gossip, Rumor, and Privacy on the Internet*. Yale University Press, 2007.

Solove, Daniel J. "Why Privacy Matters Even if you have 'Nothing to Hide'." *The Chronicle of Higher Education*, May 15, 2011. https://www.chronicle.com/article/Why-Privacy-Matters-Even-if/127461.

Stein, Joel. "How Trolls Are Ruining the Internet." *Time*. Accessed November 6, 2018. http://time.com/4457110/internet-trolls/.

Stryker, Cole. "The Problem With Public Shaming." *The Nation*. Accessed December 12, 2018. https://www.thenation.com/article/problem-public-shaming/.

Taigman, Yaniv, Ming Yang, Marc'Aurelio Ranzato, and Lior Wolf. "Deepface: Closing the Gap to Human-level Performance in Face Verification." In *Proceedings of the IEEE Conference on Computer Vision and Pattern Recognition* (2014): 1701–8.

The British Medical Journal. "The Whipping Post and the Pillory." *The British Medical Journal* 2, no. 2013 (July 29, 1899): 299–300.

The Chosun Ilbo. "Real-Name Online Registration to Be Scrapped." *The Chosun Ilbo*, December 30, 2011. http://english.chosun.com/site/data/html_dir/2011/12/30/2011123001526.html.

The Washington Post. "Transcript of Mark Zuckerberg's Senate Hearing." *The Washington Post*, April 10, 2018. https://www.washingtonpost.com/news/the-switch/wp/2018/04/10/transcript-of-mark-zuckerbergs-senate-hearing/.

The Week. "Not on Facebook? You're Probably a Psychopath." *The Week*. Accessed July 1, 2016. http://www.theweek.co.uk/facebook/48363/not-on-facebook-youre-probably-a-psychopath.

Thompson, John B. "The New Visibility." *Theory, Culture & Society* 22, no. 6 (2005): 31–51.

Titcomb, James. "Mark Zuckerberg Confirms Facebook is Working on Mind-Reading Technology." *The Telegraph*, April 19, 2017. https://www.telegraph.co.uk/technology/2017/04/19/mark-zuckerberg-confirms-facebook-working-mind-reading-technology/.

Trottier, Daniel. "Interpersonal Surveillance on Social Media." *Canadian Journal of Communication* 37, no. 2 (2012): 319–32.

Turkle, Sherry. *Alone Together: Why We Expect More from Technology and Less from Each Other*. New York: Basic Books, 2012.

Tuttle, Howard Nelson. *The Crowd is Untruth: The Existential Critique of Mass Society in the Thought of Kierkegaard, Nietzsche, Heidegger, and Ortega y Gasset.* New York: Lang, 1996.

Twenge, Jean M. "Have Smartphones Destroyed a Generation?" *The Atlantic*, September 2017. https://www.theatlantic.com/magazine/archive/2017/09/has-the-smartphone-destroyed-a-generation/534198/.21.

Twenge, Jean M. "Why Teens Aren't Partying Anymore." *Wired*, December 27, 2017. https://www.wired.com/story/why-teens-arent-partying-anymore/.

Uhls, Yalda T., Minas Michikyan, Jordan Morris, Debra Garcia, Gary W. Small, Eleni Zgourou, and Patricia M. Greenfield. "Five Days at Outdoor Education Camp without Screens Improves Preteen Skills with Nonverbal Emotion Cues." *Computers in Human Behavior* 39 (2014): 387–92.

Valkenburg, Patti M., Jochen Peter, and Alexander P. Schouten. "Friend Networking Sites and their Relationship to Adolescents' Well-Being and Social Self-esteem." *CyberPsychology & Behavior* 9, no. 5 (2006): 584–90.

Van Dijck, José. *The Culture of Connectivity: A Critical History of Social Media.* Oxford: Oxford University Press, 2013.

Wagenseil, Paul. "Your Privacy Is Gone. You Just Don't Know It Yet." *tom's guide*. Last modified July 31, 2017. https://www.tomsguide.com/us/privacy-lost-defcon25,news-25558.html.

Walsh, Paul. "Walter Palmer Speaks: Hunter Who Killed Lion Will Resume Bloomington Dental Practice." *Star Tribune*. Last modified July 29, 2018. http://www.startribune.com/walter-palmer-speaks-hunter-who-killed-lion-will-resume-dental-practice-tuesday/325185401/.

Ward, Adrian F., Kristen Duke, Ayelet Gneezy, and Maarten W. Bos. "Brain Drain: The Mere Presence of One's Own Smartphone Reduces Available Cognitive Capacity." *Journal of the Association for Consumer Research* 2, no. 2 (2017): 140–54.

Warner, Michael. "Publics and Counterpublics." *Public Culture* 14, no. 1 (2002): 49–90. Project MUSE.

Warren, Samuel D. and Louis D. Brandeis. "The Right to Privacy." *Harvard Law Review* (1890): 193–220.

Weil, Andrew. "Turning, Turning to the Sound of 'Allah'." *The New York Times*, July 13, 1975. https://www.nytimes.com/1975/07/13/archives/turning-turning-to-the-sound-of-allah-the-whirling-dervishes.html.

Weissman, Jeremy. "P2P Surveillance in the Global Village." *Ethics and Information Technology* 21, no. 1 (2019): 29.

Wilson, Timothy D., David A. Reinhard, Erin C. Westgate, Daniel T. Gilbert, Nicole Ellerbeck, Cheryl Hahn, Casey L. Brown, and Adi Shaked. "Just Think: The Challenges of the Disengaged Mind." *Science* 345, no. 6192 (2014): 75–77.

Winnick, Michael. "Putting a Finger on Our Phone Obsession Mobile Touches: A Study on Humans and their Tech." *dscout*, June 16, 2016. https://blog.dscout.com/mobile-touches.

Wong, Julia. "Former Facebook Executive: Social Media is Ripping Society Apart." *The Guardian*, December 12, 2017. https://www.theguardian.com/technology/2017/dec/11/facebook-former-executive-ripping-society-apart.

Zhao, Shanyang, Sherri Grasmuck, and Jason Martin. "Identity Construction on Facebook: Digital Empowerment in Anchored Relationships." *Computers in Human Behavior* 24, no. 5 (2008): 1816–36.

Zuckerberg, Mark. "Building Global Community." *Facebook*, February 16, 2017. https://www.facebook.com/notes/mark-zuckerberg/building-global-community/10103508221158471/.

Index

Abrash, Michael, 89
Airbnb, 111
Albrechtslund, Anders, 113
alienation, 43; of automaton conformity, 46; in digital body, 35–39
Allen, Anita, 137
anonymity, 14, 70, 71, 145; in public, 147
Apple, 146
apps: dating, 105; social media, 83; use of, 30–31
Aquila, 95
Argentina, Right To Be Forgotten, 149
Atick, Joseph, 92
augmented reality (AR), 88, 89, 113
automaton conformity, 27, 43, 78; alienation of, 46

Baker, William F., 91–92
behavioral psychology, 29, 30
belongingness, 49–52
Benn, Stanley, 140
Bentham, Jeremy, 95–97, 108
Bernheim, Douglas, 33
Bowling Alone (Putnam), 27
Boyle, Susan, 72–73
"brain drain," 45
Brandeis, Louis, 139, 140
branding, 38

Brin, David, 142; *The Transparent Society*, 141
British Medical Journal, 68
"Building 8," 93
"Building Global Community," 52
Buzz social networking service, 153

Cacioppo, John, 50
Cagle, Lauren, 86
Calvinism, 26
camera glasses, 145, 146
CampusReform.org, 86
Canary Mission, 85
capitalism, 26, 155
captology, 30
CareerBuilder, 111
Carr, Nicholas, 46
case-files, 105, 110–11
CBGB, 128–29, 133
Cecil the Lion, 65–66
Chesky, Brian, 111
China, 115
The Circle (Eggers), 153
civilization, 9–10
civil rights movement, 48
Clearview AI, 91
close-knit community, 133
Cohen, Julie, 130
COINTELPRO, 90

collective identity, 33
commercial ICTs, 90
commercial recording devices, 146, 156
commitment, 47–49
communal organizations, 27
communitas, 49
community: commitment and, 47–49; direct involvement in, 49; experiments in living as, 131; privacy and, 128–34; public and global, 52–54
community resistance, 127
conformity, 18–22, 95, 97, 115
congressional hearing, 156
Content ID, 148
contextual integrity, 135, 136
control: authoritarian form of, 78; flow of information, 87; institutionalized via process of examinations, 103; mass conformity and, 95; P2P surveillance and, 101, 105, 107, 108, 110, 115, 122, 125, 128, 144, 150–54, 157; primary psychological mechanism, 71–72; social, 69, 70, 84, 102, 140
copyright, 146, 147, 149
corporal punishments, 69
The Corsair, 58–59
crowd conformity effects, 32–35
crowdsourced feedback, 109
crowdsourced Panopticon, 95–98, 108. See also individual entries
The Crucible, 78
cyberspace, 109–10
cyborgism, 93
Cyborg Unplug, 146

DARPA, 93
dating app, 105
decision-making, 94, 95
DeepFace, 91
DEF CON 25, 2
demetricator, 155
Der Tagesspiegel, 114
Dewey, Caitlin, 107
digital disconnection, 49–52

digital information, 87, 92, 148
digitally connected crowd, 22
digital media, 16, 18
digital permanency, 18
digital public, 110; *versus* monarch, 76
digital reputation, 111
digital rights management tools, 147–49
digital Ring of Gyges, 10–14, 18, 141
"digital scarlet letter," 79
digital technologies, 96
disciplinary power, 101, 108; characteristic of, 102–3; culmination of, 103; elements of, 105
disciplinary societies, 101–2
Discipline and Punish (Foucault), 66
disproportionate punishment, 67, 77
distraction, endless buzz of, 45–47
dopamine, 29
Dopamine Labs, 29
Doyle, Tony, 145
Dreyfus, Herbert, 43–44, 50, 102
Dugen, Regina, 93

Eggers, Dave, *The Circle*, 153
envy, 55–59
Esposito, Roberto, 49
EU: guidelines against social media job screening from, 150; Right To Be Forgotten, 149, 155
European Middle Ages, 25, 66–67
exposure, 18–22
EyeTap, 146

Facebook, 16, 30, 33–34, 50, 57, 87, 93, 95, 115, 142, 143, 148, 151, 153, 154; facial recognition software, 91; self-censorship on, 34
The Facebook Effect (Kirkpatrick), 13–14, 132
Facebook f8 conference (2017), 88
Facebook Live, 90
faceprint, 91, 148
face-to-face interactions, 39, 51
facial recognition, 135; software, 91; technology, 92, 147
fear of missing out (FOMO), 32, 110

Index

feudal caste system, 25
FindFace, 91
Floridi, Luciano, 92, 130–31
Fogg, B. J., 30
Foucault, Michel, 67, 68, 77, 95–98, 101–4, 108, 124, 125; *Discipline and Punish*, 66
Frankl, Viktor, 44, 45
freedom of behavior, 132
freedom of choice, 121
freedom of speech, 124
Freud, Sigmund, 8–10, 12
Fried, Charles, 131
Fromm, Erich, 25–27, 35–38, 104, 125
The Future of Reputation (Solove), 150

GamerGate, 11, 12
Gen Zers, 17
Gertz, Nolen, 153
Gibson, William, 1
Glaucon, 8, 11–13
global community, 52–54, 136
global public, 76
global village, 79; public shaming and humiliation in, 72–74
Godkin, E. L., 13
Goffman, Erving, 39
Google, 74, 76, 78, 89, 94, 95, 110–12, 149, 153, 155
Google Glass, 89, 92, 135, 145, 146
Grand Theft Auto and Call of Duty, 11
Grosser, Benjamin, 155
group conformity, 25
group-oriented identity, 34
group privacy, 130, 131
groups, public shaming, 70–72
Gutting, Gary, 102, 103

Hampton, James, 122, 123, 126
The Harris Poll, 111
Hartzog, Woodrow, 130
Harvey, Adam, 147
#HasJustineLandedYet, 73
Hawthorne, Nathaniel, *The Scarlet Letter*, 69–70
hierarchical surveillance, 110

historical public shaming, 78
Hoover, Herbert, 90
human behavior, 12–13, 103; natural law of, 104
humiliation, 59, 66, 68, 69, 72–75, 78, 79, 154. *See also* online shaming
hyperconnected digital crowd, 49

idiosyncratic communities, 140
individual identity, 47
individual isolation, 27
individuality/individual freedom, 25, 26, 44, 48, 122, 124; and community resistance, 127; information on, 94; preserve liberty of, 133
information and communication technologies (ICTs), 3, 4, 14, 17, 31, 51, 52, 71, 74, 83, 88, 93–95, 98, 114, 139, 144, 153, 157
'in real life' (IRL), 34–35, 92, 113, 149; public shaming in, 66–70
Instagram, 31, 153, 154
Internet, 12, 65, 85, 91, 96, 112, 148; individual's information on, 113; mechanism of rating and following on, 32; remove information from, 149; resistance to, 3; and social media, 16, 37, 50, 54; transparency and hyperexposure on, 14
Internet age, 10, 28
Internet anonymity, 12
Internet architecture, 30

Johnson, Jeffrey, 131

Kazaa, 15
Keats, Danielle Citron, 79
Kierkegaard, Søren, 43–45, 47–50, 53–59, 122–24, 126, 127, 157
Kirkpatrick, David, *The Facebook Effect*, 13–14, 132
Korea Communications Commission (KCC), 142

LeCun, Yann, 148
leveling, 55–59

Live360, 93
livelihood, 111–12
live-streaming services, 90
Lulu, 105–7
Lyon, David, 16

Mann, Steve, 145–46
Marcuse, Herbert, 151
Marder, Ben, 94
marketing orientation, 35
Marx, Karl, 35
mass media, 50, 53, 59
mass surveillance systems, 84
McLuhan, Marshall, 71, 91
"mechanisms of escape," 26
micro-penalty, 105, 108–9
Mill, John Stuart, 20, 21, 27, 34, 157; "On Liberty," 18–19
"mind over mind," 108
mind-reading technology, 93
"mixed reality," 146
Molotov, 135
monarch: digital public *versus*, 76; public confession, 77
Moor, James, 145
morality, 13; *realpolitik* view of, 8
moral perfection, 26
Musk, Elon, 93
mutual commitment, 49
mutual transparency solution, 141–44

NameTag, 92
The Nation, 13
negative reinforcement, 29, 32
net of normality, 124–28
networks, 113; public shaming, 70–72
Neuralink, 93
New York Times, 65
nihilism, 44, 45
1984 (Orwell), 94
Nissenbaum, Helen, 135
Nock, Steven, 70
nonconsensual recording, 144; privacy violations of, 143
normality: knowledge of, 104; notions of, 103; observations of, 104; pressures of, 127; program of, 125; resisting net of, 124–28
normalizing gaze, 103, 105, 110

obscurity, 109, 130
Oculus, 89
offender, 68, 69, 76–77, 79, 83, 142
Oksala, Johanna, 104
Old Row Instagram, 85
"On Liberty" (Mill), 18–19
onlife, 92–93
online crowd, 33, 38
online economy, 30
online mob harassment, 152
online personality market, 37
online pornographic sites, 10–11
online public shaming, 66–70, 75–79, 83, 113, 143
online shaming, 59, 152. *See also* humiliation
operant conditioning, 29, 30
Orwell, *1984*, 94
over-reflective process, 55, 56

Palihapitiya, Chamath, 151
Palmer, Walter J., 65–66
Panopticon, crowdsourced, 95–98, 108. *See also individual entries*
Parker, Sean, 29, 151
PassengerShaming.com, 85
passionate commitment, 43, 44, 48, 49
Peeple, 107
peer-to-peer (P2P) examination, 105–11, 122, 128
peer-to-peer (P2P) surveillance, 84, 105, 115, 122, 123, 125, 128–30, 136, 137, 140, 141, 144, 148, 153, 157; blocking device, 146; chilling effects of, 151; crowdsourced Panopticon, 95–98; culture of, 155; current examples of, 85–88; future of, 88–95; harms of, 155; impact of, 152; limit effects of, 146–47, 150; privacy in public violation, 135; privacy violations of, 143; radically transparent society of, 132–33;

robust protection from, 147; scope of, 145
peer-to-peer (P2P) surveillance-free environment, 145
People, 28
PeopleofWalmart.com, 85
Periscope, 90
Perkins, Robert, 48, 57
personal behavioral change, 151
personal information, 131, 152; extraction and usage of, 156; online, 147
personality market, 35–38
personality package, 36, 125
personally identifying technologies, 148
personal ownership, 149
personal social media, 151
Pettit, Philip, *Republicanism*, 74–75
Pew Research Center, 34
physical isolation, 46
Pizzorno, Alessandro, 124
Plato, *Republic*, 7–8
Pokémon GO, 89
police surveillance system, 84, 90
political movements, 43
Pornhub, 10–11
Portwood-Stacer, Laura, 115, 151, 152
positive reinforcement, 29, 39
powerlessness, 27
The Presentation of Self in Everyday Life, 39
prison incarceration, 68
privacy, 14, 93, 123; and community, 128–34; in public, 134–37; zones of, 145
"privacy/anonymity zones," 146
privacy-eroding technologies, 93
privacy-protecting legal tools, 150
privacy violation, 130, 139; online, 156; of P2P surveillance and nonconsensual recording, 143
"private session" mode, 15
Project Loon, 95
Protestant Reformation, 26
psychological torture, 69, 70, 79

public, 52–54, 58; becomes vast bureaucracy, 124; exposure by, 123; in global village, 76; identity status, 121; online shaming and humiliation, 75; privacy in, 134–37; rise to P2P surveillance, 153
"public by default," 16
public confession, 77
public figure, 139, 149, 150
public opinion, 19, 21, 22, 39, 44, 45, 53–55, 72–77, 80, 83, 84, 97, 98, 106, 108, 115, 126, 127, 143, 144
public shaming, 59, 142, 154; in global village, 72–74; from groups to networks, 70–72; in IRL village, 66–70. *See also* online shaming
public torture, 77
Putnam, Robert, 28, 31; *Bowling Alone*, 27

quantification, 105, 109

Rabinow, Paul, 102
Rachels, James, 132, 133
radical exposure, 134
radically transparent society, 155; of P2P surveillance, 132–33
radical transparency, 13–14, 18, 136, 153, 154; proponents, 133–34, 141; in Silicon Valley, 132
ranked distribution, 105, 109–10
ranking, 105, 109
rating, 105, 109
real-name identification registry, 142
real-name policy, 142–43
Real Name Verification Law, 142
realpolitik view, of morality, 8
real-world commitment, 48
real-world community, 128
recording-enabled smart devices, 83
Reddit, 152–53
reflection, 55, 56
religious movements, 43
Republic (Plato), 7–8
Republicanism (Pettit), 74–75

reputation, as continual and compulsory inspection, 111–16
"reputation economy," 111
resistance, 144–57
"restaurant analogy," 142
revolutionaries, 47–48
Right To Be Forgotten, 149, 155, 156
"The Right to Privacy," 139
"right to publicity," 150
Ronson, Jon, 80
Rothman, Jennifer, 150
Rousseau, Jean-Jacques, 134
Rule, James, 84, 94
Rumi, 125, 128, 140, 141

Sacco, Justine, 73–74, 79, 94–95
sama ceremony, 126
Sarkeesian, Anita, 11, 12
The Scarlet Letter (Hawthorne), 69–70
schadenfreude, 58, 59, 69, 73, 77
Schmidt, Erich, 13
Schoeman, Ferdinand, 131
search engine companies, 149, 155
search engines, 74
self-actualization, 48–49
self-censorship, 34, 86, 87, 90
self-estrangement, 35
self-worth, 37, 38
Selinger, Evan, 130
sexuality, 10
shameful class, 105, 110
shaming punishments, 76
Silicon Valley, 14, 18, 28–31, 89, 134; operations and financial model of, 156; radical transparency in, 132
Skinner, B. F., 29, 30
Skinner boxes, 29, 31, 32
Skinner box-like design, 32
Slate, 114
smartphones, 51, 108
Snapchat, 16, 17, 87, 93
social capital, 37, 38, 111
social control, 69, 70, 84, 102, 140
social credit system, 115

social media, 16, 31, 32, 50, 54, 74, 108, 128, 152; crowd conformity effects on, 32–35; digitally connected crowd, 22; Google and, 74; Internet and, 50, 54; as mechanism of escape, 27–32; negative resistance, 151–52; programs, 83; researchers, 33; rise of, 28; and smart devices, 39; standard metrics, 109
social media companies, 154
social networking sites, 153
social norm, 13, 33, 44, 153; violation of, 151
social unity, 48
Socrates, 8, 12, 13, 140
Solove, Daniel, *The Future of Reputation*, 150
soul/psyche, 105, 108
SoundCloud, 147
South Africa, 73–74
South Korea, 141–42; online public shaming and humiliation campaign, 72
sovereign public, 74–80
spontaneity, 126–27
Spotify, 15, 16
"The Star Wars Kid," 15, 144
status, 55–59
"Stop the Cyborgs," 145
surveillance capitalism model, 155
systems of control, 84
systems of surveillance, 84

tech companies, 156–57
technological society, 46–47
TheDirty.com, 85
Thieme, Richard, 2
Thompson, John, 87
The Throne of the Third Heaven of the Nations' Millennium General Assembly, 122, 123
traditional surveillance system, 84
The Transparent Society (Brin), 141
tribal life, 25

tribal society, 24–25
Trottier, Daniel, 86, 87, 114
Turkle, Sherry, 34, 52
Tuttle, Howard, 49, 55, 57
Twenge, Jean, 51
Twitter, 30, 71, 73, 76, 85, 143, 150, 154

UCLA, 52
unconditional commitment, 43
under-reflection, 55
United Kingdom, shaming campaign in, 73
United Nations Educational, Scientific and Cultural Organisation (UNESCO), 126
United States, 27; Right To Be Forgotten in, 156; right to privacy in, 139
unwanted public exposure, 75, 87, 130
utopian theory, 134

van Dijck, José, 114
video games, 11–12
VKontakte, 91

The Wall Street Journal, 112
Warner, Michael, 53, 54
Warren, Samuel, 139, 140
The Washington Post, 107
wearable recording devices, 146
The Whirling Dervishes, 125–26
wi-fi architecture, 96
Wired, 95
World Wide Web, 2; mass judgment on, 14–18; rise of, 28

Yondr, 145, 146
YouTube, 15, 17, 57, 73, 86, 147, 148

Zuckerberg, Mark, 13–14, 52, 88–89, 132, 153

www.ingramcontent.com/pod-product-compliance
Lightning Source LLC
Chambersburg PA
CBHW022013300426
44117CB00005B/171